Michelle Cree is a Consultant Clinical Psychologist in the Beeches Perinatal Mental Health Service, Derby, where she has worked for the past fourteen years. She uses Compassion Focused Therapy (CFT) with all of her clients and travels the country presenting talks and delivering workshops on CFT. She has also been commissioned by the Department of Health to deliver master classes to Family Nurses, a national intensive health visiting programme for young first time mothers, on using the Compassionate Mind Approach.

Series Editor **Professor Paul Gilbert** is world renowned for his work on depression, shame and self-criticism. He is the author of *The Compassionate Mind* and developed Compassion Focused Therapy.

THE COMPASSIONATE MIND
APPROACH TO

Postnatal Depression

MICHELLE CREE

ROBINSON

ROBINSON

Published in Great Britain in 2015 by Robinson

5 7 9 10 8 6

Important Note
This book is not intended as a substitute for medical advice or treatment. Any
person with a condition requiring medical attention should consult a qualified
medical practitioner or suitable therapist.

A CIP catalogue record for this book
is available from the British Library.

ISBN: 978-1-78033-085-3

Typeset in Palatino by Initial Typesetting Services, Edinburgh
Printed and bound by CPI Group (UK) Ltd, Croydon, CR0 4YY

Papers used by Robinson are from well-managed forests
and other responsible sources

Robinson
An imprint of
Little, Brown Book Group
Carmelite House
50 Victoria Embankment
London EC4Y 0DZ

An Hachette UK Company
www.hachette.co.uk

www.improvement zone.co.uk

To Jacob, Thomas and Freya

Contents

List of figures and tables   xix

Foreword   xxi

Author's note   xxv

Introduction   xxvii

I have a new baby but don't feel as I'd hoped   xxvii

So what can we do?   xxvii

How to use this book: The Three Stages of the Compassionate
Mind Approach   xxx

Stage One
Understanding Our Human Mind: Why We Struggle   1

1   **'All going well?': Understanding the influences upon our
    experience of having a baby**   3

Pregnancy   4

Birth   6

Just after birth   9

Is there always a 'rush of love'?

The hour after birth: important but not critical

Characteristics of the baby

'Maternal instinct' and learning to mother

The early days   14

   Recovering from giving birth

   A needy baby

   Support

Summary   18

2   **'Where is the joy?': Understanding how I feel after having
     a baby**   19

Anxiety   19

Irritability   21

Baby blues   23

Hopelessness and depression   23

Summary   26

3   **'I struggle to feel love for my baby': Our mixed emotions
     and how we try to manage them**   27

Depression and bonding   28

Numbing to cope   30

Traumatic experiences   32

This baby is too much for me   34

I am not sure I like my baby   37

I feel anger and resentment towards my baby   40

I am scared to love my baby   42

I feel like I am just an object to my baby   43

Summary   45

4 **Understanding postnatal depression**   47

Myths around postnatal depression   47

What are the symptoms of postnatal depression?   50

Treatment   51

Do women with postnatal depression harm their baby?   52

Will my baby be taken away from me?   52

How might postnatal depression affect how I feel about my baby? 53

Social support and postnatal depression   54

Having frightening thoughts   55

Summary   58

5 **How we are shaped: the foundations of the compassionate mind approach**   59

Finding ourselves here in the flow of life   60

Socially made self   61

'Nature's mind'   63

Normal life is marked by tragedy and suffering   63

Summary   66

6 **Our Brain: A mix of old and new**   67

Our 'new' human abilities: the good, the bad and the ugly   72

Getting into loops: what happens when the old brain and new brain interact   74

Self-awareness and self-monitoring: the impact of 'the voice on our shoulder'   77

Exercise: The power of our mind towards ourselves   78

Mindfulness: The art of paying attention to attention   81

   Exercise: Mindful coffee drinking   85

Mindfulness and compassion   85

   Exercise: Bringing compassion to mindfulness   88

Mindfulness, pregnancy and new motherhood   88

Summary   89

7   **Understanding our emotion systems**   91

Three emotion systems: threat, drive, and soothing   91

The function of emotions   92

The threat and self-protection system   93

The drive system   99

The soothing system: slowing down and social safeness   103

Our many 'selves'   110

   Exercise: Finding balance   114

Summary   116

8   **How the threat, drive, and soothing systems change in   117
response to pregnancy and new motherhood**

The threat system and new motherhood   117

Stress, inflammation, and postnatal depression   119

The drive system and new motherhood   122

The soothing system and new motherhood: soothing,   123
affiliation, and attachment

Summary   131

9 **Understanding shame**   132

What is shame?   132

Why does 'shame' exist?   133

The hard-wired fear of rejection   135

How shame traps us   138

Shame, guilt and motherhood   139

'What have you been doing all day?'   141

Summary   142

10 **Safety strategies and their unintended consequences**   144

Pulling it all together – the four-part formulation   151

Summary   158

11 **'How am I feeling, how are you feeling baby?':**   160
Understanding the minds of ourselves and others

'I have no idea how I feel'   160

The chameleon: 'I don't know who I really am'   161

'My feelings are scary'   162

'When I am upset I can't think clearly about you or me':   166
mentalisation

What helps us to mentalise? Safeness and soothing   167

Emotional Contagion: When I feel what you feel   169

'When it gets too much, I can't think properly'   170

Our babies need time to catch up when we change   173

Summary   174

Stage Two   175
Developing our compassionate mind

12 **The nature of compassion: What makes up a**   177
    'compassionate mind'?

    Six attributes of a compassionate mind (engagement
       with suffering)   183

    Six skills of a compassionate mind (alleviation of suffering)   191

    Creating patterns of compassion within ourselves   196

    How compassion shapes our threat, drive and soothing systems   198

    The benefits of compassion   200

    Summary   201

13 **Preparing the compassionate mind: Mindful awareness**   205

    Can I really change my brain?   205

    Compassionate motivation   206

    Beginning to practise   209

    Mindful awareness   213

        An empty mind?   216

        Experiment: Awareness of the restless mind   217

        Experiment: Spotlight of attention   220

    Core mindfulness exercises   224

        Exercise: Mindfulness to the breath   224

        Exercise: Mindfulness to sounds   225

        Exercise: Mindfulness to the senses   226

        Exercise: Mindfulness to the body   227

        Exercise: Bringing gratitude and compassion to the body   229

Exercise: Mindfulness to emotions   232

Exercise: Mindfulness to thoughts   233

Mindfulness 'on the go'   234

Exercise: Eating like a baby   234

Exercise: Mindfulness to the washing up   235

Exercise: Mindful walking with the pushchair   236

Summary   236

**14 Preparing the compassionate mind: Activating the
soothing system**   237

Moving from our threat mind to our compassionate mind: 237
the five stepping stones

1) Embodiment: changing your body posture to change your mind 238

   Experiment: Finding a compassionate posture   240

2) Soothing breathing rhythm   241

   Exercise: Soothing Breathing Rhythm   242

3) Mindfulness: attention without judgment   244

   Exercise: Mindfulness to the breath   244

4) Kind, warm facial expression   245

   Experiment: Neutral face, kind face   245

5) Kind, warm voice   246

   Experiment: Neutral voice, kind voice   246

15 Strengthening the compassionate mind: Compassionate imagery 248

The three flows of compassion   250

Do I need a good imagination for these exercises?   251

Creating a safe place in our mind   251

   Exercise: Safe place   252

   Exercise: 'Safe place' with your baby   254

Compassionate colour   254

   Exercise: Compassionate colour   255

   Exercise: Compassionate colour flowing out   256

Compassionate self   256

   Exercise: Imagining becoming your compassionate self 257

Focusing the compassionate self   260

   Exercise: Bringing compassion to someone you care about 260

   Exercise: Bringing compassion to ourselves   260

Compassionate image   261

   Exercise: Compassionate image   262

Summary   263

16 Strengthening the compassionate mind: Using compassionate   264
attention and behaviour

   Exercises: Compassionate attention . . .   266

     to memories   266

     to gratitude   267

     to parts of our baby   268

     to times when it is easier   269

     to using all of our senses with our baby 270

     to what connects us   273

   Exercise: Moving together – synchrony   274

Exercise: Through the eyes of my baby   274

Exercise: Compassionate attention to what we <u>have</u> done   275
all day

Examples of compassionate behaviour   278

  1) In the moment   278

  2) In the short term   279

  3) In the long term   281

Summary   281

Stage Three
Bringing our compassionate mind to our struggles   283

Introduction   285

17 Using compassionate thinking, letter writing, and imagery   287
to help with our struggles

Compassionate thinking   287

Exercise: Compassion – focused thought balancing – an example   288

Compassionate letter writing   294

  Writing to your baby   298

Using compassionate imagery with the struggling 'parts'   299
of our self

Exercise: Bringing compassion to our 'anxious self'   301

Exercise: Bringing compassion to our 'angry self'   301

Exercise: Bringing compassion to the part that struggles with   303
your baby

Bringing compassion to our baby   304

   A 'ladder' of compassion: 'compassionate desensitisation'   305

   Exercise: Bringing the compassionate self to you and your baby   307

   Exercise: Bringing the compassionate self to your baby   308

Summary   308

18 **The journey from self-criticism to self-compassion**   310

Why do we criticise ourselves?   311

What does your self-critic look like?   312

Moving from using a critical to a compassionate self-corrector   313

Critical parent, nice parent, compassionate parent?   314

When it's hard to say 'no': being nice as a safety strategy   315

Oxygen Mask Principle   316

Compassion to the self-critic   317

   Exercise: Bringing compassion to the self-critic   320

Self-criticism to keep emotions in check   322

   'Don't wake the sleeping lion'   323

If I don't have my self-critic I fear I will have nobody: 324
our need for affiliation

The journey to self-compassion: navigating the potholes   325
and bumps in the road

   Support   327

   The 'positive feeling snowball'   327

   A fear of loss of identity: 'If I am not self-critical then   328
   who am I?'

   Self-compassion as an alien experience   329

Self-compassion is an aversive experience 329

Self-criticism of attempts to be self-compassionate 330

I don't deserve it 331

Keeping a focus on where we are going 331

Summary 332

Appendix A: A twelve-week 'exercise programme' for
developing our compassionate mind 335

Appendix B: The four-part formulation 347

Appendix C: Compassion-focused thought balancing 349

Notes 351

Useful resources 365

Index 373

List of figures and tables

Figures

6.1 Our new brain and our old brain interact and influence   76
     each other

6.2 The power of our mind towards ourselves   78

6.3 Interactions of mindfulness and compassion with the old   86
     and new brain

7.1 Three types of emotion regulation system   93

7.2 Aspects of ourselves that change as we shift our   112
     emotional state

7.3 A common example of which emotional system we spend   114
     most or least time in

8.1 The six attributes and six skills of compassion   182

8.2 The compassion process   199

Tables

7.1 The impact of our emotional state   110

8.1 The four-part formulation   153

8.2 Examples of using the formulation to make sense of why   155
     we may be struggling with new motherhood

18.1 Steps from self-criticism to self-compassion   326

Foreword

We have always understood that compassion is very important for our well-being. If we are stressed or upset it is always better to have kind, helpful and supportive people around us rather than critical, rejecting or disinterested folk. However, it is not only this common sense that tells us about the value of kindness and compassion, because recent advances in scientific studies of compassion and kindness have greatly advanced our understanding of how these qualities really do influence and help us in all kinds of ways, both in body and mind. Yet despite this common sense ancient wisdom and modern knowledge, we live in an age that can make compassion for ourselves and others difficult. This is the world of seeking the competitive edge, of achievement and desire, of comparison to others who are maybe doing better than us, and of dissatisfaction, self-disappointment and the tendency to be self-critical (sometimes very harshly). Research has now revealed that such environments actually make us unhappier, and that mental ill-health is on the increase, especially in younger people.

Having a baby and giving birth can be an especially stressful time, and one where we need as much support and compassion from others as we can get. Until relatively recently, childbirth was regarded as 'women's business' where women were assisted only by other women during the birth, were treated as special and were fully supported by their female relatives for some weeks subsequently. Now it is usual to be assisted by men during the birth and women often leave hospital quickly with very little support. Certainly before the modern era of medicine, birth was a tricky process because the human birth canal is not the easiest to navigate. In fact, human females can have the most dangerous and complex birth of all primates. Modern medicine helps in times of difficulty but we can also over-medicalise and think that all difficulties can be sorted by medical procedures, pills and potions. In reality, attending to the emotional needs of the mother is central.

So it's important to recognise that sometimes, through no fault of our own, we don't have the support that we might ideally need. So when we are struggling, we need to acknowledge that, without any shame, and reach out for help to health visitors or friends. There is, however, another problem we need to watch out for. This is the fact that we live in a society that is very judgemental and we can pick that up and become harshly judgemental of ourselves. Research suggests that women with more emotional difficulties are often very self-critical, believing that they are not good enough in some way, or struggling to bond with or have any feelings for their baby. These things can easily happen, I'm afraid. It's partly in the nature of Western society to sell us illusions and dreams of the happy mother and baby playing endlessly and joyfully with each other. In reality, things could be trickier than that. So in this excellent book on compassionate approaches to the issues involved in having a baby, Michelle Cree helps us understand how we can make compassion central to our way of being. She gently explores many of the complex issues around childbirth, the changes that take place in one's body that can produce unwanted mood changes or anxiety, and how they can sometimes turn off loving feelings. She will also explore how we can get lost in loops of self-criticism through no fault of our own. And most importantly, she shows how to reach out for help if we need it by dealing with things we might be ashamed of and learning how to treat ourselves more wisely and kindly.

Compassion can sometimes be viewed as being a bit soft or weak – a way of letting our guard down and not trying hard enough. This is a major mistake because on the contrary: compassion requires us to be open to and tolerant of our painful feelings, and to face up to our problematic emotions and difficulties. Compassion is not turning away from emotional difficulties or discomforts, or trying to get rid of them. It is not a soft option. Rather compassion is the basis for the courage, honesty and commitment to do what we can to learn to cope with and overcome some of our difficulties. It enables us to do things to and for ourselves that help us to flourish and take care of ourselves – not as a demand or requirement, but to enable us to live our lives more fully and contentedly.

In this book, Michelle brings her many years of experience as a clinical psychologist, working with mothers-to-be and those who have had their baby – some with very major mental health difficulties. She also brings a wealth of experience from working with compassion-focused therapy over a number of years. She shares her experience as a national trainer in compassion approaches in this area. In this book, she outlines a model of compassion that seeks to stimulate and build your confidence so that you can engage with the difficulties you may have. Michelle will guide you through developing compassionate motives, compassionate attention, compassionate feelings, compassionate thinking and compassionate behaviour. She will show you how to become more mindful, more observant and more aware of what's going on with you, rather than being carried away by the rush of feelings that can sometimes feel overwhelming. You will explore the potential power of working directly with your body by breathing in a particular way that helps to calm and focus the body. You will practise developing a kind voice within yourself and also using postures and facial expressions to stimulate systems and your brain. You will also learn the value of developing certain kinds of compassion-focused imagery, compassionate ways of thinking and behaving. It helps to see that if we put the desire to bring more compassion into the world and into our lives, then whether we're successful or not is less important than reminding ourselves that that is our intention. It is the recognition of the value of trying to be more compassionate and then having a go that is the important thing. Many times we can't live up to what we intend (it's very easy to get disappointed, anxious, frustrated or upset – or simply forget our intention to be compassionate) but coming back to our intention helps to guide us. By becoming more compassionate, we can become less judgemental and more focused on what we're trying to do, rather than criticising ourselves for what we haven't done or can't do. With a variety of compassionate imagery ideas, you will discover that your compassion focus can be can visual or aural (e.g. imagining a compassionate voice speaking to you when you need it), and even touch or smell can be useful in enabling us to get in touch with our internal compassionate feelings and desires.

Many people suffer silently and secretly with a whole range of fears, worries and difficult emotions at this time. Some are ashamed or angry with themselves, others are fearful or anxious, and yet others can feel exhausted or dead inside. Sadly, feeling ashamed of these things can stop us from openly acknowledging them, and leads to us blaming ourselves. But if we rather see these difficult things as part of what can happen to women, we will feel less ashamed, and be more likely to reach out for help. Keep in mind that whatever you feel, whatever you think or whatever fantasies you have, other women at some point in human history (and probably many millions of them) will have had them too – so although it can be painful, you're not alone. By opening your heart to compassion for your difficulties, you can take the first steps towards dealing with them in a new way. My compassionate wishes go with you on your journey and I sincerely hope this book will give you the help that you need.

Professor Paul Gilbert PhD FBPsS OBE

December 2014

Author's note

After a number of years working in adult mental health services I had the privilege of being given the opportunity to work at The Beeches Perinatal Mental Health Service. The move was prompted after working with a number of women who said that their difficulties had begun after having their baby. Some had been struggling for many years, with one lady approaching her sixtieth birthday and still suffering with depression, originating after the birth of her first baby when she was twenty. For some this difficulty had been connected to issues around bonding with their baby, and was still having an impact on their relationship with their adult child. What was so tragic was the possibility that if they had received help in the early days of motherhood then their lives, and those of their children, may have taken a different course.

Like many of the other perinatal mental health services around the country, The Beeches provides help to women suffering with, or at risk of, developing a severe mental illness which is connected in some way to being pregnant, giving birth or having a baby. The service works with women from pregnancy (or before, if there is a high risk of them becoming ill), until the baby is one year old, if necessary. It has a small six-bedded in-patient unit where mothers can come in with their baby if they need more intensive help. It also has a team that works with women who are unwell but who do not need to come into the in-patient unit.

The service works with others who are supporting pregnant and post-natal women, and it was a comment from a health visitor that really galvanised me to set to and write this book, which had been whirling round in my mind and on scraps of paper for many years. She commented that she had begun a new job in an area that covered a relatively well-off housing estate. She spent her days visiting women in their homes and saw the same picture again and again; in each house was a woman on her own with her baby. She realised that all over this estate women were struggling by themselves for many hours a day, but when they went out with the baby they put on their 'mask', giving the impression that all was well. They often expressed to her a sense of shame in not being able to cope when everyone else seemed to be coping so well. As we will see later in the book, we have not evolved to parent in such isolation, so it is understandable how incredibly difficult this can be. Yet women often carry the blame squarely on their own exhausted shoulders.

It is this tragedy that I hope to address in this book: having a baby is complex and affected by many factors that are not our fault, yet so many women blame themselves or feel blamed. This can stop women from seeking help, preventing them not only from finding much-needed support during these important early years, but from experiencing joy and blossoming as mothers. If the trajectory can be shifted just a fraction at the beginning of the journey, we can end up in a very different place many years down the line. This is the aim of this book: to help women to be able to shift, even a tiny amount, from shaming and blaming themselves to discovering ways that will help them get through difficult times, and – by being compassionate towards themselves – truly beginning to flourish.

Introduction

I have a new baby but don't feel as I'd hoped

Wherever we turn we see having a baby portrayed as a joyous event, with pictures and television commercials of happy babies and loving mothers. Of course happiness and affection are indeed part of having children, but what if this is not our experience? The love and affection we hope to have might be replaced by feelings of panic and dread in caring for this new young life. We may be exhausted from the birth and struggling to recover while now having a new baby to look after. It may seem as if our life has lost its joy and colour. We may feel filled with anxiety and anger; or just nothing at all, as if the baby is not ours.

Sadly although these feelings are not uncommon, it can feel like we are the only one who is experiencing them. Not only can we feel alone with these experiences, we can feel ashamed that we feel this way, perhaps believing it means there is something wrong or bad about us. We might try to behave as we think other new mothers do, so we attempt to go about our day trying to care for the baby and, as best we can, keep some kind of order in the house. But in our hearts we can feel so disappointed in our experience. We might try to avoid unpleasant feelings such as shame, anxiety, or frustration and anger, by keeping busy or allowing others to care for the baby as much as possible. But the more we hide our experiences the more separate and alone we can feel. The more alone we feel, the harder it becomes to share our fears and to find a way of understanding and managing them.

Many women who have experienced these difficulties have been helped to find ways to cope and work compassionately with their disappoint-ments and unpleasant feelings using the compassionate mind approach. This book has been written to help the many women who have a baby but may not have feelings that conform to the expectations of joy and happiness as much as they had hoped; instead they have experiences of disappointment, fear, anxiety, depression and self-doubt.

So what can we do?

First, it helps to know that, in fact, experiencing difficult and unwanted feelings is not unusual around the time of pregnancy and having a new baby. It also invariably helps to understand why we have these kinds of feelings, to discover why we feel differently to what *we think* other people might feel, and where these feelings come from.

To help us here, we are going to journey into exploring the evolution of the human brain and see how these feelings can easily arise in us through *no fault of our own*. Second, we will look at how, when we reduce shaming and blaming ourselves, we can start to think about what would be helpful, particularly the value of being supportive and friendly to ourselves. This is compassion, and cultivating a form of mindful compassion is what this book is about.

Often there is a misconception about the term 'compassion'; we can feel it is about being nice, and is perhaps and bit soft and fluffy. In fact, compassion is very different from this.

We have intuitive wisdom concerning how important and helpful compassion is in our lives, especially at times of difficulty and suffering. Imagine a kind and generous person who is going through a difficult time. Maybe they have lost their job, have got into debt, or are going through a divorce. What kind of help might they need from their friends? First, they might need their friends to reach out to them and help them with their suffering. They might need them to be able to listen to them, to be sensitive to their feelings and to be able to tolerate their feelings. This helps the person to feel they can talk to their friends, and know that they will try to be empathic and understanding. These are what we call the first skills or psychologies of compassion; being open to wanting to be helpful.

So, far from being 'soft and fluffy', to be compassionate we need to be willing to turn towards what is difficult. We have an intuitive understanding of this: before anybody sets about trying to help us, we first want them to take the time truly to understand what the nature of our struggle is.

Second, returning to the above example, friends might try to be helpful by doing things; help the person look for another job maybe, or go with them to the Citizens Advice Bureau for debt management advice, or invite them round for a chat. One thing they are likely to do is to *encourage* them to face the difficulties they need to face. When they are acting as compassionate friends, they are unlikely to advise their friend to start avoiding things: 'Oh, getting a job is far too difficult. Don't bother,' or 'Just don't open any serious-looking envelopes any more, that's what I do when I owe money,' or 'This divorce is going to be far too painful for you, so don't go through with it. Just try and distract yourself. Have a glass of wine and try to forget about it.' Not at all. Compassion is often what we need, in order to develop the courage we require, to face the things that are difficult. When we think about it in terms of giving compassion to others we care about, it becomes fairly easy to see, but it's also the same with receiving compassion. If we are open to compassion for ourselves then it can help us face difficult things in new ways that help us cope.

The compassionate mind approach brings together an understanding of how our human mind can cause us difficulties but also provide us with a powerful solution in the shape of mindfulness and compassion. It teaches ways to stimulate the part of the brain connected with kindness, warmth, compassion and safeness. This part of the brain is key in supporting us through our suffering, and also in calming the part of the brain that makes us feel anxious, angry, sad and, ultimately, depressed.

This book is designed to help develop skills in a step-by-step manner that have the potential to make profound and life-changing differences to the way we view ourselves, our baby and others around us.

How to use this book: the three stages of the compassionate mind approach

Stage One: Understanding our human mind: why we struggle

Stage Two: Developing our compassionate mind

Stage Three: Bringing our compassionate mind to our suffering

We tend to blame ourselves for aspects of ourselves which we didn't create or have any control over; aspects that were designed and shaped for us by evolution and by experiences we did not choose. Unfortunately, we have been shaped through evolution and experiences to be able to criticise, shame and blame ourselves. As we will see, relating to ourselves in this way can have an extremely problematic effect on us, including making us feel beaten down, demotivated, disconnected from others, and more likely to become depressed and anxious. It also inhibits us rather than helping us to grow, flourish, and move towards the person we really want to be.

However, we have also been designed or 'wired up' through evolution to respond to kindness and compassion, not just from others, but also from ourselves, which shapes our very mind and physiology in profoundly helpful ways. When we register a sense of others (and importantly, ourselves) responding to us with an intention to help, encourage and support us, we not only feel calmer, and less anxious and angry, but we also feel more motivated, and more able to grow and flourish.

So **Stage One** is about coming to understand why we struggle as we do; to recognise that our struggles are not our fault. This is the beginning of the shift from a self-critical view of ourselves to a more accepting and ultimately more compassionate view. Stage One is therefore not just about acquiring facts and information as it may at first seem; it is the foundation for Stage Two. In other words, although Stage Two may look like the 'treatment', in fact Stage One is a fundamental part of the 'treatment'. Without it we come to the exercises in Stage Two without the necessary attributes that give the exercises their power.

Stage Two is about really building our compassionate mind, through preparing it and then strengthening it using many different means, including how we hold our body, particular ways of breathing, how we focus our attention, ways of thinking and behaving, and the particular imagery that we can create in our mind.

Stage Three is about bringing the prepared and strengthened compassionate mind to the struggles and suffering identified in Stage One, which we now understand are not our fault. Here, we are really putting our compassionate mind to work. The principles of Stage Three are similar to how we might deal with a fear or a phobia. For example, if we are helping somebody with a fear of going out of the house, we might encourage them first to stand in the hallway with the door open. We would wait until they felt more relaxed before helping them with the next step; perhaps moving to the doorway. We are therefore helping them to pair their fear (of going outside) with a feeling of relaxation. In Stage Three we are pairing our struggle, of perhaps anxiety, depression, self-criticism or bonding difficulties, with compassion rather than relaxation. So, rather than adding fear or criticism to our struggles, we are adding a sense of being helped, supported and encouraged; a sense of affiliation or 'being with' ourselves. The aim here is not just to calm or eradicate our struggles (although our compassionate mind can be very calming) but to find more helpful ways to move through our difficulties.

Read a bit then try an exercise: A twelve-week 'exercise programme' for developing our compassionate mind

When we are depressed or anxious it can be very difficult to concentrate enough to read much at all, let alone when we are trying to care for a baby too. At the back of this book is a guideline called 'A twelve-week exercise programme for developing our compassionate mind'. This offers a way of bringing in the exercises from Stage Two as you read Stage One. Having a go at the exercises brings the understanding of Stage One alive, and the more of Stage One you read, the more powerful the exercises become. I suggest mixing the reading of a little of Stage One with trying a practice. The 'exercise programme' suggests an order in which to try the exercises.

Once you have read the book it is worth revisiting exercises you tried earlier on as you are likely to experience them differently. You may of course prefer to read Stage One first and then attempt the exercises. This works well too. The key is to find the most helpful way for you.

A note on assumptions made in the book

For ease of writing it is assumed that the primary carer for the baby is the baby's biological mother, and that her partner is male. Families can of course be complex structures. The primary care-giver may be the mother, father, grandparent, aunt, adoptive parent or foster-carer for example. There may be a sole care-giver or one supported by a partner of the same or different gender. The mother may have conceived from a donor. Difficulties of looking after a new baby, such as disappointment, numbness, postnatal depression, anxiety and bonding difficulties can, however, occur with anybody who is caring for a new baby, and the principles described in this book can be used by all.

The terms 'bonding' and 'attachment' are often used interchangeably. In the book these have been separated out to distinguish the different processes; 'bonding' has been used to denote the process by which the mother connects to her child, and 'attachment' to denote the child's connection to the mother (or others).

A note on case examples used in the book

Examples used are the result of amalgamating the experiences of real people and changing names and details sufficiently to protect anonymity.

A note on seeking additional help

This book will focus on how we are feeling and coping with life after having our new baby. It is not focused on providing a specific diagnosis, such as depression, as this is best carried out face to face with someone trained in diagnosis, such as your GP. Diagnosis can be helpful because it helps people recognise that there might be something happening to them that they can seek help for. Most GPs and health visitors will be familiar with the changes of mood and emotions associated with childbirth and whether or not extra help is necessary. The most important thing if you think you might be suffering from something like depression or anxiety, is to reach out to others, and to go and talk to your GP or Health Visitor about your feelings without shame. As you will see throughout this book, feelings of depression, anxiety, closing down and so on, both in pregnancy and after having a baby, are not uncommon at all.

Understanding Our Human Mind: Why We Struggle

1 'All going well?': Understanding the influences upon our experience of having a baby

There can be many reasons why we are vulnerable to having difficulties around the time of a new birth. For example we may have felt uncertain about whether we wanted a baby or not, the baby may or may not have been planned, we may have financial worries or concerns about our job, or we may not feel supported. Perhaps we are living away from family and friends because of work. Maybe our own childhood was difficult or unhappy and this is having an impact, particularly now we have a baby. We will also see that the human brain can cause a lot of difficulties around the time of pregnancy and having a baby. So the reasons why we might struggle are many, but they are not our fault.

As we will see throughout this book, our mind and our body are inextricably linked. Our thoughts affect our body, and our body affects our thoughts. One of the functions of our emotions is to give us a bodily response to our thoughts. But of course we are not just affected by what is going on inside of our body, but also by what our mind and body detect in our environment; basically do we feel safe or unsafe? So if we feel supported and cared for by those around us, for example, then we can feel calm inside. If on the other hand we do not have much support or have people around us who criticise us, then we can feel anxious, angry or sad inside. When we then become pregnant we have enormous changes going on inside of us; not just changes in our hormones and the physical structure of our body, but a whole other person growing inside us! In addition, we become particularly susceptible to the circumstances in which we live and the people around us. It is no wonder our mood and emotions can be so affected by all of this.

So let's look at some of the changes that occur during pregnancy, birth and new motherhood, and the impact that these can have on how we feel. What follows is by no means exhaustive, but rather an illustration of how complex and individual our experiences of pregnancy, birth and new motherhood are, and how there are no 'right' or 'wrong' experiences.

Pregnancy

From the moment of conception, there are major changes in many of the hormones of our bodies including progesterone, oestrogen, prolactin and oxytocin. These hormones prepare the body for the pregnancy, and later for birth and for milk production. The levels of these hormones change relatively steadily throughout pregnancy but then change dramatically and quickly once the baby is born. For some women these hormones create a sense of well-being and calmness during pregnancy, but for others these changes in hormone levels create real turbulence of emotions. This turbulence can be reminiscent of how we might feel in the few days prior to or following menstruation (often referred to as PMT – Pre-, or Post-Menstrual Tension) so we might find ourselves moving rapidly between feelings of anxiety, irritability and tearfulness. Some women report intense feelings of anger which stay throughout the pregnancy. Usually, because the hormones change again once the baby has been delivered, these feelings resolve, but it doesn't remove the fact that pregnancy can be a very difficult time for some women.

In addition to changes in hormones, the physical body has to change to adapt to this other little being growing inside of us. The body shape changes in a number of ways. Although inevitable, these changes can happen so quickly and in ways that we might not quite expect, that they can be very hard to adapt to. Even our shoes may no longer fit! This is because all the muscles throughout the body, including those in the feet, are affected by a pregnancy hormone which enables the pelvis to relax and open up during delivery of the baby. Because the hormone cannot be directed specifically to the pelvis but instead affects all the body, it can make the whole body become wider and looser. This causes changes in the body shape that we might not anticipate, like a wider back, chest and feet. It also brings strange new aches and pains. Some women are distressed by the change in their body shape, so pregnancy can be a real trial. Our baby 'bump' of course can be very visible and can attract a great deal of attention from other people, who may also wish to touch it too. This increase in attention and touch can be welcome for some, but feel exceedingly uncomfortable for others.

And what of having another person growing inside of us? This can seem to be the most strange of experiences when we really consider it. Unless we have been pregnant before, we cannot know how we will find this extraordinary experience. It can feel special and wonderful but it may also feel perturbing. Some women have described it as feeling like they have an alien or a parasite growing inside them. To some extent this is not so far from the truth; the baby is not fully part of our body, so our body has to undergo changes to prevent it from rejecting the baby as it would any other 'foreign body'. The baby also takes what it needs from us to grow, even if that means depleting the very calcium from our bones. The key here is about acceptance and understanding of our different responses rather than feeling perturbed about feeling perturbed.

Sometimes our pregnancy triggers memories of earlier experiences that our body has been through, giving us a feeling of unease, anxiety or even disgust. These feelings can on occasions make it difficult to have a sense of connection to the baby during pregnancy. Talking about them to a midwife, health visitor or even on an online forum such as Netmums (www.netmums.com) or Mumsnet (www.mumsnet.com) can be very helpful, as these feelings are experienced by many others but are not often shared when women talk to each about their pregnancies. This can give the impression that these feelings are somehow wrong, unusual or shameful, when, in fact, they are not so at all.

In addition to all of this, in the later stages of pregnancy there can be problems sleeping because of increased discomfort. This creates a general sense of fatigue, which in itself, of course, often undermines our ability to feel we can cope.

Birth

The process of birth itself is a particularly precise process in humans. While some mothers have easy births, other mothers do not. There is actually an evolutionary factor that can contribute to potentially difficult human birth experiences.[1] Humans are primates that have evolved to stand up on two legs rather than move around on all fours. This move from four to two legs gave us a number of major evolutionary advantages; for example, that now we could see much further and we have two hands free for using tools and gathering food.

But it is thought that this move to standing upright has had a substantial impact on the shape of the female birth canal; the pelvis moved forwards slightly and the birth canal narrowed slightly – and at the same time the human baby's head was evolving to become larger. The consequences of this biological shaping are that humans have the most difficult of births of any primate.

During delivery, human babies are also the only primates that need to undergo a particular pattern of rotation to fit through the pelvis. This means that the baby is facing 'backwards' in the opposite direction to the mother, making it difficult to be delivered easily by the woman alone. A human birth is the only birth in the animal kingdom that requires cooperation between the mother and others to vastly increase the chances of a successful delivery. Whereas non-human primates seek solitude for birth, humans seek assistance.

Historically, the role of birth attendant has always been an experienced and trusted female such as the labouring mother's own mother or aunt. It would never be a male. The attendant woman would be a quiet presence who would not be involved until needed. This particular type of presence is summed up in the term 'the knitting midwife',[2] denoting a midwife who would sit in a corner quietly knitting. The idea is that she would be calm, silent and focused on her knitting with just half an eye on the labouring mother, signifying faith in the woman to birth without the need to be 'hovered over'. This was because labouring women, like most animals, prefer to birth where they feel safe but unobserved. It gives the mother's brain the very best conditions within which to produce the hormones needed to birth.

Being observed, talked to, asked questions, experiencing noise, bright lights, and feeling unsafe – all of these switch off the hormones and slow down or halt the birth process. If we feel at all unsafe then our body instead produces hormones such as adrenalin, which prepare our body to 'fight or flee' instead of birth. This is why a woman's labour will often slow or even stop when she comes into hospital, because it is an unfamiliar place. Hence the encouragement from hospital staff to stay at home for as long as possible before coming in.

There is even a question about whether having male partners present at the birth helps or hinders the birth. Although most women say they want partners present, Michel Odent, an obstetrician who has spent his working life investigating how women best birth, suggested somewhat controversially that there is evidence that birth progresses more quickly when the male partner leaves the room. One idea about this is that men are concerned about their partner and convey this anxiety to the woman. She in turn worries about him and tries to protect him. This inadvertently places the woman in the wrong physiological state to best be able to birth. It is not clear whether this is because the partner is male, and therefore whether it would be different with a female partner, or whether this is in fact due to the particular relationship that partners have.

A major review of 15,000 births across different countries found that a woman is more likely to have a spontaneous vaginal birth, less likely to have pain relief, and less likely to have a caesarean or an instrumental vaginal birth (forceps or ventouse) if she has continuous support during the labour and birth. This support was most effective where the birth attendant was not a member of the hospital staff or the woman's social network and where the birth attendant had some training in childbirth such as a doula or childbirth educator. The important aspect therefore seemed to be providing the woman in labour with a continued presence with whom she felt confident, held in mind and safe.[3]

To add more complexity to the picture, women who have their male partners present at the birth have been found to bond better with the baby (as have the fathers) and to be more pleased with the gender of the baby. It is therefore not clear whether overall it is better to have partners present. But what we do see is the subtle effect of so many factors in the birthing process that can have an impact on the birth and bonding, without us perhaps quite realising it, but which women can blame themselves for, when it is not their fault at all.

So what about during the birth itself? The best position to deliver the baby is upright or squatting. The most difficult position is on your back as the baby no longer has gravity to help them and also has to move up and over the bony protrusions within the mother's pelvis. Birthing on the back was encouraged to make it easy for physicians to be able to see what was going on when assisting in delivering the baby. Thankfully, now that the anatomy of the woman and the process of birth are better understood, this practice is far less common. But again, where births were difficult, women often blamed themselves or their bodies for not being able to birth properly when in fact the difficult birth was caused or contributed to by the birth position that they were encouraged to assume.

We see, then, that there are many factors that make human birth very difficult, particularly in these days of having to give birth in unfamiliar environments, with strange equipment and unfamiliar people in attendance. A traumatic and painful birth might occur, therefore, because the way we birth in modern times can inadvertently disrupt what has already been made a tight squeeze by evolution.

For many people, when they think about birth, they think about pain. The two are considered to go hand in hand. The problem is, when we are scared, including being scared in anticipation of pain, our muscles contract to prepare us to fight or flee, which makes childbirth more difficult and more painful. But we can't terrify ourselves into being calm! Instead, we can find it helpful to have an understanding of just what it is we fear, how this is not our fault (we don't choose what we are scared of) and what will help us to feel we can best manage our fear. What is important is that we don't feel we are to blame for the pain we experience, or for our struggle in bearing the pain.

Just after birth

Is there always a 'rush of love'?

> *Rather than a 'rush of love', it is common to have a feeling of indifference towards our newborn. Feelings of warmth and love can take time.*

Let's move on to what happens after the baby is born. There is an assumption that mothers experience overwhelming love when they first hold their new baby. In actual fact 40 per cent of first-time mothers and 25 per cent of women with two or more babies reported a feeling of indifference[4] (and this figure may in reality be much higher than the reported figure). This was particularly so for mothers for whom rupture of the membranes was performed during labour, in women who experienced pain that was more severe and worse than expected, and in those who had more than two doses of the painkiller pethidine. The research found that initial indifference tended to last for around three months and was rarely present at six to twelve months (where it continues for longer this may be caused by an interaction with other factors, such as believing that this natural course of events indicates something wrong with oneself, which can lead to a sense of shame, and contribute to postnatal depression). The authors of this research suggested that delayed bonding may in fact be an evolved response which holds off maternal investment in a newborn until the newborn's survival is more assured.

When we experience pain or a traumatic birth then the hormones connected with stress and threat such as adrenalin and cortisol are increased, which suppress the hormones required for bonding and milk production, such as oxytocin. The mother needs time to recover and to be looked after, which then allows the body's response to stress and threat to be reduced enough to allow for the bonding and milk-production hormones to be produced. In fact after a difficult birth, for example where there is a long pushing stage or an emergency caesarean section, milk production can be delayed by a few days. This can also occur when fragments of the placenta remain undelivered after birth, because it is the full delivery of the placenta that switches on the hormones for milk production.

The hour after birth: important but not critical

Because giving birth can be so exhausting, the temptation might be to remove the baby completely after delivery so the mother can rest. In fact, the time just after birth and contact with, and proximity to, the baby are important in helping the levels of oxytocin to increase in both the mother, and the baby. There may also be cultural differences in terms of how we *expect* to feel after birth. Studies have found that in many countries indifference to the new baby just after birth is in fact the normal response, occurring while the mother recovers from the exertion of the birth. Meanwhile though, the baby is born with a multitude of reflexes that enable it to move up the mother's body of its own accord to find the nipple and start suckling, and a number of characteristics, such as large eyes and chubby cheeks, to increase the chances of it being viewed as endearing by the exhausted mother.

The hour or so immediately following birth seems to be an important time in many ways. Mothers are more likely to develop closer, more sensitive bonds and to be able to breast-feed for longer if the baby is given unswaddled and unwashed to the mother straight after birth with minimal separation time (of course, this isn't always possible – see below). The smell of the unwashed mother helps the baby to find the nipple and begin to suckle. This suckling releases oxytocin in both the mother and the baby, which helps the baby and mother to gaze at the eyes of each other, to experience mutual feelings of warmth and love, and to be calmed and soothed. The suckling also helps the placenta to be delivered and the womb to contract, so reducing the chances of a post-partum haemorrhage. The skin-to-skin contact and the holding of the baby in the 'nest' of the mother, formed by the mother's arms, body and breasts, also regulate the baby's body temperature and help to calm the baby after the birth. In fact rather than crying after birth, as is so often assumed, a baby can spend up to an hour just gazing, usually at their mother, in a state of quiet alertness, as if the two are getting to know each other.

The baby, just like an adult, will prefer a direct, friendly eye gaze from people, rather than eyes shut, averted, unresponsive or looking 'through' them. Already the baby will have a preference for the mother's voice through hearing it in the womb, and within one to two days the baby will recognise the mother's face. The baby will also have a preference for the sing-songy 'baby voice' we instinctively use with babies (sometimes referred to a 'motherese' or 'parentese') rather than the voice we use for other adults. So right from birth our baby is primed not only to want to be held close and to feed, but to be focused on and regulated (calmed down, soothed or engaged in fascination) by social cues.

If this time is unable to happen for any reason, perhaps because the baby has to be taken away for a while through health concerns, then it can take longer for the mother to bond with her baby. However, although this hour after birth is important, it is perfectly possible to develop a strong bond even if it is missed completely (we only need to look at the strong bonds that develop between adoptive parents and their adopted children to see that bonding is not dependent on this first hour, it just provides lots of factors that facilitate the process of bonding). The key is proximity to the baby, and reducing the worry about bonding, as worrying suppresses the hormones that help bonding.

Characteristics of the baby

Of course bonding isn't just a one-way process from the mother to the baby. The baby also influences this process. This two-way relationship between the mother and the baby is called a *reciprocal* relationship whereby the mother influences the baby and the baby influences the mother. This is so marked that it is argued that, as in the womb, the mother and baby still act as one organism even once the baby is born. In fact some suggest we should call this the 'mother-baby'. We must therefore remember the part that the baby plays in the bonding process. For example, when the baby is born they may initially not be very responsive, may be sleepy and may struggle to suckle. This may be caused by a difficult delivery and certain types of pain relief given to the mother, such as an epidural. The baby will therefore need a little more time to become alert enough to suckle. However, initially it can be harder for a mother to develop feelings of warmth and love for an unresponsive baby. Again this is normal, and just needs time.

Sometimes babies are very unsettled and hard to soothe. It may not be clear why this is. It can be related to a difficult birth, medication taken during pregnancy, or in some cases just a very sensitive temperament. This has been found to be the case, too, for very premature and low birth-weight babies.[5] These babies are more likely to develop what are termed 'disorganised attachment' strategies where the baby cannot find a clear way to get the care they need. In addition, babies who never seem to stop crying may have their eyes shut, body rigid and fists tightly closed, and may find it hard to experience the soothing cues of even the most highly attuned care-giver.

Such babies can be very challenging because they can leave a mother feeling helpless, distressed and inadequate. However, although they can initially be very difficult to care for, it seems that these very sensitive-seeming babies often in fact do very well and are able to develop secure attachments over time if they are parented with warmth and sensitivity as much as possible. To be able to give this kind of parenting in such difficult circumstances, however, care-givers need a great deal of support.

The message really is that pain, trauma, worry and concern can hinder a woman's recovery and the development of the bond with the baby. Being looked after, helped, calmed, soothed and reassured, and being given as much unpressurised time with the baby as she is up to, will help the woman recover and bond with her baby much more quickly.

'Maternal instinct' and learning to mother

First-time mothers across the animal kingdom often find it trickier to bond with their baby and tend to be a little less sensitive and attentive compared to those who already have offspring. This includes humans and is perfectly normal. We tend to understand this with animals and make allowances accordingly, for example deliberately taking newborn pups or lambs to an unsure mother. With ourselves though, we have an expectation that we will instinctively 'know' how to parent perfectly. This is not the case. Mothering is not a completely instinctive and natural process as we may have been led to believe. Although evolution has provided the mother and the baby with many mechanisms to help the mothering process along, it is also highly dependent upon the environment within which mothers find themselves. For example, as with all new skills, we need help from somebody more experienced to teach us. This is thought to be one of the reasons why new mothers seem to have a yearning to have their mother close by, even when they have had a difficult relationship with her. If we don't have such support and guidance, we can really struggle.

> *The ability to mother is not completely instinctive. It is dependent upon many factors.*

In addition, among a whole raft of environmental factors, to be able to mother effectively, the woman needs to feel she is safe, well-resourced in terms of food and care, accepted, and supported by those around her. This is a crucial point. The belief that a woman possesses all that is needed to mother her baby, and that once she gives birth this instinct gets switched on, is a culturally held view and can unfortunately be very harmful. Many pregnant women fear that this may not happen and suffer much anxiety worrying about what will happen if it doesn't. Once the baby is born women wait with bated breath to see if the 'maternal instinct' comes, and can experience shame and guilt if it doesn't. Sarah Blaffer-Hrdy in her book *Mother Nature*[6] looks at the complexity of mothering and how much it differs across cultures. She explains that in human mothers, like mammalian mothers, nurturing emerges bit by bit, as a consequence of so many factors. These factors include our genes and the biology of our body. But they also include a highly sensitive response to our environment and the influence of others around us.

> *Mothers need looking after and time to recover after giving birth.*

The early days

Recovering from giving birth

It used to be traditional (and still is in many cultures) that in the early days following birth, the new mother would have a period of 'lying in' where she would be looked after, encouraged to rest and given the best, most nutritious food available to enable her to recover from the birth, and to develop rich, nutritious breast milk for the baby. She would be cared for by her female relatives such as her mother, sisters and aunts, who would also teach her how to feed and care for the baby. (In fact, this is thought to be the origin of the term 'gossip', derived from 'God Siblings' or 'God Sibs' for short; the female relatives would gather round the new mother and her baby for weeks, providing her with all the news of what was going on outside the room).

Although this practice is still common across the world, in many countries women often go home within six hours of giving birth with very little help. What is more, women are faced with images of celebrity mothers who, within days of giving birth, show no evidence of ever having been pregnant, or of being in the process of recovering from birth, or indeed of looking after a newborn. The message implies that the job of women is to carry the baby during pregnancy but that they must then, as quickly as possible, carry on as before. Very little recognition seems to be given to the momentous event that has occurred to her and her body, or to the fact that she is now doing her best to raise a whole new life.

The body takes a long time to heal after birth, particularly if the birth was difficult, if the mother is trying to breast-feed, and if she is exhausted. She also needs the recognition, the appreciation and the care that was afforded by the process of 'lying in' to mark the sheer importance of what a new mother is doing.

A needy baby

And how are things at home with a new baby? This can be one of the most challenging times because of the constant demands and the chronic lack of sleep. If we think about what has happened for the baby, just before it was born it was having all of its nutritional needs met by a very efficient placenta. There was no waiting for food and the baby was continually held in a safe, warm environment. The needs of the baby do not suddenly change now they have been born. In fact, they are now hungrier than before because they are growing so rapidly. The baby's ability to self-soothe or be soothed by the face and voice of others is only just beginning to be developed and they therefore depend on feeding and being held to calm themselves in the early weeks after birth. This state of calm is crucial for growth, development, health and learning (in fact, this is true in adults as well as in babies, as we will see later in the book). In the early weeks the baby likes to stay close to the breast to suckle as a means of comfort as well as nourishment.

If we look at the animal kingdom again, we can begin to really appreciate the size of the task a human mother has in terms of feeding her new baby, whether breast-feeding or bottle-feeding. Mammals' milk is made up of differing amounts of carbohydrate, fat and protein according to whether the young of a particular species are primarily kept close to the mother or at a distance. For example, in animals where the newborns are hidden in burrows while the mother goes out and hunts for food, the milk is high in protein and fat. This keeps the newborns feeling full for longer so they can wait quietly for her return rather than protesting loudly and attracting predators. However, for a newborn of a species that has evolved to be constantly held or kept near to the mother (this includes humans) the milk is much lower in protein and fat so the infant can only go for short periods before it is hungry again. It is considerably higher in carbohydrate though, to grow the rapidly developing infant brain. This means that the human mother who is breast-feeding is in effect still acting as the placenta for the baby, hence the almost continual feeding through the day and night, particularly in the early days. As the breast milk is of course coming from the mother, she also needs to be well nourished. So here is the problem; how does a new mother keep up with feeding her baby, trying to rest so she has the energy to provide carbohydrate-rich milk, and feed herself? She must have help. And this is how it seems we have evolved.

Support

It seems we are not designed to be the sole care-givers for our baby. As Sarah Blaffer-Hrdy in her book *Mothers and Others*[7] suggests: 'continuous care and contact mothering is a last resort for primate mothers who lack safe and available alternatives' (p. 85). Therefore as human primates we have evolved to share care of our offspring with others, unless there is no other choice.

> *We have evolved to need others to help us to look after our baby.*

Imagine for a moment what it might have been like as a new mother during the thousands of years we lived on the African Plains. We would have lived in small groups of up to 150 people. The new mother would never have been alone. She would never have had to take the enormous steps we have to in modern society to ask for help. The birth of a new member of the group would have been celebrated and cherished, particularly as the baby would be genetically related to the others in the group; therefore, helping the baby to grow and flourish would directly benefit the success of the group. The women of the group would be on hand to find and prepare food for the new mother, to take turns holding and sometimes wet-nursing the baby, and doing whatever they could to help the mother and baby become healthy and robust as quickly as possible.

This is where we really come to understand the crucial role of grandmothers. It is now suggested that the time in history at which mothers became able to live beyond their menopause was a key point at which the human species was able to accelerate in terms of both brain development and numbers.[8] For a grandmother, her offspring were now independent of her and of childbearing age themselves, and because she was menopausal she was not competing with her daughter for a mate. The grandmothers were available instead to put their time and energy into helping to feed their daughters and grandchildren.

This meant that their daughters did not have to wait until their children were independent from them before they could have another child – a factor that appears to be unique to humans. Other primate species have to wait for as long as eight years before their offspring can fend for themselves, allowing them to have another baby. Humans could have children considerably more rapidly than other species. But the only way a mother could provide the massive number of calories required by a growing child as well as a growing baby was if another person was also finding and providing food. Help for the mother had now become not just useful, but vital.

Given then that human mothers and babies have evolved to need others to enable them to flourish, it is not surprising that so many new mothers are struggling in modern societies where they live separately from female relatives. This starts to make it more understandable why new mother-hood is often difficult and postnatal depression so common. It becomes clearer that this is not the fault of new mothers but the consequences of trying as best we can to give birth and then bring up a baby in a modern environment for which we have not evolved. This is really brought home to us by the fact that the single biggest predictor of postnatal depres-sion (apart from having previous depression) has been found, again and again, to be lack of social support.

Summary

The process of pregnancy, birth, and the early days of new motherhood is incredibly complex. The mother and this new being are interacting at many levels, both influencing the other in an intricate dance. Furthermore, what is going on around the woman, in terms of external influences, also has an impact on this process. We are only just discovering the many different aspects that can have a bearing on the mother and baby at this important time. What is clear, though, is that tragically so many women feel somehow to blame when things do not turn out as hoped, when it is not their fault at all. If we can remove the shame and the blame, we become much more able to move to a position of 'We didn't choose to be where we are now, but given that we are, what will help us to move forward?'

2 'Where is the joy?': Understanding how I feel after having a baby

> *We have evolved to experience anxiety more easily and to a greater extent when we become mothers.*

However you look at it, giving birth is a very major event which has a huge impact on a whole range of bodily systems and stimulates many different feelings. For some women, who have had a difficult birth, this can be a time of physical pain and exhaustion but also of upset and intense disappointment too, particularly if we feel our body or indeed our mind has let us down. This cocktail of fatigue, physical recovery from birth, rapid and massive changes in hormone levels after birth, and our feelings towards our self and our baby after birth has a significant effect on our mood. Hopefully, we can feel joy, relief, happiness, even elation, but there can be more difficult emotions too. In a moment we will look at some of the common more troubling feelings we may experience following the birth of our baby with suggestions concerning their possible cause. Although these feelings can be horrible they don't just exist to make us miserable, they have an important function. If we can start to look at them differently then we begin to relate to ourselves differently for experiencing them. Rather than further shaming and criticising ourselves for becoming anxious or down we start to appreciate that these feelings are in fact related to evolved ways of keeping ourselves safe and to biological changes of pregnancy and new motherhood.

Anxiety

In the wild, having a baby is quite a dangerous time. New babies are a real draw for predators as they are such easy prey. Similarly, in our distant history, a new mother recovering from birth and encumbered by her breast-feeding baby was particularly vulnerable and dependent upon other members of her group to protect and help her. It makes good evolutionary sense for a new mother to experience an increase in general feelings of anxiety and foreboding, which enables her to have a heightened vigilance to threats. It also makes sense for her to feel anxiety when she is not in close proximity to those who can protect her. Nowadays, of course, this kind of risk to our baby is thankfully unlikely, but the human brain is designed for living thousands of years ago. This is why mothers can struggle to switch off from worrying, even when the baby is asleep. It also explains the great anxiety many women feel when their partners return to work, and why women can be wary of strangers or those they do not trust who want to hold the baby.

This is also why women can sometimes feel increasingly anxious in the twilight hours or in the early hours before the sun comes up, because this was one of the riskiest times in terms of predation. The fact that many women say that being alone in the dark of the night trying to console a distressed baby is one of their hardest times to deal with makes perfect sense when we think of the risky environment in which our brain evolved; a noisy baby, particularly during the hours of darkness, placed both the mother and baby at great risk by potentially attracting predators. Even if they have their partner right next to them asleep in the bed, the mother can experience a sense of deep dread and foreboding until her partner is awake. Logically, we might think there is no point in two people being awake with the baby at the same time, particularly if the partner cannot feed the baby. But when we appreciate that our brain operates under the logic of millions of years of development in very risky environments, then our seemingly strange, illogical feelings start to make complete sense. When our partner is awake with us in the night we might notice a huge sense of relief and a drop in anxiety because our brain registers that we are now much safer from predators. This also fits with the relief many women feel when the sun comes up, because now the risk of predation would have dropped dramatically.

There are of course other reasons for becoming anxious, which are related to how we feel about ourselves and whether we feel we are up to the job of mothering, for example. We can feel overwhelmed by the responsibility of looking after a new baby, or believe we will not be able to protect our baby or do the right thing for them. Often these beliefs and feelings in our body can be traced back to origins earlier in our life such as times when we had responsibility for the well-being of a parent when we were just children and the responsibility was therefore overwhelming. We will look at these in greater detail later in the book. The important point for now is that the feelings we experience arise for a reason. They arise when our brain thinks we are being threatened in some way; as we shall see, feelings of anxiety and depression are a way in which our brain has evolved to protect us.

The trouble is, these mechanisms evolved over the millions of years of living very differently to how we live now. When we experience anxiety and depression in modern times these may not feel very helpful at all. But once we understand why these feelings happen, and that they are not our fault but rather the consequence of the way our brain has been set up, then we can look to what will best help us with these feelings.

Irritability

When the baby is born, and when we breast-feed, there is a surge in two hormones; oxytocin and prolactin. Oxytocin promotes closeness between the baby and the mother and gives a feeling of warmth and love. Prolactin is involved in milk production, but also in maternal behaviours, and gives a mellow feeling of calmness and contentment. Interestingly, prolactin is produced after orgasm in both men and women and is thought to shut off sexual desire so that there is a period of tranquillity, contentment and, in the case of men, sleep, after orgasm. Prolactin works in conjunction with, but opposite to, the hormone dopamine, often termed the 'reward' hormone. When prolactin increases, dopamine decreases and vice versa. Dopamine gives us the buzz of excitement and energy that motivates and drives us. It is connected to the reward system and is the hormone that makes us want more and more of something, for example achievement, praise, cake, chocolate, crisps or wine! Prolactin works in the opposite direction to dopamine and gives us that feeling of contentment once we have eaten the chocolate or drunk the wine, etc. It is a kind of 'Ahh, that's better, I've had enough. There is nothing more that I need right now' feeling. It therefore helps the mother to focus on her baby rather than on doing other things.

However, both oxytocin and prolactin have an interesting and unexpected flip-side. As well as encouraging closeness, warmth and calmness with the baby, they also create hostility towards outsiders. This is what we see in nature where a mother with her newborn is much more aggressive even than a male if she feels her baby is threatened, which explains why, for example, we do well to avoid a field of cows if they have their calves with them.

Both hormones also increase in men who live with their pregnant partners, so they too become bonded with and protective of their offspring. Indeed, prolactin is sometimes called the 'protect and defend' hormone. So although we may feel contentment when we are nursing or holding our baby, there can also be an increase in irritability if there is any sense of unease about the baby's safety, such as when we are living in a neighbourhood that feels slightly unsafe, or when we have relatives or visitors in the house with whom we don't feel entirely comfortable. This is also why women can have such a dilemma over who looks after the baby if they are returning to work. We are programmed to share the care of our offspring with people with whom we feel safe; in evolutionary terms, these would have been our kin. Now, because of our often separate lives, we may not have access to, or indeed have the psychological closeness, to the extended family. This forces us to leave our baby with people we might not feel entirely comfortable with.

Irritability may occur, of course, because of extreme fatigue, but it can also be caused by the pull of having to go and do things rather than just being able to nurse and care for our baby. This is particularly so where there is little help, meaning we are faced with washing to do, meals to prepare, and tidying up, on top of trying to care for the baby. These feelings of irritability can disappoint us if we'd hoped to feel full of love, calmness and contentment when our baby arrived. We can also feel guilty when our irritability gets directed at the baby as the cause of our tiredness and the chaos in the house. How different might we feel if we had somebody who could help us with all these demands?

Baby blues

Perhaps one of the most common sequences of feelings following childbirth is what is often referred to as the *baby blues*. The baby blues occur in nearly all women roughly three to four days after giving birth and is characterised by an increase in tearfulness, anxiety, mild depression, sensitivity to criticism, and a temporary drop in feeling bonded with the baby. Once the baby is born there is a massive and sudden drop in the hormones responsible for keeping the pregnancy going and for delivering the baby. There is also an increase in hormones concerned with milk production. The 'baby blues' corresponds with these hormonal changes and the milk 'coming in'. Here a woman's breasts become engorged and white milk replaces the yellow colostrum. Colostrum is produced just prior to delivery of the baby ready to provide the baby with antibodies, high levels of nutrients, and a mild laxative. This laxative helps the baby produce its first meconium stool, which clears out the baby's digestive system. Once these hormones settle and the milk has come in then usually the woman feels more settled in mood. This more settled feeling can take up to about ten days to arrive.

Hopelessness and depression

Giving birth can be immensely fatiguing, especially for those who haven't been sleeping too well in the weeks or days before delivery. It also, of course, has a huge impact on the body, which requires time to heal. This recovery occurs more quickly in mammals, including humans, when we feel safe and looked after, allowing us to shut down and retreat as much as possible to conserve energy for healing ourselves and for feeding our infant. If we do not have supportive people around us and if we feel unsafe, this can lead to a dip in mood, feelings of aloneness, anxiety, and can eventually lead to postnatal depression.

> *Postnatal depression creates bodily feelings within us that give us the sense that we are bad, to blame, shameful and wrong. These can be so strong that they feel like facts rather than bodily sensations.*

The rates of postnatal depression differ dramatically across different cultures and seem to be linked most strongly to the degree of support provided to the new mother rather than to characteristics of the mother. Other factors that contribute to postnatal depression are previous episodes of depression, a poor relationship with one's partner, financial difficulties and having a lower socio-economic status.[1, 2]

Postnatal depression is not due to some inadequacy or defect within the woman, but sadly the way depression plays out in us can make us believe this is the case. It affects our thinking so that we view the world and ourselves as hopeless and it directs our attention to anything negative that might confirm this. It also passes over any positives that might disconfirm this. It is as if we have been made to wear depression 'glasses' which only show up the negative. Depression reduces our motivation and our interest in life. It affects our ability to have positive feelings, so what was previously rewarding to us no longer gives us any pleasure. Food and drink seem bland and unappetising, activities we loved seem pointless, and what is particularly hard is that relationships are no longer rewarding either, including relationships with our partner and our baby. We feel listless, heavy and lacking in energy, so caring for the baby seems like an impossible feat.

Depression can cause early morning waking even when the baby is asleep, so depriving us of much-needed sleep. It also removes us from social contact, so we feel an urge to hide away from people and even answering the door or the telephone can feel impossible. But social contact is the very thing we need to best recover from depression. This is why it can be such a difficult condition to recover from, particularly if we are relatively isolated.

Depression looks very similar in most people, with many also experiencing anxiety alongside the depression. This consistent picture has proved intriguing. Is it just some kind of awful glitch in humans or does it have some kind of function? One idea is that depression has some kind of protective function. This can seem a strange and improbable idea because depression appears so unhelpful and sometimes so destructive. However, it seems to be very closely linked to our social relationships with others, as we have seen.[3] It is more likely to occur when we feel alone, unsupported or not as valued as others. If we look at animals in the wild or even domestic dogs and cats, an animal in the presence of a stronger, more dominant animal will avert its gaze, lower its body and stop fighting. We do the same when we feel not as good as somebody else, particularly if we feel ashamed. We look down, lose energy rapidly and even find it hard to speak. Our brain has selected this behaviour as a way of signalling to a more dominant individual that we are not a threat to them. It selects it automatically before we are even consciously aware of it.

Depression may take this further by removing us completely from a potentially threatening group of people, sending us in effect to retreat into our 'cave', perhaps waking us in the early hours to be alert at a time when we would be at most risk from predators, but reducing our appetite and our motivation so that we do not move out of the cave while we may still be at risk from a dominant other.

We see this mechanism in animals, but it might also have served us well when we lived in small groups, because our retreat would have been clear to see by the rest of our group, prompting our kin to come and care for us, feed us and protect us until we felt strong enough to re-join the rest of the group. This is likely to have reduced the length of this retreat period dramatically. However, when we live with very little support it is difficult to reach out and ask for help when depression is compelling us to do the opposite. This may be why postnatal depression is so much rarer in close-knit communities.

Although understanding the possible evolutionary mechanism behind depression does not change its devastating effects, it can help to remove any 'depression about depression' we may be experiencing. If we can see that it is not a consequence of a flaw within us, but rather may be an evolved protective mechanism that unfortunately does not work so well in communities where we live separately from one another, then we stop attacking ourselves, and instead can gently help ourselves to recover and to reach out for help.

Summary

We are only just beginning to understand the full complexity of having a baby and how this impacts upon us emotionally. Reactions we may regard as problematic may in fact be evolved responses to looking after a newborn in what, for thousands of years, was a highly risky environment. We have evolved to have a more highly developed sensitivity to threat, whether to ourselves, our newborns or those we rely on to help keep us safe.

Having a new baby means that we need to rely more on others to help us, so how we feel in relation to others becomes more important and acute. In addition, aspects of life that we rely on to keep us on an emotional 'even keel' can be undermined (sleep, for example) or even disappear for a while (hobbies, time for ourselves), particularly where social support is limited. What makes this harder is when we criticise ourselves for our emotional reactions.

The message, as ever throughout this book, is that bringing understanding, acceptance and kindness to ourselves, rather than attacking and shaming ourselves, will have a fundamental impact on our emotional state and our ability to get through these difficult times.

3 'I struggle to feel love for my baby': Our mixed emotions and how we try to manage them

We have seen just how complex the process of bonding is. We know it can be affected by the birth itself and by interventions during the birth. The complexity is so great that we probably only know a tiny amount about what is involved in the development of a bond between a mother and her baby. For example, in many animals smell is a crucial component in bonding. Where the sense of smell is affected in the mother then she may reject her baby entirely.

This may be the case in human mothers too; we can recognise our baby's smell within a few days of birth, and in fact our baby is already used to our smell from the amniotic fluid. In effect the mother and baby 'imprint' on one another, just as a mother and baby seal or ewe and lamb do. The smell of a baby's head and neck are often cited as one of the most pleasurable smells, and in some societies the new baby is passed around, each smelling the baby, as a way of bonding the baby to the whole group. But what if our sense of smell or our olfactory system is compromised in some way? To what extent might this affect the bonding process? And what other factors might be involved in the bonding process which science isn't even aware of yet?

Once a mother and baby begin to spend time together then the bond develops and grows due to the influence of many factors, including hormones such as oxytocin and dopamine. However, for some women that bond doesn't seem to come. They describe a sense of disconnection and numbness. One woman who was referred to me said:

> Don't get me wrong, I look after her and protect her and I do think she is a sweet little thing, but she doesn't feel like she is my baby.

If somebody came to the door and said 'Excuse me but I think you have got my baby by mistake', I wouldn't be surprised and would hand her over straight away.

> *Bonding can occur at any time, even after a long period of not being able to.*

It is not a case of just not being bothered about the baby; many women seek help specifically because they are so worried about this numbness. It causes incredible concern and also sometimes a sense of shame, as if there is something wrong with or bad about her. Who knows how many women struggle along without telling anybody? Certainly, there are women who give accounts of living most or all of their lives feeling numb towards one particular child, but often having strong feelings of love and warmth towards another. Thankfully, there are also many accounts of where these feelings became 'switched on', or where a tiny spark of warmth appears, which grows and grows over time into strong feelings. What is clear is that it is never too late. The boat is never missed.

We will look at some ideas that may give some clues as to why there can be this numbness or disconnection, but the answer will be specific to each woman and her baby.

Depression and bonding

We can experience a sense of numbness and disconnection when we are depressed. Some people say that even when they are with people it is as if they are watching them from outside of a bubble; there is a sense of something separating them.

With depression our sense of joy and interest in anything, including the people close to us, is shut down. As mentioned earlier, one of the effects of depression is to damp down the motivation or reward and 'positive feeling' systems in the brain. This gives us a feeling that previously meaningful or enjoyable activities seem pointless and bland. Unfortunately, this can also include our relationship with our baby. Surprisingly, in non-depressed women, even a baby's cry switches on the reward system. But in depressed women the reward system remains unstimulated.[1] This makes it incredibly hard for a depressed mother to summon the energy and motivation needed to meet the relentless demands of a baby, particularly when she experiences no pleasurable feelings at the end of it.

Depression also makes it very hard to respond to subtle cues and changes in the faces of other people, and to accurately gauge what they're thinking. It tends to focus us on threat and the potential impact of that on ourselves. We are more likely to see threat, criticism and rejection in other people whether it is there or not. Depression can make mothers perceive that when their baby cries in their arms it is because the baby doesn't want to be with them rather than because the baby's tummy hurts or because they want milk, and when the baby turns away during an interaction with the mother she assumes this is because the baby doesn't love her rather than seeing that babies regulate their excitement or effort of an interaction by turning away to calm back down for a moment.

As if this wasn't hard enough, the tension and worry that the mother feels when she holds her baby in case her baby rejects her, then gets transmitted to the baby. The baby then does indeed start to feel uncomfortable with her and to add insult to injury proceeds to settle quicker in the arms of somebody else who is quite relaxed, therefore seeming to reinforce the beliefs of the mother. This is sadly a very common scenario in postnatal depression and the situation can spiral downwards very rapidly, particularly if the people around the mother unwittingly take the baby more and more believing this will help her.

> *Sometimes we can feel so depressed that we need others to help care for the baby. It is important to have times of physical closeness to our baby when possible to help bonding.*

We will look at a number of ways of increasing the bond between ourselves and our baby later in the book, but proximity to our baby is key. Even if we are depressed and not up to the day-to-day care of our baby it is important to keep as much contact between us as we are able to manage. This might mean initially just watching our baby play without physical contact, if physical contact feels too difficult. Proximity can be increased over time as both mother and baby feel more comfortable within each other's company. This stimulates the production of oxytocin in response to each other, which promotes feelings of warmth and connection and so keeps the bond going.

As oxytocin levels rise, this can help to lift the depression, which is one of the reasons why breast-feeding can help with postnatal depression. (Breast-feeding that isn't going well may not be helpful, and this is where help from the midwife, health visitor and specialist infant-feeding advisors – such as those from your local La Leche League (www.laleche. org.uk) or sometimes provided by your local hospital or health visiting service – is so important).

As the depression lifts then feelings of warmth, love and joy return. However, for some the numbness is more specific and may arise in relation to one particular child. There may be strong feelings of warmth and love to, say, the first-born but not to the second-born, or vice versa, and these feelings seem to persist. This is what can be so perturbing. In fact some requests for help have come from women who describe 'falling in love' with their new baby, which has then highlighted to them how little they feel for their first-born. So what might cause this very specific switching off of feelings towards one particular child?

Numbing to cope

First, it is helpful to understand why we numb. Numbing is a normal and adaptive bodily response (although it may not feel very helpful). It is a way of shutting down action in the body when the action is no longer having any effect. So, for example, if a crying baby is left alone in a room it will eventually stop crying. This is partly because crying is a high-energy activity and the body will conserve energy if the behaviour is not working. But also, importantly, if we think about a baby animal crying in the wild, a continual crying will alert other predators, so stopping crying could save its life. This shutting down is an automatic response.

> *We have evolved the ability to become numb. It can serve as a protective mechanism when we feel overwhelmed.*

We can also become numb in situations where we feel very scared but cannot control what scares us. So, for example, if we live in a danger-ous area but cannot move away, we become shut down, or numb, to the fear, and this enables us still to function, albeit in a very tense and hyper-vigilant manner. Likewise with caring for somebody enduring a long and distressing illness. Our body cannot keep operating with high levels of distress so it shuts down to conserve energy and to prevent unsuccessful behaviours. We can then become numb towards that person. This numb-ness doesn't mean we aren't bothered or distressed. Just the opposite; it occurs because of our distress.

> *When we feel safe with others, and with ourselves, we have less need to numb. We can experience a greater sense of safeness when we come to understand and accept why we are struggling.*

Numbing as a safety strategy may become particularly tuned up in us as children if we experience high levels of distress over long periods of time that are not resolved. We may then find ourselves more likely to numb in response to relatively lower levels of distress compared to adults who didn't have such experiences. So, for example, if we find ourselves with a very colicky baby who cries loudly day and night, eventually all of us may find ourselves shutting down our emotions towards our baby. However, for some this numbing or shutting down will happen much more quickly because it has become a more highly developed way of responding to stress.

Numbing can be an automatic response and is not our fault. Once we understand that it is a response to threat rather than some flaw in ourselves, we can then set about trying to identify the threat, and understand what will help us to feel safe. A sense of safety can come just through developing an understanding and acceptance of why our minds are behaving as they do. When we feel safer, this tones down the need for the numbing response. Then we are much better able to turn our attention to our relationship with our baby.

We will look in more detail later in the book at how we respond to threat, what helps us to feel safe, and how to bring warmth and joy into our relationship with our baby. For now we will look at some of the aspects of having a baby that can trigger a numbing response so that we can recognise that it is an understandable response to threat rather than something wrong or deficient in us. We do not always appreciate how certain situations can cause us to feel under threat, or how the mind can react to earlier memories triggered by an apparently innocent situation, without us fully being aware of this.

The message here is that, even though you may not think particular circumstances should be sufficient to cause you distress, should you experience numbness towards your child it may well be because your brain has detected some kind of threat. This can occur even if the source of the threat is initially hard to fathom.

Traumatic experiences

One circumstance that can trigger numbing as a protective process is having a traumatic experience. A 'traumatic experience' is not easy to define. Generally, it refers to powerful emotional experiences, commonly of fear, that seemed overwhelming and often involved a sense of being alone or unprotected. Sometimes feelings of shame can be part of the experience of trauma. It might be an experience where we felt that great harm or even death might come to us or to somebody we care about. Looked at in this way, an experience of trauma with high levels of pain, feelings of being out of control, and fears for one's own safety and/or that of one's baby can, for some women, be part of the actual birth experience. After such an experience we can develop a range of symptoms and difficulties that are sometimes referred to as 'Post-Traumatic Stress Disorder' (PTSD).

When experiences are very overwhelming it can be difficult for us to process them and so they stay in a kind of unintegrated, unprocessed state. If we imagine our mind as a filing cabinet, usually memories get 'filed away' or processed. We can typically pull out or retrieve these memories when we want to – for example, if someone says 'Where did you go on holiday last year?' – but they are not there in our mind on a day-to-day basis.

Overwhelming, traumatic memories are held in a kind of 'to do' file and pop into our mind during the day and perhaps at night in the form of dreams or nightmares. Unlike the 'filed away' or processed memories, these memories are vivid, often with lots of sensory information such as smells and sounds. They can sometimes feel so real it is as if they are happening again in that moment.

'Filed away' or processed memories are 'time and place stamped' so we have a sense of how long ago and where they happened. Unprocessed or overwhelming memories do not have this sense of time and place; hence they can seem to be happening at this moment as intrusions or flashbacks. These intrusions typically come with heightened emotions and arousal such as irritability, anger, anxiety or fear. Because we do not know when these intrusions are going to happen we can live in an increased state of threat, which causes us to feel generally more irritable, angry, tense and apprehensive.

We might also have a sense of numbness. In extreme cases this can be felt as a form of dissociation where we feel as if we are living in a dream or that things around us are unreal. It can also lead us to avoid reminders of the trauma, which, if it was a traumatic childbirth, may include people who ask us about the birth, and even avoidance of our baby. (For more information about trauma and how to deal with it from a compassion point of view see Deborah Lee's book *The Compassionate Mind Approach to Recovering from Trauma* in this series[2]).

It has been found that there may be more women experiencing PTSD than was first realised after particularly traumatic births. What constitutes a traumatic birth is unique to each individual. It is the *perception* of harm coming to ourselves or our baby that is key, even if we later discover there was in fact no danger.

Not surprisingly, people who have had rather traumatic backgrounds may be more sensitive to experiences of trauma. Indeed, particularly for people who have experienced sexual abuse, birth itself, especially where it requires intervention, can trigger unwanted memories. So, when we come to having a baby, as with any event, we also bring to it a history which can help us through or make it much harder for us, through no fault of our own. It is very important then that we take experiences seriously and don't try to blame and shame ourselves if we are struggling.

If you wonder if you may be experiencing any of the symptoms of PTSD then go and see your GP; there are now very effective psychological treatments available specifically for PTSD.

This baby is too much for me

When we are feeling exhausted, low, or feeling overwhelmed by the prospect of looking after a new baby, particularly if we have little in the way of support, we may begin to feel the baby is better off being looked after by someone else. Sometimes this can lead to a turning down, or a shutting off, of our feelings towards the baby.

If we return to considering the process of caring for our offspring from an evolutionary point of view this can offer some potentially helpful insights into why we may shut down from our baby when we feel it is too much for us. You may be familiar with how animals sometimes abandon their offspring. One idea is that we, like many other animals, have evolved mechanisms that motivate us to invest or disinvest time and effort into a particular infant. These processes can be governed by whether or not there are resources and an environment to support them. Systems in our brain can therefore turn on bonding but also turn it off, which allows us to disinvest in a baby if we do not have the resources to care for them. This is very important because of course we find it's not uncommon for bonding problems to arise in mothers who may have little support around them, have financial worries, or even be experiencing domestic violence.[3]

Earlier we looked at how a human baby needs huge resources to keep them alive and flourishing until they are independent. They require the help of others to support the mother. If that support is not there, or the environment is impoverished, or the mother feels too physically or mentally depleted and lacking in help to be able to nurture the baby, then we, like many other animals, may then feel an urge to abandon the baby. This also appears to be more likely if the baby is disfigured in some way or born with a serious illness.

What we do not know in humans is how much this is a conscious, apparently 'rational' decision and how much it is a more reflexive threat response whereby our brain selects a kind of 'don't attach, abandon' set of responses when the costs to the mother and her other offspring of raising this infant with limited support are much too high. Of course this is not to condone the abandonment of infants, but instead to remove the shame from women who are wondering what has happened to their 'maternal instincts', and to make sense of urges to leave the baby on the steps of the local church. It points to solutions, such as responding to our innate need for wide social support, rather than shaming women into hiding away their thoughts, feelings and urges.

We might perhaps think that only early humans abandoned their babies, but it is in fact seen across history and cultures. Abandonment, particularly through exposure, where the baby was left outside in the hope it would be taken in by someone else, was widespread in Roman times and up until the late Middle Ages. Around this time provisions were made in many countries for specific places, such as a hospital, where babies could be left and provided with care.

> *The reasons why we may struggle to feel bonded to our baby are many. However, they are rarely due to a conscious choice not to bond. Often it is due to factors in our current environment or from our past. It can also be caused by postnatal depression.*

In modern times we still struggle with these age-old dilemmas. We offer terminations of pregnancy, place children up for fostering and adoption, and give children to other family members to bring up; sadly, also, child abuse and neglect are still prevalent. In many countries (including a number of European countries, Japan, China and the United States), provision is currently made, by providing a glass incubator with a mattress in it in the walls of some hospitals, for women to give up a new baby anonymously.

In about half the cases where mothers of abandoned babies were identified, key factors in the decision to abandon the baby were that the mothers were under twenty years of age, and/or had given birth a number of times in quick succession, and/or had a lack of support. A key factor, particularly in countries with limited welfare provision, was poverty. It is not clear, however, whether the decision to give up the baby was instigated by the mother or her partner.

The point about this is to help us understand that some of our feelings towards babies may be regulated by 'rational decisions', but we may also be at the mercy of quite ancient evolutionary mechanisms that we share with other animals. Although it can be painful to realise that our brains can turn off bonding systems, it's important to recognise that it's through no fault of our own that this can happen.

It's not just a lack of resources or fears about being able to care for a baby that can turn off one's bonding systems. Indeed, many women who are fully supported and resourced can still feel numb and disconnected. An often-voiced expression of shame is that the baby was planned and wanted, and is well loved by their partner, other family members and even friends, but the mother herself cannot feel anything at all for her baby.

We may never know what has caused this for a particular woman, but what emerges again and again is that women do not wake up one morning and choose to feel nothing for their child. It usually causes worry, shame, a quest to try to 'switch on' the feelings, and a motivation to try and protect the child from ever knowing this state of affairs. But once we reduce the feelings of shame and fear that create an urge to hide away or react with panic, we can approach the struggle compassionately, seeking to understand the nature of our difficulty sensitively and without passing judgement. From there we can consider what might help, such as allowing time to be a healer, reaching out for support and help where we can find it, talking to the health visitor or our doctor in an open way, and joining support groups, perhaps on the internet such as through Netmums (www.netmums.com).

Shame always closes us down to seeking help, so as we reduce it we open up the possibility of reaching out for the support we need.

I am not sure I like my baby

So what else could be causing this shutdown in feelings? As we have seen, there are the 'here and now' circumstances of the birth itself, such as a traumatic birth, or interventions that may initially disrupt or slow the bonding process, such as a caesarean delivery or the use of some forms of pain relief such as pethidine. We have also looked at how a lack of social support, and depression, can tone down our ability to bond with our baby. In addition, we bring to the relationship our particular genetic makeup and temperament, and also the experiences we have had through life which have shaped our biology and strategies and instinctive responses to other people.

Let's consider genetics, and particularly temperament. We are born with particular tendencies that govern how we interact with the world. So some people may be naturally shy, cautious, need time to assess a situation before responding, and be very sensitive to changes. Others are more outgoing, confident, wanting to explore, and can manage change while staying 'on an even keel'. These tendencies appear to be genetic and are reasonably stable throughout life although we now know that even our genes can be changed to some extent by deliberately toning up or down particular characteristics of ourselves, and also through the parenting and environment in which we develop. This is called 'epigenetics', where our experiences and our environment actually switch on or off certain genes.

When we have children we can find that each of them has their own very different disposition or temperament. These may fit well with our own temperament, or might not fit at all. Some mothers have described how one child seems like their 'sunny' child who 'lights them up' when they are around, and the other their 'cloudy' child with whom they feel irritation or disconnection for reasons that might not be particularly clear.

This 'lack of fit' between a parent and child is actually a very common experience. It has been researched over the years, with figures ranging from 30 to 65 per cent of mothers saying that they preferred one child over another.[4] Some researchers have argued that it may well be universal; that a difference in preference is inevitable. We may try to love and care for all our children equally but we may find it easier to like one child compared to another. In fact, we can like some aspects of our children and not other aspects, and can move in and out of particular feelings for our children throughout their lives, and even throughout the day, as indeed our children will do with us. The key is to remember that love is complicated and means very different things in different contexts – and when it comes to parental love it is not the same as liking our children.

Sometimes we can have a sense of similarity to our children and feel close to them but sometimes our children seem very different from us; they like different things and have different values so naturally we feel less close. Some children we might find easy to talk to and others more difficult; one child may have an easy temperament, another be moody. This is just the way it is. We may not like how our child looks, be reminded of bits of ourselves or others that we intensely dislike, or be disappointed that we have a boy when we so wanted a girl, or vice versa.

As we will see throughout this book, we bring compassion to ourselves by first being honest about our feelings and then recognising why they are not our fault but that we want to deal with them honestly and compassionately. We need to understand and appreciate our own disappointment and emotional struggles; perhaps our own grief for the child we wanted but didn't have, our own guilt at not being able to feel love for this baby, our anger towards this baby because she or he has taken the place of the one we wanted. We understand that we really didn't want or choose to feel this way and it is not because we are bad or wrong, but because we are experiencing painful feelings that are entirely understandable.

Once we understand some of the biological, evolutionary, social and personal historical reasons for what is happening to us we can stand back without blaming ourselves, and seek instead to do what we can to help the situation. This includes taking a position of understanding, acceptance and kindness towards ourselves, which can then move us from threat and fear to feeling held, safe and soothed.

> *We find it easier to think more broadly, and to come up with creative solutions when we feel safe and soothed, rather than when we are in threat.*
>
> *Try the exercises in Chapter 14 ('Preparing the compassionate mind: Activating the soothing system') to experiment with the impact that a changing physiological state has on our thinking.*

As we will see, when we can make the shift from shaming and blaming to viewing ourselves with kindness and understanding, we have *physically* moved from one bodily state to another. When we do this our mind is able to look out into the world in a different way; it no longer homes in on threat, but has a wider, more open perspective.

Now we are better able to see our baby not just as a source of threat and pain, which triggers our numbing response or turns down our positive feelings, but as somebody with whom we might in the future want to develop a caring relationship. Cultivating compassion provides us with a strength and determination to find a way through the difficult feelings that can inevitably crop up along the way.

I feel anger and resentment towards my baby

We can idealise mothers as 'Madonnas' who are unfailingly loving and giving towards their baby. In reality of course a mother is still a person in her own right who will continue to experience the full range of emotions including anger, frustration, rage and resentment. It is normal to experience a mixture of emotions towards one's baby. This is often referred to as 'maternal ambivalence'.[5, 6] The difficulty arises when we seem to be 'stuck' in a difficult emotion and it is beginning to affect our relationship with our baby. Here it can really help to talk about these feelings, with other mothers, with the health visitor or with a counsellor or therapist.

There are many factors that may contribute to feelings of anger and resentment towards one's baby, including circumstances where the baby was unplanned, where either parent was not fully behind the decision to have a baby, where the pregnancy was difficult, the birth frightening, or where the early days of new motherhood were exhausting and overwhelming or marked by mental or physical illness. We may feel furious at our baby for bringing such harm or disarray to us, our lives and our relationships: 'If you hadn't come along everything would be all right.'

Sometimes our baby becomes the focus of rage, which is really at ourselves or others. One woman explained:

I realise that I put all my anger onto him [her baby] because it seemed clear at the time that it was since I got pregnant with him that I have felt so trapped. But actually now I realise I am furious with myself for being so stupid and getting pregnant. I feel like I have messed everything up, not just for now but forever.

This quote also hints at what might drive our anger and rage; often real fear that we might not be good enough, that we are not 'up to the job' of mothering, that we might harm or not be able to protect our baby, that we have taken a decision that might in some way harm ourselves (for example by making us ill, exhausted, anxious or depressed) or harm relationships that are important to us. Having a new baby can sometimes feel utterly overwhelming.

Often behind anger and rage there is also sadness and grief; at doors that now seem shut, at lives we are no longer leading, at the sense of ourselves that we seem to have lost, at relationships that have changed, and even at memories of past relationships that have been triggered off again by this baby.

Sometimes the resentment is because we feel so needy and we see that our baby is using up the care that we are so desperate for ourselves. We can feel jealous, as if they are our rival, but also there can be a deep panic that without the care we need we will not manage or, indeed, survive. These feelings might arise from experiences when we were young when perhaps care was scarce, or when there was a sense that love was finite and could 'run out', or could be taken away and given to somebody who was considered to need it more. Or they may occur because circumstances around the baby mean we are more needy than usual, or because existing illnesses mean we may need care, but the people who would usually support us transfer their support to the baby. Even if we feel well-resourced and cared for, just the realisation that our needs will now take second place to those of our baby can be very difficult to come to terms with.

These feelings of rage and anger can be very scary indeed, particularly when we see their strength in relation to the powerlessness and vulnerability of our baby. The key here is to bring understanding rather than shame to ourselves. We can fear that if we don't beat our rage down with the stick of shame we might do some serious harm, but it is actually understanding, warmth and compassion that bring down our rage.

I am scared to love my baby

We can also numb or disconnect when allowing ourselves to love our child involves high stakes. If we have had an experience of the fragility of life and lost somebody we loved, for example, perhaps a parent, grandparent, sibling or a previous baby, through miscarriage, stillbirth or death at an older age, then letting ourselves love our baby can feel very scary indeed. We may have had a termination of pregnancy earlier in our life and feel guilt, and grief, and pain as this baby becomes full of life. Perhaps we have had experiences of loving people who then left us. Or perhaps the very existence of this baby has had such a fragile start, maybe through IVF treatment, or a difficult pregnancy and birth, that it is difficult to believe they are really here, and here to stay. Finally having a baby in our arms, who has been desperately longed for, can provoke a response of numbing ourselves or shutting down our feelings. It is as if one's breath is being held for fear of causing such pain again, should we allow in love for our baby and then lose them.

> With sadness and grief, as with any other emotion, we don't have to 'open the floodgates' completely. Instead we can 'thaw' gently, experiencing our emotions a little at a time.

Once again we see that numbing, disconnecting or turning down positive feelings is the mind's way of responding to threat. Here the threat is of loss and the fear that we will not be able to bear the pain of such loss. The way through is by taking it slowly, step by step, allowing ourselves to gently 'thaw' over time, while treating ourselves with compassion rather than shaming and blaming ourselves. (Russell Kolts used this analogy in his work using compassion-focused therapy (CFT) with people struggling with their anger; see his book *The Compassionate Mind Approach to Managing Your Anger*, Robinson, 2012, for further details of his work. He had noticed instructions on a packet of frozen prawns warning that they should be thawed slowly, as trying to speed up the process could lead to the prawns losing their shape. He felt it applied to us too!)

> *Bringing understanding rather than shame to ourselves is key in managing our anger.*

I feel like I am just an object to my baby

Many parents find the first six weeks or so with their baby particularly hard, especially if there is little support. This is not just because of the chronic lack of sleep and high physical demands of looking after such a helpless and dependent being, but also because there is very little feedback for all this effort. Parents often express something to the effect: 'I know I shouldn't expect a reward and should do it because I love them and they need me, but I am finding getting nothing back really hard.'

The reason we find this hard actually makes a lot of sense when we look at the particular makeup of humans. We have a whole system within our brain and body which is designed to calm us down when we feel safe. What primarily makes us feel safe is social feedback, which we pick up from the eyes, voice tone and head movements of other people. The quickest and most powerful form of social feedback to make us feel safe is a genuine smile that incorporates the muscles around the eyes causing them to 'crinkle up'. We also respond to a kind, warm voice tone.

Unfortunately, this social response system takes a long time to develop in a baby, and although our baby responds to our face and voice, they cannot smile until about six weeks. Until this time, the social signals that we rely on to tell us we are on the right track, and which make us feel good and want to carry on doing what we are doing, are not there in our baby.

> *Mothers need 'feeding', both physically and socially, particularly when their baby is young.*

What can make this lack of positive feedback even harder is when the baby feeds and feeds. Many mothers, particularly breast-feeding mothers, describe feeling like 'nothing but a feeding machine'. The relationship is stripped back to a very primitive, animal-like state of providing food and safety, while the whole social aspect of being human is largely absent.

It can be very difficult to get through this stage and this is where the mother needs to be 'fed' by others around her, not just in terms of good food and care for her, but with social responses too. The smiles, the re-assurance, the affirmation from others, are particularly important during the early weeks when there are few positive social signals coming from the baby.

Joan Raphael-Leff, a psychotherapist who has worked for many years with new mothers, identified differences in parenting styles that can also impact on how we experience parenting our baby. She noted two particu-lar styles, which she called 'Facilitators' and 'Regulators'.[7] Facilitators allow themselves to be guided by their baby whereas regulators prefer to be more organised and in control, setting up a routine for their baby, for example. Most of us are a mix of both, but for some of us, particular periods during the journey of motherhood, such as the early days, can be especially testing. We can feel like we have lost our identity and have become mere objects to a baby. We may crave adult company and the time and space to be able to do whatever used to make us feel 'ourselves'.

This time is often difficult for most parents, but it is even more so for those who have had previous experiences, perhaps as children, where they were treated more as objects than as discrete individuals with their own mind and needs. Uncomfortable feelings of rage and fear from such past experiences can be triggered off, usually without us realising it, because the mind has registered similarities between the current and the past situation. If we had to shut down these feelings in the past to protect ourselves (particularly where rage in a child would be met by even greater rage from a parent) then we might find ourselves automatically shutting down now. This is because our rage at being treated like an object (this time by the baby) has been conditioned to trigger an automatic anxiety in us, which can lead us in turn to automatically numb our feelings in order to protect ourselves and others.

Usually, this passes when the baby begins to smile at us. But we need to hold in mind that we may sometimes find it hard to provide a great deal of care with very little feedback. This is not our fault. It is an indication that we need to give ourselves particular support and kindness during such times; to experience our rage without acting it out and without shaming ourselves for it, instead bringing a wise understanding and reaching out to others for help if we can.

Summary

- Although giving birth can be a joyous occasion, what we are addressing here is the fact that many women have rather different experiences that may involve fear, anxiety, sadness, anger, problems of bonding with her baby, or a sense of numbness. By understanding some of the many influences that affect how we feel, we begin to see that these are indeed very sad and tragic experiences but that they are not our fault – we certainly don't choose to feel this way.

- Compassion means that we turn towards our suffering and try to understand it as honestly and openly as we can. When we do this we see that the human mind is very difficult because of the way it has evolved and that, as a consequence, many of our feelings can get turned on and off, or up and down, by all kinds of situations. So, for example, we've seen that there are evolved mechanisms that can interfere with our ability to bond and feel connected to our baby and these in turn can be linked to our experiences, our social environment, and the amount of support and care there is for us.

- In addition, our feelings can be linked to our own personal histories of being parented when we were children. Sometimes, for example, we can be fearful of loving our baby because of the fear of losing them, or we can be fearful that we will not be good enough mothers. The key thing is that, whatever our feelings, they are understandable and do not mark us out as some abnormal or bad mother. Rather, we share these feelings with many millions of other women around the world and the more open we can be about them, the more able we are to reach out and talk about them to our health visitor, GP, internet support forums, friends or family. Compassion is all about being honest about how we feel and then doing what we can to address it – which can include reaching out to sources of help.

4 Understanding postnatal depression

Myths around postnatal depression

Earlier in the book we saw that we can experience a whole range of emotional difficulties. Sometimes these difficulties can become intense and cluster around loss of positive feelings and depression. The term and the concept of postnatal depression is becoming more widely known and consequently it is now easier (though sometimes not easy) to seek and receive help. However, there are some myths surrounding postnatal depression that may cause hesitation in asking for help. In this chapter we are going to explore some of these myths. (For more information about postnatal mental health difficulties, go to the excellent Royal College of Psychiatry website: www.rcpsych.ac.uk/healthadvice/problemsdis orders.aspx).

Myth one: Postnatal depression only develops once the baby is born

In fact in about a third to a half of women the beginning of what is regarded as postnatal depression starts in pregnancy[1, 2] (particularly in the final three months) with symptoms such as low mood, irritability, tearfulness, feelings of hopelessness, and anxiety.

Myth two: Postnatal depression is characterised by tearfulness, low mood, and lack of motivation

That can be one presentation, but depression is also closely related to anxiety and irritability and they commonly occur together. We may therefore find our predominant experiences are of feeling restless, irritable, worried and angry. Another common emotion is detachment; of feeling things to be slightly unreal, including feeling that we can't really make a connection to our baby.

Sometimes though, rather than feeling detached we may want to hang on and cling to a baby more, perhaps for comfort or a feeling of being loved, perhaps through a fear of losing the baby, somehow, or of the baby coming to love another person more. We may feel we want to give our baby away, not because we are detached from it, but because we feel so inadequate and desperately want the baby to be loved and looked after by somebody we believe is better than we are.

We will be looking at some of the typical experiences of postnatal depression below but the point here is that depression takes many forms; for some of feelings of tearfulness and inadequacy, for others of loss of energy, while for others it may be marked more by fear, anxiety and anger.

Myth three: Postnatal depression can arise 'out of the blue' once a woman has given birth (the difference between postnatal depression and postpartum psychosis)

In a small minority of cases women can become severely unwell in the days or weeks after giving birth with a postnatal illness called postpartum or puerperal psychosis. This is different from postnatal depression and is very rare (occurring in one in every thousand women as opposed to ten to fifteen in every hundred women who experience postnatal depression[3]). There appears to be a genetic link to postpartum psychosis and so a woman may be at greater risk of it if a close female relative such as her mother or sister experienced severe mental illness, such as psychosis, bipolar disorder (manic depression) or psychotic depression, arising shortly after giving birth.

It is not known what triggers postpartum psychosis and it can seem to come 'out of the blue'. For those at genetic risk it may be triggered by severe lack of sleep and/or by the rapid drop in hormones that occurs in the days following birth. There is also an increased risk for those who have had previous experiences of postpartum psychosis, bipolar disorder or schizophrenia (so the GP and midwife should be informed of these, preferably before you become pregnant, and even if you feel well, so that you can be monitored and given any necessary help by the appropriate services).

Symptoms include mania – where there are racing thoughts, difficulty sleeping, restlessness and agitation – but also depression – where you become very withdrawn and don't want to see anybody. There may also be delusions – where you believe things that aren't true, for example that you have won the Lottery, or that your baby is the devil. You may hallucinate, seeing or hearing things that aren't there. You might also experience rapid changes in mood.

Postpartum psychosis is considered a 'psychiatric emergency' because it is difficult for a woman to look after herself and her baby safely when she is experiencing this. It means that medical help needs to be sought immediately (the same day, through your GP or Accident and Emergency department) and in most areas in the UK a woman can be admitted to a specialist psychiatric unit, called a Mother and Baby Unit, with her baby (for more on this, see the 'Treatment' section below). Despite this being such a severe illness, it responds well to treatment with medication.

Unlike postpartum psychosis, postnatal depression for many women arises in the context of her current and past experiences rather than being a 'disease' that has come upon her for no reason. There may be some genetic risk of postnatal depression, but this is still unclear. Rather than coming 'out of the blue', there are usually indicators that a woman may be at risk of postnatal depression. Risk factors include: previous episodes of depression, depression during pregnancy, relationship difficulties, financial worries and lack of support.

Myth four: Postnatal depression is just 'the blues' and will pass of its own accord in a few days

It is very common for new mothers to experience a transient dip in mood, or mood swings, roughly three to four days after giving birth, this being caused by the dramatic drop in the hormones progesterone and oestrogen, responsible for maintaining the pregnancy. You may feel tearful, irritable, low and anxious at times. This can pass by the time your baby is about ten days old and does not need further help. If these feelings persist for more than two weeks and don't seem to be helped by getting sleep, rest, recuperation time, sunlight, good food, gentle exercise such as gentle walking, and social support from family, friends and a health visitor, then make contact with your health visitor, health visiting service or GP. They can check whether or not you have postnatal depression.

What are the symptoms of postnatal depression?

So let's have a look at how postnatal depression actually manifests itself. It affects about ten to fifteen in every hundred women who have had a baby, although rates may actually be much higher. The symptoms are similar to depression that occurs at other times. These symptoms, which can vary from mild to severe, can include:

- Feeling low and tearful most or all of the time. This may be worse at particular times, such as the morning or evening.

- Irritability or anger towards your family, baby and/or yourself.

- Tiredness and a reduction of energy and motivation (new mothers are usually tired but postnatal depression can cause this to be more extreme).

- Loss of enjoyment or interest in aspects of your life that you usually take pleasure in. This may include an inability to enjoy your baby.

- Difficulty in falling asleep despite feeling tired, or waking early in the morning even when the baby is asleep.

- Losing your appetite or starting to eat more in an attempt to make yourself feel better.

- Negative thoughts and feelings of guilt; you may find yourself thinking negatively about yourself and those around you, such as thinking that you are a bad mother or that your baby does not love you.

- Anxiety. You may worry that you cannot cope, or that you will inadvertently harm, or be unable to protect, your baby. You may worry that there is something wrong with your baby or with you, and that you will never get better.

- Suicidal thoughts. You may have a sense of hopelessness and believe that your family and baby would be better off without you. Discuss these thoughts with your GP or health visitor. If you have a strong urge to harm yourself then contact your GP, out-of-hours GP service or NHS 111 (dial 111), or call your local Accident and Emergency department, which is open twenty-four hours a day.

Treatment

With all treatments it is very important that you stay sensitive to what helps you. Some women find medication can be very helpful, but others can experience unwanted side effects. Your GP can discuss with you which medications can be taken during pregnancy and while breast-feeding, and if they don't suit you then discuss this with your GP to find out about alternatives. Talking therapies are also helpful, either with or without medication.

Many areas have a local perinatal mental health team for women who are experiencing severe mental health difficulties in the late stages of pregnancy or up until one year after having their baby (exact criteria will vary from service to service). Your GP can refer you to such a service. In some areas your midwife or health visitor can also refer you.

You should also be referred for assessment if you are well but have experienced a previous severe mental illness, particularly if this occurred around the time of a previous pregnancy.

If you become so unwell that you no longer feel you can care for yourself or your baby at home with the support of your family and your health visitor, your GP may recommend that you are admitted to a Mother and Baby Unit. These are small specialist units where a mother can go with her baby. Here the mother is treated by a team specialising in the treatment of mental illnesses that occur in pregnancy and shortly after childbirth. The mother is given as much or as little support as she needs in caring for her baby while she recovers.

Do women with postnatal depression harm their baby?

This is a common fear but its occurrence is extremely rare. Many new mothers and fathers may at times feel so tired and frustrated that they feel like hitting or shaking their baby. Very few act on this. If you do feel you could harm your baby then tell your GP or health visitor, who can help you, or who can refer you to services that can help. Don't let shame, or maybe fear that your baby will be taken away (see below) or that you will come under scrutiny, stop you from doing this. These fears are common and understandable (see below), but these kinds of problems, associated with depression and other mental health difficulties, are well recognised now and the services are there to be helpful to you and your baby.

Will my baby be taken away from me?

This is an extremely common fear and can be a real barrier to seeking help. Postnatal depression is understood by GPs and health visitors as temporary and treatable. Rather than them taking the baby away, it is now seen as important to keep the mother with her baby as much as possible, which is why Mother and Baby Units have been developed around the country. It can, however, be difficult to care for yourself and your baby while you are depressed, so you may need extra support during this time. Family support can be crucial. Lack of available support is one of the most significant factors thought to contribute to postnatal depression. When you feel depressed it can sometimes feel particularly hard to ask for help. If you do not have this, it is important to tell your GP and health visitor. They can put you in touch with organisations, such as Homestart, which can help, and they can also increase their own involvement with you.

How might postnatal depression affect how I feel about my baby?

Postnatal depression may affect your relationship with your baby in different ways:

- You may or may not feel love or affection for your baby as much as you hoped.

- You may find it hard to understand the needs of your baby.

- Caring for your baby may feel effortful and joyless.

- You may feel angry and resentful of your baby.

- You may blame your baby for your postnatal depression.

- There may be little or no impact from postnatal depression on your relationship with your baby.

- In fact you may find that your baby is a positive factor in your life. Many women say that the routine and physical contact of caring for their baby helped them through their depression.

Once women feel less depressed they often find their relationship with their baby improves. This used to be assumed to always be the case.

Treatment was focused solely on the mother and was stopped once the mother felt better. However, it is now understood that a substantial proportion of women still struggle with their relationship with their baby even once the postnatal depression has lifted. Because they are given the message that all should be well now, they can feel ashamed that they are still experiencing difficulties with their baby. This is becoming more recognised by services, and there are increasing numbers of groups, and interventions such as baby massage and so on, that focus on the mother and baby relationship.

The relationship between postnatal depression and difficulties with baby bonding are still not fully understood; either may cause the other, they may arise irrespective of the other, as one improves the other may improve, or one may improve without having an impact on the other. This is why this book focuses on the compassionate mind approach to both postnatal depression and baby-bonding difficulties; they can be intertwined, but may also need a separate and specific focus to help alleviate them.

Social support and postnatal depression

As we have considered earlier, research has repeatedly found that one of the key contributing factors to postnatal depression is lack of social support, particularly from our partner or close family. This makes sense when we think of how, for almost the entire history of human beings, we have lived in social groups where a baby and new mother would be cared for by the extended family and social group. Earlier in this book we referred to how Sarah Blaffer-Hrdy, in her ground-breaking book *Mothers and Others*,[4] notes that we are unique among the great apes in sharing care of our offspring. She argues that this may be one of the reasons for our evolutionary success; we could reproduce much more quickly once others were able to help us feed, carry and protect our young. However, in Western societies, mothers often care for their offspring and themselves completely on their own for long periods of the day. As we shall explore later, our minds are not designed for such isolation. An important step in moving out of depression, or preventing it from taking a severe hold, is therefore to seek out support; from our GP, health visitor, relatives and friends, networks of new mothers at groups, and on the internet (sites such as 'Netmums' and 'Mumsnet').

Self-compassion helps us to reach out whilst depressed.

Reaching out for help and connecting with others is an important part of the 'treatment' of depression.

As we will see in this book, this seeking out of support is a 'treatment' for postnatal depression in itself. However, the very nature of depression is to take us out of social contact. So reaching out to others is directly going against what our depression is driving us to do. It therefore requires the mustering of a great deal of understanding, tenderness and strength to reach for the telephone or step outside the front door. This is our self-compassion.

Having frightening thoughts

If we stop for a moment and just attend to and notice our thoughts we may become aware of, first, just how many thoughts we have. In fact the human mind is often awash with all sorts of thoughts and fantasies, some of which we choose but others which are simply intrusions. Second, our thoughts are often focused on something we are planning or wanting to do, or on something that is bothering us. Third, usually this concern is about the past, or the future, rather than the present moment. Later we will explore how we can become mindfully aware of this but not overly engage with the hustle and bustle of our mind.

For the moment, though, we can notice that most of these thoughts just come and go and we do not think anything more about them. However, some of our thoughts can surprise or even shock us. Examples of such thoughts include imagining not stopping our car at a zebra crossing and running somebody over, or pushing somebody in a river while they are looking in the water. These thoughts pop into our mind for many reasons and are normal for both adults and children.

There is an excellent book about this called *The Imp of the Mind: Exploring the Silent Epidemic of Obsessive Bad Thoughts*, written by Lee Baer and published in 2002. It is written for people who have obsessional sorts of difficulties and worry about the kinds of thoughts they have. However, it's also very useful for mothers who are having thoughts that they find difficult to understand or that upset or alarm them. Once again, it helps us to recognise that these experiences are not at all uncommon.

Worrying thoughts and intrusions may often occur when we become aware not just of our own vulnerability to being harmed but also of our power and ability to harm others. We will look later in the book at how we have evolved as social animals and the degree to which we have developed a highly imaginative mind. This means we have the capacity to play out the consequences of our actions on others over and over again. We can create some horrifying scenarios. Indeed, people make a lot of money out of this capacity by writing films and books of extra-ordinary violence and cruelty, which sell in their millions because people are drawn to them by a morbid fascination.

Such intrusive thoughts can increase during pregnancy and after child-birth, often focused around harm coming to our baby. The thoughts might be about harm caused by ourselves or others. These thoughts can take the form of 'what ifs . . .' such as 'What if I pushed the baby's head under the water while I bathed them?' or 'What if I dropped this chopping knife on the baby?' or 'What if I sexually abuse my baby while changing their nappy?' These thoughts are incredibly distressing and can be a source of horror and shame if we mistakenly believe that they come from some dark and evil intent within us. The important question here is *'What is my motivation or intention towards my baby?'* Is our intention to harm the baby, or is it to go through scenarios in our mind to make sure we *prevent* harm coming to the baby?

When we look at the intention behind these intrusive thoughts we see that they are in fact driven by the brain's increased motivation to protect our baby, by our increased sense of responsibility once we become pregnant or become a new mother, and by our realisation of the potential harm that could come to such a vulnerable being. (See *Dropping the Baby and Other Scary Thoughts: Breaking the Cycle of Unwanted Thoughts in Motherhood*, written by Karen Kleiman and Amy Wenzel (2011), for a fascinating book which specifically addresses these intrusive thoughts).

The idea is to understand these thoughts as normal (albeit distressing) thoughts, which we can let come and go, just as we do all of the hundreds of other thoughts that pass through our mind. If we pick out particular thoughts for special attention then we reinforce them and make them stronger in our mind. Some of the techniques that we will look at later, particularly the skills of mindfulness, can be incredibly powerful in helping us to allow distressing thoughts to come and go while bringing kindness and support to ourselves through compassion.

> *Mindful compassion (noticing thoughts with kindness and understanding, and then letting them pass), rather than shame, reduces distressing thoughts.*

If you feel that actually you do have a strong sense of *wanting* or *intending* to hurt yourself or your baby, for example where you feel so low that this seems the only solution, then it is vital that you seek help immediately by contacting your GP, GP out-of-hours service, the NHS on 111 (available twenty-four hours a day, every day of the year) or your local Accident and Emergency department. It is surprisingly common for women to reach these depths and we see many women in our Mother and Baby Unit who feel this way. Thankfully, as much as it may feel at the time like a permanent and inescapably awful state, with help, support, listening and perhaps medication, it does in fact pass.

Summary

We've seen that there are a lot of myths about postnatal depression. While baby blues are relatively common, postnatal depression is not so common, but when considering how it may present, it is more prevalent than many realise. However, the very severe forms are actually quite rare. All depression should be taken seriously, especially if it lasts longer than ten days to two weeks. It is well recognised medically now and there are many ways to help.

One of the core issues is that when mothers begin to experience feelings outside of the supposed 'joyful norm' they can become frightened and ashamed of what is going on inside them, whereas in actual fact the experiences are sadly painful but common. Depression itself by its nature takes us out of social contact, but when we feel shame, too, then it can be very hard indeed to reach out for support and to find that others share our experiences. Yet support is a key 'treatment' for depression. This is why developing self-compassion is so important; it is what helps us to develop ways to help and support ourselves rather than shaming ourselves when we are struggling, it enables us to feel worthy of reaching out to others, and it supports us when we find this difficult.

5 How we are shaped: The foundations of the compassionate mind approach

We might think that after all of these millions of years of evolution our brain must have reached perfection. Although the brain is indeed amazing, through the nature of evolution it has actually developed in a way in which it can end up creating real problems for us.[1] When we have difficulties with certain kinds of emotions such as anxiety or anger, have difficult intrusive thoughts and ideas, or feel disconnected from others such as our baby, we can believe that we shouldn't be feeling these things. Rather than seeing them as unfortunate, sad and tragic ways that our mind can respond to certain situations, we think they indicate that there is something wrong, broken or bad about us. This can lead to a sense of shame and blame, and a belief that if others saw these 'flaws' within us they would become equally judgemental and as a result wouldn't want to know us. This is very common, and when people consider being more compassionate to themselves one of the initial struggles is often with that inner nagging voice telling them: 'Yes, but if you really knew what went on in my head you wouldn't think that I deserve compassion.'

While the fact is that things go on in our heads that can be pretty difficult and indeed unpleasant – just look at the way humans have treated other humans throughout history – it is very unlikely that anything in our head hasn't been in the heads of millions of others throughout history. We feel the way we feel because of the way our brains have evolved and the way the nature of life has shaped our brains.

By understanding how our minds have evolved and how they have developed throughout our lives we can see that actually these struggles are shared by other human beings; that what we thought disconnected us actually connects us.

Finding ourselves here in the flow of life

If we could watch a speeded-up recording of the life on our planet, from its beginning, millions of years ago as single cells floating about in the sea – then, after an exceedingly long time, to fish, then reptiles, then mammals, and then more specifically humans, and then to the present day – we would see the gradual unfolding process of the flow of life. Different species emerge and change slowly. So, for example, we share a common ancestor with chimpanzees dating back six million years ago, and even with turtles, going back to five hundred million years.

Evolution is a process of gradual change while maintaining some of what has gone before. Our brains and our bodies have been designed in the evolutionary flow to function in certain ways. Like many other animals, we have four limbs, we reproduce, we eat and we defecate. We have brains designed to pursue certain things such as food, safety and finding a mate. Our brains are also designed to become anxious when threatened, and angry when thwarted. Like many other animals, we are also motivated to care for babies – but also, as we will see, like in many other animals these evolved systems don't always work in quite the way we would hope.

We also know that each life form, be it a plant, an animal or a human, blinks into existence, grows, flourishes for a while and then gradually decays and disappears. In its short time of existence (in the case of humans, our lives are only about 25,000 to 30,000 days long) each life, as noted above, has very similar goals, which have been refined through evolution; basically to feed, stay safe and reproduce. No life chooses to come into existence and neither does it choose the circumstances in which it appears. Cats don't choose to be cats, zebras don't choose to be zebras, no human chose to be a human – and no human chose to be male or female with a particular set of genes.

> *We can end up blaming ourselves for aspects of who we are which have been developed through evolution, and are not our fault at all.*

So we, like other living things, have just 'come into existence' in this flow of life with genes that build our physical forms and make possible certain motives and emotions. These have been shaped for us by evolution. We don't choose them, and as well as serving important functions they can cause us real difficulties, as we will see. They also profoundly affect our sense of ourselves.

In other words we have inherited a brain and body that has primarily been built by evolution rather than by us. However, we can come to believe that the side effects or unintended consequences of how we have evolved are somehow our fault when in fact they are not our fault at all.

Socially made self

If we think about ourselves and our lives, we didn't choose the part of history, the part of the world or the social structure into which we arrived. We could have appeared as early humans living on the savannah, into a very poor family during the Middle Ages, into an incredibly wealthy family during modern times, or into a violent drug gang. Though we don't choose the circumstances and social conditions in which our existence will be shaped they will have a profound effect on the person we become. Nor do we choose which gender we are, whether we are first born or last born, how we are parented or what our mother ate during pregnancy, but these, along with many other factors, will all shape us without us having any choice in this at all. The person we are now is just one of the many possible selves that we could have become; and this was not of our choosing and not our fault.

So we can do a sort of experiment here. Imagine that I was born to a loving family but while I was in hospital as a three-day-old baby I was kidnapped by a violent drug gang and brought up in that environment. What kind of Michelle Cree do you think would exist today? If we think about that for a moment we can imagine that the Michelle Cree who is a psychologist writing this book would be very unlikely to exist. But what version would exist? The chances are that it would be a much more aggressive one, who is perhaps less interested in others, and who may have experienced and instigated some awful things.

So the fact of the matter is that we are all only particular versions from many possible versions of ourselves. This is not our fault. As humans we can, however, choose to consider which version we would like to be, and to work towards becoming more like this. This book is about how we go about creating a more self-compassionate version of ourselves.

We now know that our backgrounds can even influence our genes. So, for example, genes that 'mop up' stress hormones after a stressful event appear to be switched on when we are cared for as babies but remain switched off otherwise. This means we are more likely to stay feeling anxious even after a stressful event has passed if we have not had a lot of sensitive and affectionate care as babies. Crucially, it also seems that we can influence this switching on and off of our genes even when we are adults, and this is part of the basis for the 'training' aspect of the compassionate mind approach. A key part, though, is not just how to change ourselves but how to be able to understand and accept the extent to which we have been shaped without choosing this at all.

This understanding is important because so many people with psychological and emotional difficulties have a real sense of personal blaming and shaming, when in actual fact so much of what creates our pain – even the versions of ourselves that we become – is outside of our control.

It's easy to misunderstand this issue of reducing blaming and shaming. Even though it is not our fault that we are the way we are, it does fall to us to do what we can to heal and bring compassion to ourselves and indeed to others. So, for example, it might not be our fault if someone knocks into our car while it's parked perfectly appropriately in a car park, but if they drive off it is only us that can get it fixed – it becomes our responsibility to sort it out. It is not our fault if we have inherited a greater risk of heart disease or Type 1 diabetes, but it is our responsibility to maintain the best lifestyle we can, given those increased risks.

So compassion is a way of thinking about the consequences of our behaviour and how we would like to move through life as best we can. On the whole, shaming and blaming rarely helps us, and usually makes our struggles even worse, whereas beginning to understand our pain and difficulties and choosing to treat ourselves with compassion can helps us to live the best lives we can, despite those unchosen difficulties.

> *Our early life experiences shape us into versions of ourselves which, if we had the choice, we may not have chosen.*
>
> *With wisdom, understanding and commitment, we can shape ourselves into more of the version we would choose.*

'Nature's mind'

Sometimes we can see that our minds are not really 'our minds'; they are, if you like, 'nature's minds' because it was nature that designed them. Of course, when we personally feel anger or anxiety, joy or sexual feelings, for example, we think it is 'us' but in reality we are experiencing a mind that nature created. We are experiencing the brain's capacity for generating anger, anxiety, joy and lust. When we look at mindfulness later in the book, we will see that mindfulness is a way of us beginning to observe 'nature's mind'.

All of these insights can really help us when we are struggling with feelings of pain, depression, anxiety and disconnection, because we see that we are experiencing nature's mind up to its 'tricks'. The question then becomes: what can we do to help ourselves when we feel this way (which is what we will be focusing on in this book)?

Normal life is marked by tragedy and suffering

As humans we have the capacity to understand that we will all get old, decay and die, and that we, and people we love, may develop diseases, or be injured or killed. We know that life is impermanent, and constantly changing. Yet we also have minds which prefer predictability, stability and permanence. How often have we heard love songs talk about 'I will love you forever'? Unfortunately, there is no forever, there is only now, and the few years we are here.

Not only do we try to seek permanence but, quite understandably, we are constantly trying to avoid things we don't like and grasping hold of things we do, even though all of these are constantly fluctuating and changing. We feel driven to find a state of constant peace and happiness without any suffering, but these moments constantly change; sometimes there is peace, sometimes there is happiness, sometimes there is sadness, sometimes there is suffering. Even objects, which seem so solid and constant, decay over time. There is nothing that we can freeze in time exactly as it is. This conflict between being driven by our evolved mind to create and then keep hold of a state of happiness, and the awareness that this is impossible, can create great suffering in humans. So how do we deal with this?

Through all of history humans have understood that life often involves suffering and that it is the way in which we deal with that – in particular, how we reach out to each other and help each other on our short journey – that is central. Many religions have ideas about what happens after this life. Historically, there was a belief that suffering in this life means that we were more likely to have a better time in the next. Suffering was therefore embraced to some extent. Now, particularly in some Western cultures, medicine and modern technologies mean that we don't die in pain and of the diseases we used to; from 1348–50 the Black Death reached its peak in Europe and probably killed somewhere in the region of 70 to 200 million people. Up until a hundred or so years ago, many children died before ever reaching adolescence. In some parts of the world, life expectancy is still less than forty years. With advances in medicine, and greater wealth, we are more able to prevent or remedy some causes of suffering. This can have the unintended consequence that we begin to view the inevitable tragedies of life as something that we can control or avoid completely. When tragedy does come, as it inevitably will, sometimes we can view it as our fault in some way: 'What have I done to deserve this?'

Inadvertently, these views of suffering can add to our suffering because we react with panic, anger, resistance or self-blame to the tragedies of life rather than with acceptance that actually they are a normal part of human existence. The question becomes then not so much why these happened to us but how we can find the strength, wisdom and determination needed to help us to get through them. We will of course be driven to do what we can to try to prevent hurtful things happening but when tragedies occur, as they will, compassion means trying to face them with courage, support, kindness and strength rather than get lost in anger, fear, and ruminating about why, and how bad, it is. We will see how the nature of our mind makes shifting out of anger, fear and rumination difficult, and this book focuses on what can help us to do this. The key point here is to understand just why we might want to make this shift.

> *Wanting to avoid suffering is part of human nature. As suffering is part of life, however, sometimes we can't avoid it.*
>
> *Compassion helps us to face and get through even the most turbulent of times.*

Our lives, then, will inevitably be marked by tragedies and difficulties of some kind, which we did not choose, but have to somehow find a way of coping with. Although this thought might seem a bit heavy, such a realisation is in fact the beginning of our compassion; that we suffer, that we all suffer, but that we have not chosen this suffering. However, we can find ways to manage suffering – and sometimes even grow from it.

A confusion that often arises with the compassionate mind approach is that it will enable us to find a state of constant happiness. The problem here is that people start trying to develop compassion as a kind of Valium or happiness pill. The understandable hope is that if we could only do this or that, then we will be happy. Evidence suggests that the pursuit of happiness in itself, while a common one, actually doesn't take us very far. Part of the reason is because we then try to get rid of the things that make us unhappy as opposed to learning to ride them. Sometimes we talk about riding the waves of turmoil in our minds.

So the aim is more about how we can learn to deal with things, as and when they arise. If we were a sailor then learning how to sail when the sea is rough would be an important skill to learn. While it's pleasant to sail on a beautiful calm day we also need to be able to manage the times when the sea turns rough.

Summary

In order to understand ourselves we have to understand where we have come from, what we are made of and why. The only way to answer this is to see ourselves as part of the flow of life along with all other life forms on this planet. Our personal lives come into existence, flourish for a while, and then decay and go out. Along the way we can find many tragedies, but we can also find care, affection and compassion. It's how we cultivate and use these to deal with our own personal difficulties, and indeed those of others, that offers a path to a happier and more settled existence.

So this book aims to provide the context to help us think about our mind in a new way, so that we can stand back from it, become more observant of what is going on in our mind (because really it's what we've called 'nature's mind') and then begin to operate within it in ways that are conducive to well-being.

6 Our brain: A mix of old and new

So, we didn't choose when or where we appeared on this planet, nor many of the experiences that have profoundly shaped us. We arrive into this world with a brain that is shaped by our parents' genes and by the environment within our mother's womb. We know that the human brain evolved from early life forms. Having a little insight into how our brain has been constructed can help us understand why we have some of the problems we do – and why our brain can be so tricky for us. (You can find out more about the evolution of the human brain at http://thegreatstory.org/home.html).

David Sloan Wilson, in his 2007 book *Evolution for Everyone*[1], points out that as humans we need to look back many millions of years to understand our unique attributes as we possess attributes now that we acquired from the great apes, the primates, 600 million years ago from the vertebrates, and even right back one and a half million years ago to the origins of life. He reminds us that we even share with round worms the same gene that controls our appetite!

This evolutionary journey is reflected in the development of our brain. Emerging from our spinal cord into the first part of our brain is an area that evolved with the reptiles and is sometimes called the 'reptilian brain'. This is hard-wired for basic survival and reproduction, so it is concerned with getting food, finding a mate for reproduction, and staying safe by fleeing, freezing or fighting. For the most part, reptiles don't care for their young in any sophisticated way. Although it is the case, for example, that crocodiles can carry their babies gently in their mouths to the water, this care-giving behaviour is short-lived, it not being long before the young crocodiles have to go it alone.

The next major adaptation came with the evolution from cold-blooded reptiles of warm-blooded mammals. The same basic instincts for feeding, reproducing and staying safe were retained but were slightly modified, particularly concerning care for young.

The part of the brain that creates mammalian psychology is sometimes referred to as the *limbic system*. As we are mammals, too, we still have all of the impulses of the reptilian brain, but we also have the motivation to seek closeness rather than distance for protection. One of the central evolutionary developments is this process of being able to care for another. Mammalian mothers have the capacity to be attentive to the needs of their infant and provide food, warmth and closeness. They can also be responsive to distress calls. So, our ability to pay attention to the distress of another and to respond to that distress probably began many millions of years ago with the arrival of mammals that cared for their offspring. And, just like us, the care-giving system in all mammals will be affected by many influences that, in certain contexts, can amplify or reduce these abilities.

As mammals, with mammalian brains, we have offspring who stay close to their mother rather than having to venture out and survive alone soon after they are born. This allows them time to be taught skills rather than just having to rely on instinct, and, as we see from watching bear cubs or baby monkeys on nature programmes, or watching puppies together, it also enables them to play. Play is not just a delight to watch, it is also part of another important function of the mammalian brain – social communication and connection – and it is this ability that is thought to be one of the main reasons for the success of mammals as a species, and humans in particular.

With our instinct for living closely in groups rather than being separate comes many advantages, but it also brings with it a whole new set of problems to be overcome. As humans, we know that living in close proximity can be stressful and complicated. One of the ways of developing some kind of stability in a group is by having status hierarchies. Again, we see this repeatedly played out on nature programmes, with our pets, and of course with us as humans.

Mammals, in comparison to reptiles, have a much more complex way in which status operates. For the most part, reptiles are territorial and if they fight over a resource (which may be food but may also include things like a male or female with which to reproduce) then the losers simply move away. Mammals on the other hand have sophisticated ways of evaluating their relative strength in comparison to others and form what are called status hierarchies. Here, the weak tend to be submissive and non-challenging to the stronger. By having these status hierarchies it means that groups can be reasonably stable and cohesive and not constantly fighting over every resource – in other words, each animal in a group knows their place.

This concern is very much part of our human psychology, too, and so we can also get caught up in comparing ourselves with others and judging ourselves to be superior or inferior. Indeed, we have many ways of comparing ourselves to others, such as whether we are more or less attractive, likeable, important, valued, richer, thinner . . .

We may try not to be so caught up with this, but the instinct to be constantly judging ourselves and others, keep an eye on where we are in the social hierarchy, is very strong indeed; once again, then, being judgemental is something we shouldn't judge ourselves for – it is not our fault.

> *We have evolved to judge, compare and be concerned with where*
> *we are in social hierarchies*

Even motherhood isn't immune from this instinct for social comparison; we can speculate, for example, over how 'good' or 'bad' a mother we and others are. Because being high up in a social hierarchy has, throughout evolution, signalled greater safety and access to better resources, we can experience very strong reactions when we detect we are rising up or dropping down a social hierarchy. This is partly why arguments about 'stay-at-home mothers' versus 'working mothers', or 'breast-feeding' versus 'bottle-feeding mothers', can create such strong feelings. We want to be sure not just that we are doing the very best for our children, but also that we are considered a worthy member of our group by others. If we feel inferior and looked down upon by others, this can be the basis of shame, which signals to us that we are in potential social 'danger'; for many years of our existence as humans, being in danger of being cast out of the group put us at a very serious survival risk, particularly for those who were mothers with a dependent baby. We are therefore hard-wired to pay very close attention to our position in the social hierarchy.

We see this the world over because it is a basic part of how our brains are built. Understanding how we have evolved to judge, to compare, and to experience shame can help us to accept our instincts rather than further shaming and judging ourselves for being at their mercy. This awareness of these natural processes and instincts then enables us to learn a different way of relating to ourselves and others, which we will be learning to cultivate in this book.

As well as giving us the ability to organise ourselves by social hierarchies, the mammalian brain also afforded us another important development, which we draw on in the compassionate mind approach. It is the way in which mammalian evolution gave rise to our ability to be close to each other and in some contexts be calmed by that closeness. With reptiles, closeness usually signalled threat, so with mammals there is a whole physiological system concerned with distinguishing whether a particular type of closeness is threatening or safe, and if it is safe then making it rewarding in some way.

We have evolved to be regulated by the social signals from others.

We are calmed and soothed when we detect safeness in others through physical contact, facial expression and voice tone.

So not only does our mammalian brain enable closeness, but it incorporates a new system within the brain which enables us to feel peaceful and calm when we feel close and safe. Closeness that is assessed to be safe has now become linked to hormones such as oxytocin, which enable us to experience pleasure but which also calm us down and soothe us. So monkeys will groom each other, enabling them to experience closeness as calming in what otherwise could be a stressful group environment. When babies become distressed it is being held close that soothes and calms them. We share this mammalian brain with pets we may have such as cats and dogs. This is why the relationship between them and us can work so well, because both of us are hard-wired for closeness, and feel calmed and settled when experiencing the warmth and physical contact of the other.

With the evolution of mammals there was a change in what is called the parasympathetic nervous system. This is the part of the nervous system that calms down the heart rate and aids digestion and physical healing of the body (sometimes called the 'rest and digest' system). With mammals a new branch of the parasympathetic nervous system developed, which is involved with this whole care-giving system. It is activated by skin-to-skin contact, but also by the detection of safeness in the voice tone and facial expression of others. Therefore mammals have evolved this ability to be calmed or aroused – in other words, regulated emotionally and physically – through relationships with others. We will be looking at this in more detail shortly.

The evolution of mammals, then, opened up the capacity for a two-way responsiveness in terms of care giving and care receiving; not only do we have the capacity to be caring towards others and responsive to their distress, but we also have the capacity to be *responsive* to that caring by being calmed by it and experiencing a feeling of safety. So compassion has the quality of both giving and receiving care.

Our 'new' human abilities: the good, the bad and the ugly

About two million years ago our primate ancestors began to evolve capacities for much more advanced intelligent thinking; we evolved capacities for imagining, anticipating and planning. We began to evolve language and the ability to use symbols. We also evolved a capacity for different kinds of self-awareness and self-identity. As far as we know, no other animal reflects on itself like we do, wondering, for example, whether its fast heart rate means it is having a heart attack, or looking into a watering hole and wondering if it has put on weight lately!

This part of the brain, sometimes referred to as the neocortex, has the ability to look back into the past, learn from it and imagine the future so that we can plan and play out possible scenarios in our mind without actually having to act them out. So, for example, we could try out different concoctions of ice cream flavours in our mind. Would lemon and cherry work? What about chocolate and toast? Or beef and potato? We can have a physical reaction to these because we can bring different images and sensations together and integrate them in our mind. We don't have to go to the trouble of making them to find out what might work and what probably wouldn't.

Then we get to the very newest part of our brain in evolutionary terms, called the prefrontal cortex. This resides at the front of our brain just behind the forehead. This part was thought to be uniquely human but it now looks as if we can't take all the credit because mammals such as dolphins, elephants and great apes also have it too. However, in humans the prefrontal cortex is much bigger in relation to the rest of the brain and shares many more connections to other parts of the brain compared to other animals.

The prefrontal cortex is involved in social decision making, working out right from wrong, sorting out conflicting thoughts, and deciding how best to behave, so guiding our thoughts and actions according to our internal values and goals. It is also involved in the calming down or suppressing of all of the evolutionarily older parts of the brain. It begins its development in the third trimester of pregnancy but doesn't finish its development until we are about twenty-four or twenty-five years of age. Unlike a two-year-old, we learn to suppress, for example, an urge to stamp and scream when we disagree with somebody, or to run away if we see someone we don't want to speak to; when we are two years of age the prefrontal cortex isn't developed enough to prevent our temper tantrums. This long length of development outside of the womb means that the prefrontal cortex can be shaped by the environment we are in during our childhood, adolescence and young adulthood.

> *Neuroplasticity: we can shape our own brain.*

This amazing ability of the brain to respond to and actually be shaped by influences such as the environment in which it is operating is called 'neuroplasticity', a concept that has given rise to phrases like 'neurons that fire together wire together'[3] and 'use it or lose it'. Each experience, thought, feeling or physical sensation triggers thousands of neurons in the brain, creating a neural network with links between the neurons. If this is repeated, the links get stronger. This is how a particular smell might trigger a memory of a person or place, for example, or how our fingers seem to 'remember' a particular action such as how to tie a shoelace or play a piece of music. If we stop the practice, the links become weaker.

Although our brain is being constantly shaped by experiences that happen to us, we can also deliberately shape it ourselves. The exercises in this book are designed to stimulate the neurons involved in giving and receiving care. So we can actively develop our own compassionate mind. The more we practise the exercises, the stronger the connections will become. The stronger the connections, the easier it becomes to trigger off the set of neurons that give rise to feelings of safeness, soothing, calmness and stability.

Of course, the entire brain continues to be shaped by experience throughout our lifetime, but the prefrontal cortex is the part that is particularly shaped by the circumstances of our lives. Understanding the time it takes fully to develop helps us to appreciate the difficulty that children and young adults can have in controlling their impulses or in being able to plan for the future rather than just living for the moment. It is now thought that the adolescent brain experiences a huge reorganisation of the prefrontal cortex,[4] and for a while adolescents may actually drop back in their capacity to be empathic, until they emerge, like butterflies from a chrysalis, with a brain that can now comprehend a much broader worldview.

In understanding human nature we can see just how the interaction between these parts of the brain creates difficulties for us. We often blame these difficulties on personal flaws within ourselves when they are in fact 'glitches' created through evolution.

Getting into loops: what happens when the old brain and new brain interact?

As humans, we have our old brain, which we now know is principally the same in most animals; it is basically wired up to help us to stay alive until we reproduce. As with reptiles, we have the motivation and the capabilities to look out for predators, to stay safe by fighting or running away, seeking out and protecting our own territory, finding food and water, and ultimately finding a mate and reproducing. We can see just how territorial we are if we look at how we react if someone sits in 'our' seat, parks in 'our' parking space, or if we are told we have to share a desk at work. Even though we might be able to tell ourselves that it doesn't matter if someone sits in the seat that we normally sit in (we will see that this is actually our 'new brain' talking), our old brain still registers a sense of discomfort about it because it perceives this as a potential threat to our territory.

As well as our territorial old brain we have our new brain with its imagination and ability to plan. So, when our old brain fears our mate has been unfaithful, for example, our new brain, fuelled by anger and hurt in the old brain, can use its imagination to get back at our partner in really creative ways. Likewise, the new brain can take on old-brain anger and anxiety over territorial disputes between neighbours concerning fences and shared driveways, these potentially growing quite heated and vengeful. And, of course, what about war and the weapons of war, including the nuclear bomb? This is where we can see the terrifying effects of putting our new brain to work in responding to an old-brain urge to protect territory and group identities by creating weapons and strategies for widespread destruction.

A key problem we face with this awkward brain of ours is that the old brain is fast and automatic, acting before we are conscious of it.[5] Although we may feel as if we are driving our brain, in fact research is increasingly demonstrating that much of the activity within our brain is not within our conscious awareness at all. We are therefore driven by our old brain often without being aware of this fact at all.

> *Our brain drives* **us** *much of the time.*

So we begin to react to threat before we are consciously aware of the threat. For example, if we see something that looks a bit like a snake when we are out for a walk in the countryside, what is the first thing we do? We might jump with fright, freeze or run. However, this response will be set off in us *before* we become fully aware of seeing the 'snake', just as we will pull our hand away from something hot before we are fully aware of the heat. This is why it can be so hard to calm down our anger or anxiety once it has got going.

Figure 6.1: Our new brain and our old brain interact and influence each other

From Gilbert, *The Compassionate Mind* (2009), reprinted with permission from Constable & Robinson Ltd.

For example we may notice a pain in our chest. Our new brain may have the fleeting thought 'Could this be the start of a heart attack?' Before we know it, our old brain has registered this fear and has started up the 'fight or fright' response. Now our heart has started beating faster. Our new brain might think 'My goodness, now what is happening to my heart? This really might be a heart attack!' which of course then alarms the old brain even more. We can see just how quickly and easily we can get caught in these loops between the old and new brain.

We can really see the impact of this interaction between the old and new brain if we imagine not having our new brain. We can see this in animals. Let's take the example of a gazelle which has just escaped from the jaws of a lion. What does it do once it has escaped and the lion has disappeared? Well, it simply calmly goes back to eating. If *we*, however, had just escaped from a lion, what would we do? Well, we would certainly be thinking about it for a very long time! We might imagine all kinds of awful scenarios. We would probably lie awake ruminating on it; worrying about the lion coming back, or thinking that we had better get fitter and even more nimble in case we end up in that situation again. We might even consider how it affects our self-identity: 'Will people think I am a rubbish mother because I was more interested in finding a patch of juicy grass rather than watching out for lions?'

Self-awareness and self-monitoring: the impact of 'the voice on our shoulder'

This is a key quality of the new brain; it gives us a sense of self-awareness in a way that no other animal has. As we mentioned before, as far as we know monkeys don't sit worrying about their appearance, how they are getting on as parents or what others think of them. Humans can do this, of course, because we have a capacity to have an objective view of ourselves. We may have a sense of pride if we think others view us positively. However, we can also view ourselves in a self-critical way if we think that we may have been viewed negatively by others. This criticism switches on our old brain, making us feel anxious, angry or even disgusted with ourselves.

Below is a wonderful little exercise that can really help to give us insight into the capabilities of our human brain; how this can cause great problems for us, but also offer a solution too.

Figure 6.2: The power of our mind towards ourselves

Stimulus – Response

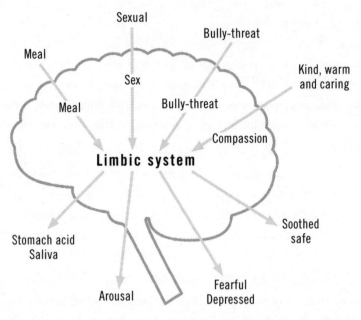

From Gilbert, *The Compassionate Mind* (2009), reprinted with permission from Constable & Robinson Ltd.

Exercise: The power of our mind towards ourselves

1. First, just bring your attention to how your body responds while you are waiting for your favourite meal to be cooked. You can smell it and you are hungry. You might notice that your stomach rumbles and you salivate as your body gets ready to eat (see Figure 6.2).

2. Now, what does your body do if you imagine your favourite meal? It does exactly the same thing; you salivate and your stomach might rumble. So our brain treats our imaginings as if they are real. Whatever is in our imagination therefore has the same impact on our body's response as if it were real.

3. Let's think about another example; what happens in your body when you see someone you are attracted to on TV or in a film? Now be honest! We experience arousal in our body (to skip the details!)

4. And what happens if we fantasise about that person? Again, our brain reacts just as if the fantasy is real and our body responds accordingly. This is why fantasy can be such an important part of a sexual experience.

5. This time, think about what happens in our body when someone criticises or bullies us. We might feel anxiety, anger or the urge to cry.

6. What happens in our body then when we criticise or bully ourselves? Here we start to see that our brain does not differentiate whether the critic is outside of us, or our own voice. Our mind (the threat system) registers it as an attack on us and triggers a protective response such as anger (attack back or humiliate), anxiety (urge to run, freeze, or submission), or disgust (wanting to get rid of the part that puts us at risk of rejection; for example, by cleaning our hand repeatedly).

7. We can now take this on a bit further and note how we feel when we register genuine kindness and warmth from another person towards us. We might notice our threat system trying to intercept this because of memories of being hurt by those we thought were kind. But if we can just imagine putting this fear next to us for a moment (like acknowledging the fear of a child, not pushing them away but having them close, and letting them know we will listen more fully to their concerns in a moment) and allow ourselves to really feel that kindness and warmth, what do we feel in our body? We might feel, calm, happy, peaceful, contented, safe, soothed.

8. So what happens in our body when we are kind, warm and caring to ourselves? Again, our protective threat system may jump in first, and we will turn to this in more detail later, but if we can again set this aside and really allow ourselves to feel the warmth, kindness and care in our own voice, how does our body respond? As in the previous examples, it will respond just as if this is another person being kind to us and we will feel soothed, reassured, contented.

> *Our mind responds to the social signals we send to ourselves, as if they were coming from another person.*
>
> *We can therefore trigger our threat response through self-criticism, but trigger our soothing/safeness response when we use a kind, warm voice tone and facial expression towards ourselves.*

This exercise demonstrates so powerfully the importance of the voice we have 'on our shoulder'; when the critical voice pipes up, our threat system is activated. When the compassionate, supportive, soothing voice on the other shoulder speaks, our soothing system is activated, which, as we now know, calms the threat system. How we speak to ourselves; the tone of our own voice and the facial expression we use towards ourselves; has the power to stimulate our brain and body in radically different ways. We also know that whatever we practise wires our brain in particular ways ('neurons that fire together, wire together') so when we criticise ourselves we wire up and strengthen the threat system a little more. When we are compassionate and kind to ourselves we wire up and strengthen our soothing system.

So, our capacity to have a sense of self and to be self-monitoring can be helpful but it can also be a source of great pain and upset when our judgements become negative. It is one of the biggest sources of difficulties for humans – our own self-monitoring and self-judgements can be harsh or unkind.

Our minds are set up to pay much more attention to the negative than the positive. We are therefore much more likely to dwell on the negative aspects of ourselves and to lose sight of the positive. This is because of the 'better safe than sorry' strategy that has evolved within the mind over millions of years of evolution. It is therefore not our fault that we do this. However, we can learn to rebalance this negative bias to some extent by teaching ourselves to pay real attention to the positives too (See Rick

Hanson's book, *Hardwiring Happiness*, referenced in 'Useful resources' at the back of the book).

> *We have evolved to focus on the negative more than the positive to keep alert to danger.*
>
> *However, we can train our brain to take in and be shaped by the positive too. This can have a powerful effect on our mental well-being.*

However, we can learn to train up our 'compassionate mind', which, as we see, can have a profound impact on us at many different levels.

Mindfulness: the art of paying attention to attention

Our brain has another capability that is believed to be unique to humans: mindfulness. This is our ability to mentally step back and become aware of the processes of the mind and body. This ability will be one which we will make great use of in the compassionate mind approach.

There are a number of definitions of mindfulness. One is 'paying attention in the present moment on purpose without judgement'.[6] A simpler one is 'observing without judgement'. Mindfulness enables us to pay attention to attention.

So why might paying attention to attention be so important? Well, it's because what we pay attention to becomes bigger in our mind and what we are not attending to fades out of our mind.

Exercise: The spotlight of attention (1)

One exercise that demonstrates this is to sit in a chair and focus for a while on your left foot, maybe for ten seconds or so. Take a breath and shift attention to your right foot. Take a breath and shift your attention to your thumb rubbing against the tips of your fingers. What you might notice is that when you are paying attention to your left foot you are not aware of your fingers. When you are paying attention to your fingers you become less aware of your feet. Attention is like a spotlight, brightening up some things while putting other things into darkness. So where our attention falls affects what comes into our mind.

Here is another exercise.

Exercise: The spotlight of attention (2)

Sit comfortably in a chair and bring to mind a memory of you laughing – maybe somebody had told you a good joke, or you are watching something really funny on the television. Remember who you were with, what was happening and how funny the joke was. Notice what happens in your body and in your face in particular. Then, after ten or fifteen seconds or so, bring to mind a memory of a mild frustration in your life, nothing too major. Again stay in that memory for ten to fifteen seconds. And then, finally, focus on a memory of one of the best holidays you've ever had.

As you remembered the joke you probably felt a sense of fun again and you may even have noticed your face smiling. All that would have disappeared, though, when you focused on your frustration, being replaced by a very different body experience and emotion, only for this to change again as you shifted your attention to the memory of your best holiday.

This exercise is a simple way of demonstrating to us that our attention is very powerful and can be moved around. Where our attention settles will have a very powerful impact on our body and the emotions we have. This means we have to be cautious about our attention because it's so influential in stimulating our bodies and emotions.

> *What we focus our attention on can cause a physiological response within us.*
>
> *We can learn to feel calmer and more supported just by choosing where we focus our attention*

We saw another example of this in the exercise where we imagine eating some really delicious food. If we think of food, we may well find our stomach rumbling and our mouth salivating. What about if you imagine cutting a lemon in half and licking the lemon juice? Sometimes we can get quite a strong physical reaction to this even though the lemon only exists in our imagination.

It's quite amazing to realise that an image we are creating in our mind on purpose can have such a powerful impact on our brain, which in turn triggers sensations and reactions in our body. So what we think about, remember and imagine can affect us physiologically.

In this book we are going to be using this natural quality of our brains to keep track of where our attention goes and to help us to focus on themes, images and ideas that are highly conducive to well-being and calming.

What we have seen is that where our attention goes, so does our body. Our attention tends to follow the negative more than the positive; for example, we will focus on one negative comment rather than five positive ones. Emotions are very powerful controls of attention. Anger or anxiety can easily take hold of attention and we are likely to ruminate on the triggers for anger and anxiety, so fuelling our feelings even more. We can, however, learn the skill of mindfulness; of noticing how our mind has perhaps settled into thinking about the negative comment, which is making us feel angrier or more anxious, and then deliberately shifting our attention to the positive comments. We learn to notice what our mind is up to, paying attention to attention.

Learning to become more mindful

A crucial piece of knowledge in developing mindfulness, and which mindfulness itself helps us to understand, is that we only ever exist in the present moment. We are never in the moment to come or in the moment just gone – only in the now. Once we move into the 'future', then that of course becomes the present moment.

We would notice how special is each present moment if we fully lived there. Unfortunately, we usually don't. We live in our new brain, which is always on the go, wanting to think this, plan that, and worry about something or other. As we have seen, what we focus on, what we think about and what we are attentive to will affect our bodies – so all that worrying and planning will pull us away from the present moment and might create feelings of tension and anxiety within us. So mindfulness is partly learning to constantly wake up to the present moment – to become more and more aware of how much our new brains are thinking, planning, anticipating, worrying and fretting, and how this is stimulating our bodies in ways that aren't helpful. Often the present moment is just fine, and can be quite wonderful, but we are not aware of that because we are worrying and ruminating. Sometimes the present moment is not fine, but we need to be present to be able to best respond.

There are a number of ways in which we can begin to become mindful. For example we can focus on our physical sensations of breathing. Or we can be mindful by allowing the attention to settle on one of the senses. We can try this right now; in this moment we can become fully aware of all the colours, shapes and objects around us, really observing how the light falls on them, the textures and the shapes. We can then switch our attention to the sounds around us – really listening to whatever sounds exist in this present moment. Rather than analysing them, labelling them or judging them in some way, we are allowing sounds to flow in to our ears. In other words we are just experiencing sounds rather than thinking about the sounds.

Exercise: Mindful coffee drinking

Imagine being mindful of drinking a cup of coffee. We first notice how the cup feels in our hands, really allowing our hands to explore the shape and notice the warmth in the cup. Next we switch to what we can see, so the colour and patterns on the cup, and then the colour of the coffee; really noticing the colours of cream or brown as if seeing them for the first time. We let our attention settle here for a moment or two. We can then move the cup a little and observe the movement of the coffee in the cup. Notice how light is reflected off the coffee as it moves. Next we focus on smell and really allow ourselves time to focus and experience the smell of the coffee. Now, when we are ready, we can finally switch to taste and the temperature of the coffee in our mouth. Notice what it tastes like – imagine tasting it as if it's for the first time, really giving ourselves time to notice the sensation of taste.

If you do this exercise, compare it to how you normally drink a cup of coffee, perhaps noticing how little attention we usually pay to it and how much more there is to an experience of drinking a cup of coffee if we become mindful and create time to be mindful. This can be true for every experience and every moment of our lives.

Later in the book we will look in much more detail at developing the skill of mindfulness.

Mindfulness and compassion

It's important that this observing aspect is itself gentle and kind rather than harshly critical. If it's harshly critical then, of course, it is interfering with the process of mindfulness itself because it is judgemental, and mindfulness is all about being non-judgemental. So we want our attention to be held gently and kindly with support. Learning to cultivate compassion will help this.

However, it can also be that rather than just noticing where our attention goes we want to direct our attention to brain systems that can be very helpful to us. For example, if we are wanting to win a race we might focus on thoughts and images that will motivate and energise us; imagining lying on a sofa or falling over is unlikely to be particularly helpful. (In fact sports people are becoming more and more aware of just how much good sports performance is to do with our minds, not just our physical performance). It is the same with compassion – if we learn to pay attention to aspects of compassion we can begin to stimulate areas of our brain that are conducive to well-being and that help us cope with anxiety, pain and depression. There is nothing magical about this; it is simply recognising that our attention can stimulate our emotions and our bodies in certain ways.

We can put these two elements together in Figure 6.3 below.

Figure 6.3: Interactions of mindfulness and compassion with the old and new brain

From Gilbert and Choden, *Mindful Compassion* (2013),[9] reprinted with permission from Constable & Robinson Ltd.

> *We can learn to observe the activity of the mind, rather than getting caught up in it.*
>
> *We can observe this activity with curiosity, warmth and compassion.*

As we saw earlier, our new brain and old brain can get caught in loops where the worry from the new brain fires up the old brain, which further stimulates the new brain, and so on. Now, when our old brain and new brain get caught into these loops, we can use our skill of mindfulness, simply by observing the interaction without judging it or trying to change it in any way. Rather than getting sucked into the loops by ruminating on anger, anxiety or depression we learn simply to observe them. We might even say to ourselves: 'I'm caught in an anxiety loop' and simply observe it rather than get caught up in it and then find ourselves generating more anxious thoughts.

When we become an observer, though, it's helpful to try to bring that warmth and understanding to our mind as we watch the interaction. Later we will explore how we can bring our voice tones and facial expressions to help build compassionate attention for the moment.

This is the beginning of compassion. Compassion has the power to help settle the mind in ways that we will explore as we go through this book. One of the reasons for this is because compassion stimulates our brain in a particular kind of way that is different from, say, anger or anxiety. The basis for compassion comes from the care-giving and care-receiving system of our mammalian brain. This particular system has the capacity to engage with and turn down the part of the brain that generates our anger and anxiety. Here is an exercise that adds the affiliative elements of compassion to our mindful practice.

Exercise: Bringing compassion to mindfulness

Close your eyes and allow your attention to settle on the movement of your breath. If you notice your attention has moved off your breath just notice it with warmth and a friendly smile, with the wisdom that comes from understanding that wandering thoughts are a characteristic of the human mind that we share with all other humans. See if bringing this warmth and understanding feels different or not, compared to just noticing without judgement. Don't try to make it one way or another, just notice whatever you observe with curiosity and warmth.

Mindfulness, pregnancy and new motherhood

The skill of mindfulness has an important place in pregnancy and new motherhood. Ellen Langer, Professor of Psychology and her team at Harvard University, carried out some research on the impact of mindfulness training for first time mothers where they were taught to notice the subtle changes in their feelings and physical sensations each day[10]. They found that these women reported more well-being and positive feelings and less emotional distress. According to Langer 'they had higher self-esteem and e satisfaction during this period of their pregnancy and up to at least a month after birth. And this also had a positive impact on their deliveries and overall health of the newborns.'

Langer talked about how mindfulness enables us to become aware of variability and change by noticing the constant tiny fluctuations in our feelings and sensations. This counters our tendency to try and keep things constant and stable. We naturally try to do this to give a feeling of predictability and safeness, but it is an illusion, because actually we are constantly changing. By becoming aware of this constant change Langer suggests we open up possibilities in us. For example, when we believe we are in constant discomfort, mindfulness opens up the possibility that there may be times when we feel comfortable. When we believe we feel constantly unsafe, with mindfulness, we open up the possibility that there are times when we feel safe, and when we believe we feel nothing at all for our baby, we open up the possibility that there might be times when we feel tiny sparks of warmth.

In the next chapter we will have a closer look at the different systems within our brain to help us to really understand where compassion fits in and just why it is so crucial in helping us with painful aspects of our lives such as postnatal depression and struggling to bond with our baby.

Summary

1. Our brain has evolved over millions of years. Newer sections have been added to much older sections. So we have a whole range of motive and emotions potentials that are hard-wired into us. Some of these date back to our common ancestor with reptiles such as a tendency to be territorial and our capacity to fight, flee or freeze.

2. We also evolved through the mammalian line and therefore have a limbic system that provides us with the capacity for our emotions, attachment, the ability to play, and basic socialisation. The most recent brain competencies are very new and give rise to the ability to imagine, anticipate, plan, and worry as well as a sense of self and the capacity for self-monitoring.

3. The way our capacities for thinking, planning, anticipating, and creating a sense of self interact with some of the older emotion and motivational systems can be a source of great difficulty for humans, for example we can get into loops of worry and anxiety and we can become harshly self-critical.

4. Activity within the old brain can occur rapidly and automatically before it reaches conscious awareness. Our body is therefore starting to react before we have the awareness to do anything about it. It is only once it reaches awareness that we can try to have any control over it. It is therefore not our fault that we find ourselves beginning

to respond with anger, anxiety, sadness, disgust, or indeed contentment or joy. As soon as we are aware of it, then we can try to shape or change it.

5. How we respond to ourselves has a profound impact on us at many levels. We respond to the face and voice we direct at ourselves in the same way we would if it was somebody else relating to us in that way; when we criticise ourselves we can feel beaten down, anxious, and depressed, when we are kind, encouraging, understanding and compassionate to ourselves, we feel safe, settled, and more able to function well.

6. We try to shape our response using the abilities of the prefrontal cortex. So we might decide that although we feel angry, this isn't the response that we want to give. We might for example, decide to try to respond with compassion instead. This is our prefrontal cortex recruiting the new brain (thinking and imagination) and the mammalian brain (attachment and soothing) which calms the reptilian brain (fight or flight).

7. Mindfulness is our ability to be able to just observe the activity of other parts of our mind, without judging them at all. So for example we can just observe our thoughts arising and disappearing, the rhythm of our breathing, and our emotions ebbing and flowing in our body.

8. Mindfulness has been shown to have a wide range of physical and mental benefits. It also forms the basis of the practice of compassion because it helps to stabilise our minds and because we learn how to do compassion training 'mindfully'. It helps us to really understand the nature of our mind which brings with it a kind acceptance rather than criticism. It also allows us to be aware of which reaction we find ourselves in, to enable us to choose a compassionate response instead if we wish.

7 Understanding our emotion systems

Three emotion systems: threat, drive and soothing

In previous chapters we have seen that we are like other animals to the extent that we share basic desires and motives in life. These include: to stay safe, to eat, to find comfort and to accumulate resources. We also have a number of *social* motives to do with our relationships to others. These include to have status rather than feeling we are inferior, to feel accepted rather than rejected, to feel a sense of belonging rather than being an outsider, to have friends, to find a sexual partner, and to reproduce. We also know that humans in particular have an interest in caring and helping each other and indeed studies suggest that this is an important source of meaning for us. These basic social motives are the guides to how we live our lives and relate to other people.

In this chapter we are going to explore emotions because it is the emotions that give 'fuel' to our motives. Our motives are hard-wired so that we 'know' instinctively that something is important. Our emotions however help us to 'feel' in our bodies that it is important. Without emotions motives would have nothing to propel us along. Emotions are like the 'petrol', while our motives are the direction in which we want our car to go. So for example I might say that I am motivated to care for my baby but that I am not affected emotionally by whether my baby is flourishing or ill. As we can imagine, it would be very difficult for me to keep going giving my baby the care he or she needs without emotions, particularly when caring for a young child is so hard.

We can see in this example that it is the emotions which can also interfere with our basic motives. For example when we get depressed, our ability to experience positive emotions such as enjoyment and pleasure gets toned down. If these emotions and feelings are not there it can then be extremely hard to even want to care for ourselves, let alone a baby. It is our emotions that help to give motives a sense of meaning and purpose; without them we can feel that things are meaningless and pointless.

We can think about the relationship between our motives and emotions using the concepts of a game that children play where they are guided to a hidden object with the words 'colder, colder, warmer, warmer!' As the child hunts around they are guided towards the object with shouts of 'warmer, warmer, colder!' and when they move further away from it they are warned with shouts of 'colder, colder!' Our 'negative emotions' of anger, anxiety, disgust, and sadness are equivalent to 'colder, colder', signalling some kind of threat or blocking of our goal. 'Negative' emotions are therefore warning emotions. Our 'positive emotions' such as happiness, joy, and excitement signal getting closer to our goals. These are equivalent to 'warmer, warmer'.

The function of different emotions

As have seen above we can look at our emotions in terms of their function, so for example the function of threat emotions are to warn us about things and take defensive actions whereas the function of more positive emotions is basically to indicate that we are doing okay and to keep going. Our emotions can roughly be put into three main categories in terms of their functions:

1. Those that are focused on threat and self-protection.
2. Those that are focused on doing and achieving.
3. Those that are focused on soothing, contentment and connection with others.

> *Our innate motives give us direction. Our emotions help us to* **feel** *that these motives are important to us.*

These three emotion systems are represented in diagram 7.1 as three circles which interact with each other). This 'three circle' model is an important part of the compassionate mind model and will accompany us through the book.

Figure 7.1: Three types of emotion regulation system

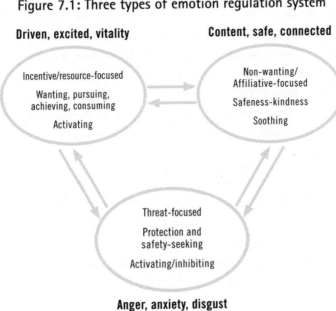

From Gilbert, *The Compassionate Mind* (2009), reprinted with permission from Constable & Robinson Ltd.

The threat and self-protection system

Let's start by looking at the threat-protection system as this is likely to be the one that has brought you to this book. Throughout life we are confronted by different types of threats and therefore we have different types of emotion. So threats that could harm or damage us typically produce anxiety making us want to flee or hide. Threats to do with things getting in the way of our goals for example (which might include ourselves or other people getting in the way) produce frustration and anger. Threats associated with some kind of fear of contamination can be associated with disgust. Sadness can also be seen as a link to threat although it's more to do with a reaction to a loss.

Let's think about that gazelle again that we came across earlier in the book, quietly grazing this time. The part of the brain concerned with threat detection is keeping an eye, an ear, and a nostril open for the slightest hint of danger. If any potential danger is detected the gazelle might stand still in a state of heightened awareness, and then flee if the lion attacks. We can see this in ourselves. Imagine going to a new mother and toddler group when we are feeling a little shy and unconfident. We might notice that we would be in a state of elevated anxiety, where we might scan for 'danger' in the form of hostile faces, or being seen as an outsider where we might be ignored or judged. We might really feel like running out of the room or 'fleeing'.

Anger on the other hand is a different type of threat emotion which arises when we feel thwarted and blocked or when we feel people have treated us unfairly for example. Rather than having an urge to run away, with anger we want to engage with the threat, perhaps by arguing, or even fighting. Interestingly mothers of many species can become more aggressive especially in contexts where they think others might be harmful to their babies. So when we have a baby we might find that we experience anxiety and anger much more easily than before.

When we are anxious we often become more irritable as well, and find it easy to experience full-blown anger. Imagine a scenario where we are trying to get out of the mother and toddler group quickly because we are overwhelmed by anxiety and someone has blocked in our buggy with their buggy. We might feel like throwing their buggy out of the way. This is because it represents a threat to our chances of getting to safety. As we will see, anger and anxiety usually come together. Where there is anxiety we can look for anger, where there is anger, we can look for anxiety or fear behind it.

> *The emotions of the threat system help us to take action to stay safe.*

When we experience a threat, usually the part of our nervous system called the sympathetic nervous system is activated. This is an energising system that prepares us for action and it does so by speeding up our heart rate and transferring blood rapidly to our muscles away from our digestive system to give us the strength to fight or flee (this is why when we are anxious or angry we can experience stomach and digestive problems). Sometimes, however, even when we are in higher states of threat arousal, we can experience more inhibition in our bodies, as if we are being held back in some way rather than activated. Here we are more likely to be submissive than aggressive and we can feel like our body has lost energy and feels 'collapsed'. Our voice also quietens and we become passive and withdrawn. This is the 'fright' response. If the emotion is one of disgust, we can have a sense of wanting to stay away from what we feel disgusted by. Disgust typically centres on bodily fluids, products and odours. Sometimes we can find the vomit or poo from our baby rather 'disgusting'. Our threat responses therefore include freeze, flight, fight, fright and disgust.

'Better safe than sorry'

A key point to recognise with threat emotions is that they are often very easily activated – we can be immersed in an emotion almost before we even realise it has been activated. This speed of reaction has evolved within us to help us stay safe. So, as we saw earlier, if we were enjoying a stroll through the woods on a summer's day and came across a snake, we might jump, freeze or shout out before we had time to check properly whether it was a snake or, in fact, a stick. This is because when our brain detects a potential threat it uses a 'better safe than sorry' strategy and starts a threat response automatically within us, even before the information reaches our conscious brain. This saves us from wasting precious time wondering whether it is a snake or a stick while in the meantime we have been bitten.

In other words, we begin a freeze, flight, fight or fright response even before we are consciously aware of it. This is an important point to remember if we find we are criticising ourselves for our initial reactions. So, when we suddenly feel angry after our baby accidentally bashes us on the head with a wooden block, or when we feel like crying in front of somebody who has criticised us, it is not our fault. We cannot change this first reaction. We can only take control of it once we have become consciously aware of it, and even then this is hard to do, So, while giving us sensations and emotions that are unpleasant and difficult, such as anger, anxiety and disgust, the threat system is actually, in its own simple, unsophisticated way, doing its best to keep us safe, even if sometimes this means mistaking something safe as unsafe.

Freeze, flight, fight and fright

As we have seen, we can have different threat responses, and these are rapid and automatic. It is thought that animals and humans go through a sequence of threat responses according to the proximity to the threat.[2] For example, the gazelle that detects the lion will freeze first of all. This is because animals have evolved to detect movement, so a good first response is to keep still. Then if the lion starts to run towards it, it will run. If the lion gets hold of it the gazelle will fight by struggling. But if it cannot get free it has one last threat response sometimes called the 'fright', 'flop' or 'sham death' response. This is where it becomes floppy or 'tonically immobile'. One theory for this 'fright' or 'flop' response is that if the attacker believes its prey is dead it might relax its jaws, giving the prey a chance to escape. We see this in a mouse that is in the jaws of a cat. It appears dead, but the moment the cat drops it, it 'comes back to life' and runs off. People who are being attacked may find that this response switches on automatically when the brain detects that it would be dangerous or impossible to fight or run.

The body's ability to respond to some kinds of threat with a decrease in muscle tone rather than the increase involved in freeze, fight and flight is involved in the submission response. This system can get activated when we are threatened by people bigger and scarier than ourselves such as our parents when we are children, people who bully us at school, or if we are sexually, physically and emotionally abused. It is also thought to be involved in the experience of shame, which is where we feel put down in the mind of another person who we see as important as or more dominant than ourselves. We can respond by casting our eyes down, feeling that we want to 'disappear through the floor', wanting to curl up, or having very little energy. These are automatic signals of submission designed to prevent the other person from attacking. We see this system in many animals too. It is thought to be involved in depression. As with the other responses from the threat system, we do not choose to respond in this way; it is our mind rapidly selecting the best response to keep us safe.

Baby notes

There can be many occasions when our threat system is activated when we have a new baby, creating feelings of anger, anxiety and even disgust within us. We now see that it is hard to control feeling these as they begin rapidly and automatically before we are consciously aware of them. Instead, if we can learn to understand, and show compassion towards ourselves, when we feel these emotions arising within us, then we can develop a little space around the feelings. This allows us to be less likely to act reactively to the cause of the threat and even enables us to calm down our anger, anxiety and disgust.

Sometimes it is clear why we have become flushed with these feelings when we are with our baby; we may be incredibly tired and worn down, or feel helpless and frustrated with a baby who has cried for hours. But sometimes the strength of our feelings seems out of proportion to what has happened. This can be because a particular moment with our baby may bring up memories of something that has happened in the past.

Our baby can of course be a wonderful source of learning for us. We can learn a lot about our own emotions by watching our baby. Babies are still unselfconscious so they generally do not hold back their emotions. They also show their emotions throughout their body so making them much clearer to spot. As babies get older we can notice which signals tell us whether our baby is feeling anger, or anxiety or disgust. We start to learn about our baby from these signals.

> *Naming emotions can help to calm them.*

We can also start to name these emotions for our baby. The naming of emotions is a very important process. As our baby gets older it helps them to identify what they are feeling. It also helps the child to feel they are having an understandable, universal experience rather than that something nameless, strange and without form is occurring in their body. It has been shown that when we give a name to a threat emotion, it calms down activity in the part of the brain that detects threat. For example, if we see a picture of an angry person, the part of the brain that detects threat (called the amygdala) becomes activated. But as soon as we label the emotion 'anger' the amygdala 'calms down'.[3] Naming threat emotions perceived in our baby can calm not only us, but also our child as they become older.

We can begin naming emotions even before we think the baby can under-stand them. Just the tone of our voice and our facial expression can calm our baby (and ourselves). This is because – given how far other people can be significant sources of threat or safeness to us – our amygdala has evolved to be particularly sensitive to facial expression and voice tone, which is why our baby (and ourselves) can be so rapidly alarmed, or soothed, by our voice tone and facial expression.

This is a two-way process. When we pick up threat signals of anxiety, anger or disgust in our baby, these signals automatically create responses within us too. Because these happen so fast we need to use our mind-fulness skills to replay and slow down the interaction and to observe it without judgement. This enables us to be curious about what happened. We might find that we have very different thoughts and behaviour towards our baby depending on whether we detect anger, anxiety or disgust in them. Perhaps we feel concern and care towards them when they are scared but anger towards them when they are angry. These are normal responses. But if we can become more aware of our responses, then we may be able to choose other ways of responding which were not available to us when we responded without awareness. We might, for example, want to try to respond to anger with understanding.

> *Mindfulness gives us a chance to notice and then to change our responses.*

All this helps us understand the value of mindfulness; we learn to be observant about what arises within us and as we do so we become able to label our emotions. Ideally, we become curious about what arises in us rather than judgemental. The point is that our emotions have been generated by deep brain processes that sometimes we really don't want. Non-judgement allows us to choose to act in the way we do want. There are many times in life where we learn to override anxiety – for example, taking a driving test, doing an exam, going out on a first date, or going for an interview – if we gave into anxiety every time it arose, we wouldn't do anything. In a way, then, life is about learning *to notice what we feel but choosing what we do*. Noticing your threat system at work can be very helpful.

The drive system

Let's take a look now at the first of the two 'positive' emotion systems: the drive system (see top left-hand circle in Figure 7.1).

Life is, of course, more than dealing with threats, and a number of emotions activate and energise us to go out and secure the things we need and want, such as food, a partner, a job, a home, even buying a new pair of shoes. For the most part, drive emotions can feel pleasant or at least are associated with the anticipation of some pleasurable emotion. Imagine, for example, if we discovered we had won a million pounds. What would we feel in our body? What would our body want to do? Where would our attention be? What would our thoughts be? We might notice our heart thumping and a desire to jump up with our arms in the air, a huge smile on our face, wanting to phone people and tell them about our good news. We might think about what we could buy with the money: perhaps replace the old car, buy a new house, finally pay off the credit card, or have that dream holiday. We might feel hyped up and a bit manic, and would probably find it hard to sleep that night.

For the most part, our pleasure emotions are less extreme, typically associated with a whole range of activities related to small successes, including doing well at our job, calming our fractious baby, going out with friends, or even finally getting the kitchen tidy.

> *The emotions of the drive system are pleasurable and energising.*
> *They help us move towards our goals.*

Activated positive emotions are also associated with falling in love, including falling in love with our baby. Sometimes these emotions are described as joyful ones, or even as excitement. However, there are two major process that can interfere with positive emotions. The first, of course, is threat. Imagine we are having a wonderful time one day enjoying the weather, perhaps dozing a little in the sunshine, and suddenly we hear a shout. The threat system will turn off the positive emotions straightaway. We are wired for threat to override positive emotions.

As mothers, then, when we feel under very high levels of threat we can find it very difficult to experience positive emotions concerning our babies. That is through no fault of our own; it is simply the way the brain is wired. As the threat subsides the positive emotions can then begin to re-emerge.

Another major cause of toning down the positive emotion system is fatigue. Fatigue is a bodily state that basically tells an organism it is out of energy and needs to rest. Indeed, tiredness and fatigue are one of the major reasons why mothers of young children can find it hard to feel joy and to take delight in their children as they might have hoped. This is because the process of pregnancy, birth, recovery and caring for a young child is a long and often relentless process that can lead to extreme fatigue, which in itself can reduce the positive emotion system. If we then start criticising and blaming ourselves for not being able to delight in our child, we will trigger more threat within ourselves so inadvertently making things much worse.

Boredom can be one of the consequences of a toned-down positive emotion system. Many mothers admit to feeling bored by looking after a young child. This is particularly so if motherhood has meant the loss of aspects of life that reward us; for example work, contact with others, hobbies, even simple things like time to read a magazine or a good book.

> *Our drive system needs 'feeding', otherwise we become bored, lethargic and low in mood.*

Becoming depressed can also be a cause of boredom. Depression gives us that feeling that we really cannot be bothered about anything, that we haven't got any energy, and that we no longer experience any joy. Some people describe it as feeling as if all of the colour has gone out of life and it seems just grey. It is thought that one reason for difficulties in bonding with our baby when we have depression is because the drive system is toned down. This means that it cannot register the baby as 'rewarding' as it does in non-depressed mothers. As we will see later in this book, there may be many reasons why a mother struggles to bond with her child. However, in some women, once their depression has lifted, they find that they do begin to experience joy again, and that their feelings for their baby come on line of their own accord.

It is also important to remember that *positive emotion systems need feeding*. We don't need to feed our threat system – threat emotions will just turn up by themselves – but we do need to practise stimulating positive emotion systems. So, for example, we need to have things to look forward to in order to help keep us interested in life. This is why one of the peak times for planning a holiday is directly after Christmas; the anticipation of a holiday can help sustain us through the rest of winter.

When we start to feel bored, low or depressed, it is important that we plan things that can stimulate our positive emotion system. Two types of activity are particularly important: those that give us a sense of achievement and those that give us contact with other people. These might include going out for a meal with our partner, meeting friends, going to a mother and toddler group, or just going out to the shops. Achievements do not need to be significant to stimulate our positive emotion system. Just making the bed, or putting some washing away, can be enough. Small acts can create a kind of 'snowball effect', giving us enough energy and motivation to do something else, which then makes us feel even better.

With a baby it can be particularly important to plan opportunities into our schedule for activities that have the potential for bringing enjoyment, otherwise our world can shrink to being alone at home with the baby. Depression can also shrink our world, which is why the combination of depression and having a young baby can be particularly hard. We need to keep in mind that our positive emotion systems need to be actively fed, like our pets, or like our muscles, which need exercising to keep them toned and working well. In other words, pleasurable activities are not just 'nice' things to do, but are actually vital to our well-being and our ability to keep going.

Sometimes these activities can be hard to do because we are fatigued, feeling low or anxious. Going out with friends, for example, can become an ordeal rather than a pleasure. Nonetheless, it still important to try to override that anxiety where we can. People frequently discover that if they can override anxiety and do what usually brings them pleasure, they feel a great deal better.

BABY NOTES

The drive system can be seen very clearly in our baby as they get older. We might begin to see it first in facial expressions of smiling and then later as real joyfulness. We can watch how our child responds if we get out their favourite food or toy. Often their whole body becomes energised; they might jig up and down, reaching out with their hands *and* legs. Their face might break into a big smile and they may make lots of excited noises. We might also note that if they don't get the toy or food quickly, then the threat system takes over and they start to get frustrated and upset. The drive and threat system can be closely connected as they are both part of the sympathetic nervous system, which is linked to activation and arousal.

We can also see from how quickly our baby becomes bored, or loses interest in something they initially found exciting or captivating, that the drive system needs constantly renewed stimulation. This is a normal process called 'habituation'. As the drive system turns down and becomes too under-stimulated it can switch on our threat system to alert us to the need for more stimulation. When a baby becomes bored with a toy, he might become irritable again, signalling that he needs something new.

The soothing system: slowing down and social safeness

Dealing with threats, and going out and acquiring resources, are important tasks of life and, as we have seen, we have the motives and emotions to pursue those life tasks. But it is also vital that we are able to allow time to 'rest and digest' and generally slow and quieten the body and mind. Otherwise we would be on the go the whole time, using up valuable energy. We see this in our baby, who for the first few months will spend a lot of their time asleep, conserving energy where possible, as the stimulation of being awake for a baby, and the process of growth it is going through, use immense amounts of energy.

It turns out that when we are not under any threat and not needing to achieve or pursue anything, the body can go into a state of *peaceful contentedness*.[4] This offers a very different type of positive feeling to that of drive, and has a profound impact on our bodies and our minds. This system of contentment, safeness and connectedness is represented in the top right-hand section of Figure 7.1. Rather than energising us like the drive system, it soothes us, bringing us to a state of calmness, peace and quiescence. We will refer to it as the 'soothing system', for shorthand. It is switched on when we have what we need (the drive system is switched off), and when there is nothing we are worried or angry about (threat system is switched off).

However, it is more than that. It is activated not just by the *absence* of drive or threat, but when we register the *presence* of a sense of safeness. This sense of safeness might come from inside us or from those around us. This is why the circle in Figure 7.1 refers to 'affiliation' because it is switched on when we feel connected to others (not just to our children).

The nature of soothing, slowing and stilling

There is both a social and a non-social way we can experience contentment and soothing. They are different processes though. The non-social way is simply that we feel content with where we are, when not under any threat and when we do not want to achieve or pursue anything in particular. We are just content being in the moment with the way things are. This is a sort of relaxation. So, for example, we might feel this way when we are on holiday, lying by the pool, enjoying the sun without a care in the world. However, there is also an alert form of soothing which is very important and arises when we are preparing to do something. Imagine a diver on the high-diving board preparing to dive. For a moment they pay attention to the body and their breathing, settling the mind, creating an inner point of stillness – and then they dive. When we talk about soothing and engaging in a particular type of breathing, which we call soothing rhythm breathing, we are going to be focusing on this 'inner slowing and stilling' rather than the kind of soothing which is more akin to relaxation and in which we have floppy muscles and go to sleep.

When we consider compassion, although it is connected to what we refer to as the soothing system, it is certainly not about relaxation or going to sleep. It is about finding an inner point of stability within ourselves which allows us to think clearly and act helpfully. The compassionate mind approach is as much about the process of stilling as the process of soothing.

> *The emotions of the soothing system help us feel safe, calm and at peace.*
>
> *Our body feels settled and stable, allowing it to conserve energy, digest, and repair.*

The capacity to feel soothed is associated with affection and affiliation. For example, imagine a baby who seems a bit distressed. When they are picked up, gently rocked and spoken to in a soothing voice, they gradually calm down. What has happened here is that your caring behaviour of holding and cuddling has activated your baby's soothing system. The signals given from the cuddling and holding, and the gentle voice and facial expression, are recognised by the baby's brain to indicate the environment is safe. In fact the ability of mammalian mothers to calm a distressed infant has come about with the evolution of a particular part of the parasympathetic nervous system – one that has the properties of slowing and calming in response to the detection of social safeness. We saw above that the sympathetic system was linked to activation and energising. In contrast, this part of the parasympathetic system is linked to soothing and calming.[5] It evolved in mammals and facilitates attachment. It is a way in which the mother and the infant regulate each other's emotions.

The impact of caring signals (the basis for compassion) operates throughout life, not just when we are babies. For example, if we are distressed and people we like are kind and helpful to us, this will calm us. Being 'calmed' by the kindness of others occurs because our brains are set up to respond to it – in other words *we are designed to be soothed by caring signals from others*. It is actually quite fundamental to how our brains work. Having people around with whom we feel safe gives us a feeling of safety and contentment.

Being safe and becoming safe

Many years ago the British psychiatrist John Bowlby developed 'attachment theory'. He pointed out that all mammals require caring early in life and that the parent and infant are biologically organised for that relationship. So infants are attuned to pay attention to their mothers/ carers and, in turn, mothers/carers are attuned to the needs and signals of their infants. He suggests that the parent provides two key qualities: a secure base and a safe haven.[6] The *secure base* is what provides the confidence for the child to go out and explore. The parent is encouraging of exploration and development of their offspring. So, for example, in a new environment a child may begin to explore that environment while the parent is somewhere close – the parent's proximity gives rise to courage within the infant. If the parent suddenly disappears the child will become alarmed and will stop exploring. So there is an intimate relationship between a secure base and the ability to explore our environments and ultimately develop the courage to face things that might be anxiety provoking.

A *safe haven* is one that allows us to calm down and regulate our distress when it's been stimulated. So, for example, if a child is upset or alarmed they will immediately seek out their carer and then, depending on how the carer relates to the child, will calm down. There are physiological systems within the child that are responsive to the caring behaviours of the parent.

Imagine for a minute that a mother is sat in a waiting room and her baby is happily playing with his toys on the floor. He can explore these toys and perhaps his surroundings because his mother provides a safe base for him. Suddenly an ear-piercing fire alarm goes off for a few moments. What does the baby do? He might turn to his mother, put his arms up and show his worry in his face. He might cry. We can see that his threat system has been switched on, and it has orientated him towards his mother. He now needs her as his 'safe haven'. What does the mother do? She will automatically detect these signals, which then sets up a whole series of responses within her. Some are hard-wired and some are learned. She is likely to pick her baby up, hold him in her arms, use a soothing voice and a soothing facial expression, and perhaps rock him. Her baby's distress has switched on her caretaking system, which has the ability to understand his distress and is also wired to want to make it better. Young children will respond in a similarly care-taking manner, as this is innate within us. (As we see, though, in this book, there are many factors that can knock this innate response off course).

What happens now in the baby? If we go back to the three emotion systems we noted above, which circle has now been activated in him? The chances are he will calm down; he will stop crying, his body tone will relax, and his attention will become more open and curious again rather than focused on the threat (the noise) and the source of safety (his mother), and he may even wriggle off his mother's lap to go and play again. So his mother's actions of holding and rocking him, together with touch, warmth, soothing voice tone and facial expression, all switch on his soothing system. It is this activation of the soothing system that calms down the threat system in the baby.

Even as adults we need a secure base and a safe haven. The compassion-ate mind approach helps us to develop these in ourselves and to reach out for them in others

BABY NOTES

What helps our baby to move into his or her soothing system? If we remember the example of the diver and the state of stillness that they try to find as they prepare to high-dive off a diving board, this state will correspond to when the baby is alert but calm, often referred to as 'quiet wakefulness'. Notice how connected to safeness this state is for a baby. This might occur when the baby is in your arms or the arms of somebody who cares about them. They might be sat on your lap or exploring but with one eye on where you are. What are the signals, both obvious and subtle, which indicate to you that your baby is in their soothing system?

The soothing system: a state for openness, creativity, learning and exploring

As we have seen so far, the soothing system helps us to bear and get through suffering, and can also calm and soothe us when we feel angry or fearful. It also facilitates another very powerful state. Think about a baby trying to reach a toy that he wants. He is in his drive system. His attention is focused on his goal. Now imagine that the baby's mother walks away from him. He panics that she is going to leave him behind and crawls after her, crying. He is now in his threat system. His attention is focused on the threat. Then imagine that his mother picks him up. In that moment he feels that all is right with the world again. He is in his soothing system. As he calms down he turns his head to look out from his mother and to look around. In this state of quiescence he is able to look with open attention and an interested awareness. He has the space and broadness of view to explore, to learn and also to integrate different aspects of knowledge. This applies to us as adults too; when we find ourselves in perhaps a rare moment when there is nothing to do, no role to fulfil, and nothing very much that is worrying us, we might find that all sorts of interesting thoughts and ideas start to spring to mind. Think about which system you are in when you tend to get the best ideas. A group of people who relied on creativity for their work were asked what helped their creativity. Their answers included:

- Taking a walk outside, even in the rain.
- Weeding the garden.
- Getting up in the middle of the night when I've given up on trying to sleep.
- Knitting.
- Swimming.
- Looking at beautiful pictures in magazines or online, particularly colour and nature.
- Getting into taking photographs of my baby, particularly when I need him to sleep and he won't.
- Pushing the buggy through the park.
- Yoga.

> *We can think more clearly and creatively when we are in our soothing system.*

We might find that as new mothers we bounce backwards and forwards between the threat and drive systems, and that the soothing system seems to figure rarely. This is demonstrated so clearly in the eternal dilemma of the mother in the moment when her baby finally goes to sleep. The house is messy, she could get ahead with the dinner, put the clothes away, and so use her drive system to move her away from the unpleasant sensations being evoked by her threat system. However, what she might need most, to be able to meet the often relentless challenge of motherhood (apart from some help with all of this), is a moment in her soothing system. The soothing system is the state of restoration, repair and recuperation, and also the state which allows one to see a difficult picture more clearly and be able to resolve it more creatively. How many mothers would respond to this suggestion with an 'Okay, I will rest, but when I've just washed up the lunch things . . .'?

Our many 'selves'

Just like the weather, we are constantly changing in how we are feeling from moment to moment, and like the weather, as one aspect changes then it has an impact on many other aspects too. Whereas a weather pattern has an impact on factors such as temperature, wind speed, levels of cloud, light levels, humidity, rain, and air pressure, our emotions have an impact on our thoughts, feelings in our body, our urges or action tendencies (behaviour), images that pop into our minds, where our attention is directed, and our memories.

Imagine one scenario; discovering our baby has just learned to roll over. Let's look at how the way we are feeling at that moment might create different patterns within us.

Table 7.1: The impact of our emotional state

	Anxiety	Anger	Excitement	Soothing/content-ment
Thoughts	'Oh no, now he can roll into things and get hurt!'	'That's it – yet more things I've got to keep my eye on. As if I haven't got enough to do.'	'Yes, well done! You are so clever!' 'Wait till I show Grandma when she comes round!'	'Aah, is that better now you can move yourself? There, you will enjoy being able to do that.'
Bodily feelings	Heart racing, butterflies in tummy, breathing faster.	Heart racing, jaw tense, chest tight, breathing faster, tightness in arms, hands, tops of legs.	Heart racing, breathing faster, tingling in chest and arms.	Heart rate slowed, breathing slowed, 'warm' feeling spreading from chest to all parts of body.

Urges/ action tendencies (behaviour)	Wanting to run and get baby and put somewhere out of harm's way.	Wanting to grab baby and put in cot. Wanting to phone partner to shout about how much there is to do.	Wanting to pick baby up and dance around in excitement together. Wanting to phone partner to tell him about the baby's achievements.	Wanting to give the baby a smile and a cuddle.
Images	Baby falling off bed. Being looked at with horror by partner when he finds out.	Picking up baby roughly and dumping him in cot. Walking out and leaving partner to it.	Getting family round to celebrate baby's achievements together. Balloons and cake!	Contented baby, smiling and playing happily.
Focus of attention	On potential dangers.	On how much harder life is going to be.	On telling people.	On the baby.
Memories	Other times when awful things happened.	Other times in life when you have been expected to do things without any appreciation.	Other times when things have gone well.	Previous times when you've felt warmth and at peace.

We can represent these as 'cartwheels' (Figure 7.2) where the emotion is the 'hub' and each aspect is a 'spoke'.

Figure 7.2: Aspects of ourselves that change as we shift our emotional state

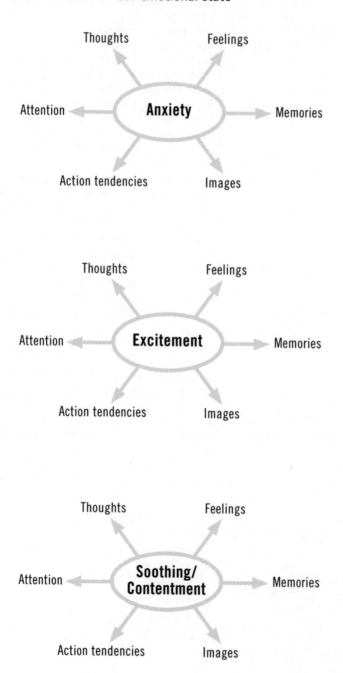

There are a number of key points from this exercise:

1. How we feel affects many different aspects of ourselves. They can be thought of as mini 'selves': for example, our 'angry' self, our 'anxious' self, our 'contented' self.

2. We can have more than one response to the same event, so we might feel excited but there might also be elements of anxiety and frustration too.

3. These mini 'selves' can respond to each other, so when our 'angry' self appears this might create anxiety within us. When we are anxious, the angry part of us might respond with frustration or contempt.

4. We saw earlier in the book that wherever our attention rests, this is what fills up our awareness and everything else disappears into the 'shadows'. What is more, whatever fills up our attention affects us physiologically. So whichever 'self' we are focused on will fill up our attention and all the others will 'disappear'. As we have seen, each self then has an effect on many different systems. So when we are angry, for example, it is difficult to imagine thinking or feeling any other way.

5. We can choose to shift our attention to different 'selves'. So although one may take our attention initially, we can consciously shift it to another, meaning we can regard one scenario from many different perspectives.

6. The threat system is quickest to capture our attention and the hardest to move out of.

7. In the compassionate mind approach we will be using our soothing system as the basis for developing a particular 'weather pattern' or 'self' of compassion. So when we are struggling, perhaps with anxiety or anger, we can then learn to shift into the calmer, more grounded, broader thinking compassionate self with which to respond to our anxiety or anger. But this is hard to do, hence the concept of having to 'train' the brain to do this.

Exercise: Finding balance

Each of our three emotion systems have important functions. They are all equally important. What is key is that they are roughly in balance, in other words that each is sufficiently developed that we can recruit it when necessary. We can begin to explore our insight into the balance we have between different emotion systems with a relatively simple exercise.

Think of the three different types of emotions we discussed. Now think about how much you live in each system. How much of your life is given over to noticing anxiety or things that are making you irritable? How often do you have intrusive worries? Then think about the things that you gain genuine pleasure from. Then think about the things that calm you and soothe you and how perhaps others support you. Now draw out the three circles according to how prominent they are in your life.

Figure 7.3: A common example of which emotional system we spend most or least time in

As you look at your diagram have a think about whether or not your emotional systems are roughly in balance or whether there is one system which is very often stimulated and one which doesn't get much stimulation at all.

The most common pattern that I see in my work is a very large threat system, a smaller drive system and a much smaller soothing system. We can see at a glance the balance of the mind. People who are suffering from depression often draw a large threat system, and very small drive and soothing systems. Those who are rather manic tend to draw a large threat system, an even larger drive system and a small soothing system.

> *Where we have a strong threat system and under-developed soothing system, we focus on building the soothing system, rather than weakening the threat system.*
>
> *This corresponds to how we would give physiotherapy to a weakened leg, rather than attempting to balance ourselves by weakening our strong leg.*

Of course these aren't static for us; we are likely to find that even from moment to moment the balance of these changes. The problem comes when we just cannot draw on a particular emotion system when we need to because it is damped down or under-developed.

Our drawing can help to clarify a way forward. As the sizes of the circles need to be roughly in balance, we can identify which systems need the most work in terms of exercising to stimulate them and therefore build them up, just like building muscles in the gym. If it is the drive system then we can consider how to put more pleasurable activities, potential for achievement and enjoyment into our lives. Often the smallest circle is the soothing system. If this is the case then we can use some of the many ways described in this book to stimulate the soothing system so that it is available to us when we are struggling. We don't need to focus on making the threat system smaller. As the threat system is regulated by the soothing system, building the soothing system gives greater potential to calm the threat system.

Summary

The most difficult and problematic parts of our minds are to do with our emotions. How many times do we think 'If only I could feel better, happier, more content, less anxious and worrying'? We've seen that part of the problem is that our brains are made up of a range of different emotion systems that can easily take us over. As we begin to understand these different emotions we can become mindful of them arising in us and then make decisions about what we want to do.

This chapter explored three types of emotion and how they affect each other. It has also highlighted that the central role for the regulation of many of our emotions is the degree to which we can find a place of slowing and stilling within us. Then we are less constantly being thrown around by drives and threats. We can do this by learning to be mindful and by breathing in a soothing way. We can also do this by learning to focus on the helpfulness and kindness of others. We have seen that mammals in particular have evolved to be regulated through positive social relationships. So it is with ourselves and others; the more we can engage with and be open to support, kindness and helpfulness, the more we will be able to work with our difficult, and at times painful, emotions.

8 How the threat, drive and soothing systems change in response to pregnancy and new motherhood

There is growing evidence that alongside the physical changes, the brain changes too during pregnancy and after the birth of our baby. What is more, these brain changes may remain for life.[1] They occur in all three of the emotion regulation systems: threat, drive and soothing.

The threat system and new motherhood

Earlier in the book we looked at how the threat system evolved to be able to detect threats and prime defensive responses. Such responses include the emotions of anger, frustration, irritability and anxiety along with behavioural responses of freeze, flight and fight. So here we are looking at how pregnancy and new motherhood might impact upon these systems.

Women experience the largest increases in sex hormones in their entire lifetime from early to late pregnancy. In addition to maintaining pregnancy and taking the body through delivery of the baby, these hormones also appear to increase sensitivity to detecting emotions in other people. One study found that women became increasingly accurate at detecting emotions in the faces of other people as pregnancy went on.[2] Moreover, they were particularly accurate at detecting the threat-based emotions of fear, anger and disgust in the faces of others. These changes may be priming the pregnant woman to be hyper-vigilant to people who may be a threat to themselves and their baby, and also to have an increased sensitivity to their baby's distress.

We might think that this increased sensitivity to 'negative' emotions in others means that women are more likely to be experiencing stress and anxiety later in pregnancy. In fact pregnant women appear to become better able to manage stress in late pregnancy compared to early pregnancy. For example, their blood pressure, heart rate and psychological distress remained lower during stressful tasks compared to in early pregnancy and compared to non-pregnant women[3, 4].

> *Our responses to threat change across pregnancy and new motherhood.*

Women who experienced stressful life events such as serious arguments, death of a family member, or serious injury[5], and even in one study, earthquakes[6] during pregnancy rated these as less stressful in late pregnancy compared to early pregnancy. The study found that those who experienced earthquakes in early pregnancy gave birth earlier than those who experienced earthquakes later in pregnancy. So early stress seems to have a comparatively greater impact than later stress.

Interestingly, when an earthquake occurred in the early weeks after delivery, this was considered to be as stressful as earthquakes that happened in early pregnancy. So it seems that late pregnancy may be a unique period where we have an increased ability to manage stress.

This picture might be very different, however, if a pregnant woman has experienced a difficult early life. There have been very few studies looking at this area; however one study[7] looked at the impact of childhood sexual abuse on levels of cortisol in the saliva throughout the day in pregnant women. (Cortisol levels increase with stress but are also important in waking us from sleep and giving us energy for the day). The study found that pregnant women who had experienced childhood sexual abuse had higher levels of cortisol at waking as pregnancy progressed compared to those who hadn't experienced childhood sexual abuse. Although it is important not to put too much store on just a few studies, it starts to give us a sense of the complex mix of factors, none of which we choose, that may influence our response to threat during pregnancy and new motherhood.

Stress, inflammation and postnatal depression

There are of course many physical changes that occur in a woman's body during pregnancy and new motherhood. There is, however, one change that is being viewed with interest as potentially a key factor in contributing to postnatal depression. Kathleen Kendall-Tackett is a proponent of what is called the 'Inflammation Paradigm for Postnatal Depression'.[8] When the body is under stress the immune system triggers inflammation throughout the body to help the body heal wounds and fight infection. What is intriguing are the consequences of the inflammation response; it causes a whole set of behavioural changes including alterations in sleep, appetite, activity, mood, energy, sexual activity and socialisation, all in the same direction as that seen in depression. And, indeed, if the stress continues for too long or becomes too severe there is an increased risk of depression.

So why is this of particular interest for postnatal depression? Inflammation levels rise significantly during the last trimester of pregnancy as part of the normal and adaptive response to pregnancy and preparation for birth. This means that if this idea is correct, then pregnancy itself can place a woman at increased risk of low mood or depression. In addition, factors associated with new motherhood such as sleep disturbance, postpartum pain, psychological stress, and trauma also increase inflammation, thereby also increasing the risk for depression postnatally.

Kathleen Kendall-Tackett also suggests that the relationship between inflammation and depression goes both ways; inflammation increases the chances of depression, and depression increases inflammation. Depression can also impact upon mechanisms that usually keep the inflammation process in check, therefore allowing the inflammation process to continue unimpeded.

As mentioned earlier, an important ingredient to add into this is the impact of previous experiences. Prior depression and traumatic experiences, including stressful early experiences such as childhood abuse or neglect, primes our stress and inflammation response so that our body reacts much more quickly and strongly to lower levels of stress. This means that pregnant and postnatal women who have had earlier depression and trauma may be at increased risk of experiencing depression and anxiety.

This theory suggests that there should be a higher incidence of depression in pregnancy and early motherhood, but research suggests it is the same incidence as for depression at other times. This incident rate was used to argue that postnatal depression was no different from depression that occurred at any other time. However, Kendall-Tackett's theory suggests that mechanisms around pregnancy and new motherhood may be more intricate than previously thought.

The conclusion from this points to the importance of reducing both maternal stress and maternal inflammation if we are to try to reduce or prevent postnatal depression. Pregnant and postnatal women really do need care and support. It isn't just that it is a 'nice' or kind thing to do; it is absolutely vital to the physical and psychological well-being of both her and her baby, and this is even more so if there have been earlier experiences of depression and trauma.

In addition, activities like breast-feeding that are going well can help because they contribute to reducing stress levels. In contrast, difficult or painful breast-feeding can increase stress levels and inflammation, which may lead to an increased risk of developing depression. Therefore it is important that women who are struggling to breast-feed receive early support. (Your health visitor, National Childbirth Trust and La Leche League can all offer advice and support). Gentle exercise, but also resting and recovering when fatigued or in pain, and getting as much sleep as possible rather than accepting lack of sleep as the lot of the new mother, are all key to reducing stress and inflammation. If we can understand this deep necessity for sleep and rest it can make it easier to raise it as an issue for requesting help.

Sometimes short-term but drastic action is required such as having somebody else look after the baby at night-times for a few nights, or sleeping in 'shifts' for example where, say, the mother goes to bed very early while her partner cares for the baby and then takes over from perhaps midnight or the early hours, or vice versa, so a good stint of sleep can be had. Sleep is so important that for some of the women admitted to our Mother and Baby Unit, we suspect a key factor in their psychological as well as physiological recovery is that they can finally get some sleep.

This also directs us towards the importance of developing and stimulating the soothing system as it is this system which can calm the threat or stress response. So, practising soothing breathing rhythm exercises, compassionate self and compassionate image exercises (which we will look at later in the book), Yoga designed for postnatal women, Tai Chi, walking in the countryside, being with people, anything that makes us feel soothed, peaceful and safe, will help in reducing this inflammation or stress response. It will also help to build resilience against future stress.

Indeed, this is what has been found by professor of psychology, Barbara Fredrickson. She looked at two types of activities from which humans experience pleasure, happiness and a sense of well-being.[9] The first is called 'hedonic' well-being, which includes activities such as eating or buying things (more closely associated with the drive system). The second is called 'eudaimonic' well-being, which results from 'striving towards meaning and a more "noble purpose" beyond simple self-gratification' such as feeling connected to a larger community (more associated with compassion and the soothing system). Professor Fredrickson found that it was the latter type of well-being that actually changes the functioning of our immune system at a cellular and genetic level. The first type of pleasure actually made our genes more likely to respond with inflammation in response to chronic stress. The second type of pleasure made our genes less likely to.

> *Being able to feel safe and soothed is important both mentally and physically for the mother and her baby.*

This brief look at some of the research gives us some idea that pregnancy and new motherhood can have an impact on our ability to manage threat, an impact that could affect us significantly but that is not our fault. Understanding this can help to increase our self-acceptance. It helps us to move more towards a position towards ourselves of 'No wonder I have been struggling so much, given all of these different changes that occur around pregnancy, the particular set of genes I have inherited, and the early experiences I have had, none of which I chose; I can just try to be the best I can, and help myself as best I can, given these circumstances.'

The drive system and new motherhood

As discussed earlier in the book, drive emotions are primarily ones connected with seeking out resources, with achievement and with getting things done. For the most part they are pleasurable and give a sense of joy, pleasure and excitement.

Changes relating to these emotions were detected in brains of mothers in the months following the birth of their baby.[10] This study found that the brain undergoes rapid changes postnatally. In fact it grows in particular areas at rates usually only seen after periods of significant learning, brain injury, illness or significant environmental change. These areas are connected to motivation and reward (the drive system), and the regulation of emotions (soothing system). A baby's smile and even a baby's cry will 'light up' this reward or drive system. Interestingly, the greater the changes in the brain, the more the mother was likely to rate her child as 'special, perfect, beautiful, ideal'.

This research is very much in its infancy. One of the key questions raised by the research is what might disrupt this process, so leaving women struggling to experience their baby as rewarding. Later in the book we will look at what we can do if this is the case for us.

The soothing system and new motherhood: soothing, affiliation and attachment

The way we attach to our babies is influenced by all three emotion regulation systems; threat, drive and soothing. For example, when our babies seem distressed or there is a threat to our baby, the threat system kicks in and we respond to that threat because we love them and care for them. When we are enjoying interacting with our babies, maybe in play, we have a sense of pleasure and joyfulness. When we are very tired or stressed, this damps down the drive and soothing system. So attachment and affiliation don't depend on any one system, but on how they pattern together. What is also important is the way in which we are able to calm both threats and drive to allow peacefulness, which also allows open attention. We can call this the soothing system simply because that's what it does. The soothing system plays an important role in attachment and, as one might expect, there are many important changes that occur in this system during pregnancy and after the baby is born.

During pregnancy the mother's nervous system responds to the movements of her baby even when the movements are too small for her to be consciously aware of them, suggesting that even during pregnancy the baby is influencing the mother and may be priming her to become alert to and tuned in to her baby. The following sections look at the role of various hormones connected to the soothing system and the impact of these during pregnancy and early motherhood.

Pheromones

Smell is often overlooked when considering the factors involved in bonding but it may have a very important role. Animal mothers will reject their young if their young are tainted with another smell or if the olfactory system in the mother is damaged. Is it possible that problems with the olfactory system of a human mother affect her bond with her baby?

Smell receptors are primed during pregnancy. Pheromones are hormones that can act outside of our body. They are passed between the mother and the baby in her womb so that by the time the baby is born the mother and baby recognise the smell of each other.[12] Pheromones are also transferred in breast milk. In addition, during breast-feeding the baby learns the smell of the mother's nipples and also her underarm area. The mother and baby, and indeed other care-givers and the baby, will be learning the smell of each other. When naming smells that we love, the smell of a newborn baby's head or neck is often mentioned. Sarah Blaffer-Hrdy in her book *Mothers and Others*[13] notes how a newborn baby is passed around, nuzzled and smelled by family members. She suggests that by sharing her baby she is sending out a signal to her 'clan' that both her and her baby will need them for help. By allowing them to hold and smell her baby she is setting in place the foundation for a bond between them and her baby.

Oxytocin

Oxytocin is a type of chemical called a neuropeptide. It is regarded as a key ingredient for attachment, not just between a mother and her baby, but between the baby and others who care for the baby and between people who have a trusting relationship.

The number of oxytocin receptors increases dramatically in a woman's brain as she nears the end of pregnancy, making her much more receptive to the effects of oxytocin.

Oxytocin surges during labour and is involved in causing the uterus to contract. There is then a further surge of oxytocin in the mother and the baby as the baby passes through the birth canal. As well as being involved in the birth process, oxytocin appears to have a role in helping the mother and baby to recognise the unique smell of each other and to produce a sense of calmness and also pain reduction when in contact with each other.

Breast-feeding within the first hour of birth produces the highest levels of all of oxytocin in what is considered to be a golden window just after birth with regard to bonding with her baby. (Bonding can occur at any point in our lives but both mother and baby are particularly primed for it during this first hour after birth).

Oxytocin contributes to creating pleasurable associations of calmness and soothing between the mother and her infant. It has a social function too: it orients us towards faces and eyes, helping us to gather information about the mind of the other person, and stimulating them to respond to us, and it increases our trust in the other person.

It is not the case, however, that all pregnant women and new mothers have the same levels of oxytocin. Moreover, these different levels can have different effects. One study[14] found that women with higher levels of oxytocin in their blood in the first trimester and in the early postnatal period engaged in more bonding behaviours with their baby postnatally, such as gazing, touching, stroking, singing to them and worrying about their safety, compared to women with lower levels of oxytocin.

It is not clear what causes different levels of oxytocin in pregnant and postnatal women. One piece of research[15] found that levels of oxytocin seemed to be connected to the temperament of the mother. Those who scored high in the trait of something they called 'effortful control' characterised by being 'compulsive, schedule driven and task orientated' had lower levels of oxytocin in their blood after playing with their baby. In comparison, those with high scores on the trait of 'orienting sensitivity' had higher levels of oxytocin. Those high in orienting sensitivity were characterised as having a greater sensitivity to moods, emotions and physical sensations and were less compulsive, schedule driven and task orientated.

The 'dark side' of oxytocin

Oxytocin is a more complex chemical than at first it seems. It has been referred to as the 'cuddle hormone' or the 'chemical of love', with the assumption being that it is directly connected to feelings of love and warmth. However, research using oxytocin in the form of a nasal spray has demonstrated some interesting and surprising results. Oxytocin was found to increase envy and gloating in a game involving winning and losing.[16] Although oxytocin has been found to increase trust and cooperation, this appears to be only towards people regarded as our 'in-group'.[17] It actually created an aggressive stance towards 'out-groups' where participants became more ready to defend if they felt threatened. The researchers called it a 'tend and defend' stance.

In another study[18] researchers asked men to recollect memories of their mothers with regard to maternal care and closeness. They found that for men who were more securely attached, they remembered being closer to their mother when they received oxytocin compared to when they received a placebo spray (a spray with no active ingredients). However, men who were *less* securely attached had the opposite effect; when they received the oxytocin spray they recalled being *less* close to their mother compared to when they received the placebo spray. The researchers wonder whether oxytocin increases activation of the attachment system and therefore brings back those memories which are consistent with an individual's current attachment style. Oxytocin therefore appears to create a bias in types of memories recalled.

Other studies also found a difference in how individuals responded to oxytocin. Oxytocin is assumed to increase trust and cooperation but a study found that individuals diagnosed with Borderline Personality Disorder (a difficulty in regulating mood particularly in relation to others, thought to arise from very stressful and unstable childhood relationships) actually experienced a *decrease* in trust and cooperation when they received a nasal spray of oxytocin.[19] This was particularly so for the more anxiously attached, rejection-sensitive participants.

Another piece of research also found individual differences in the experience of oxytocin. In this study[20] participants were taken through an exercise where they were asked to imagine receiving warmth, kindness and understanding from another being such as a person or an animal. They were given either a spray of oxytocin or a placebo. Generally, the oxytocin increased the ease of experiencing the compassionate imagery. However, those who were high in self-criticism, and lower in self-reassurance, social safeness and attachment security, found it more difficult to receive compassion emotions from the image. When asked about their experiences of the image, those high in self-criticism experienced feelings of anger, frustration, fear and sadness at not having such a person in their lives.

Oxytocin and Bonding Difficulties

These individual differences in response to oxytocin have some potentially important implications in terms of understanding differences in mothers bonding with their babies.

First, as suggested above, oxytocin may only promote trust and care-giving behaviours in people who have had secure attachment experiences themselves. For those who did not feel safe and secure in relation to attachment figures such as a parent, oxytocin may make them mistrustful and even hostile. In effect, mothers can have negative responses to their own oxytocin – but we hasten to add this is a yet to be researched area, though it is potentially very important.

> *Our early experiences can influence the physical response we have to our baby.*

As we have also seen, oxytocin may actually give us difficult feelings if early experiences were of insecure attachment (where an attachment figure is physically or emotionally unavailable, or is unpredictable). As birth, breast-feeding and physical closeness with the baby all trigger oxytocin in the mother, could this mean that mothers who have had less secure attachment experiences, or who are more self-critical or less able to self-reassure, find themselves filled with emotional responses of anxiety, anger or disgust when they are with their baby rather than warm, loving responses? Moreover, if we do find we are struggling to bond with our baby, does our baby come to feel like they are in an 'out-group' separate to us, rather than in our 'in-group'? If so, the oxytocin naturally stimulated by birth, and by the baby, could create feelings of anger and defensiveness towards the baby, and an urge to want to protect oneself and to shun the baby.

These are of course speculations that would need to be researched, but they are certainly experiences shared by a number of women with whom I have worked, who describe finding their baby scary and overwhelming.

Case Example: Alison and her baby, the 'enemy'

Alison described how she felt 'attacked' and 'assaulted' by her baby's long bouts of crying. She saw her baby as an invader into the quiet lives of her and her husband. In an effort to support his wife in her distress her husband allied himself with her against their baby, a position which became stronger and more heavily defended until a new baby came along whom they described as a 'quiet, sunny soul'. It was her profound sense of shame about her reaction to her now two-year-old, compared to her outpouring of love towards her baby, that finally brought her to seek help.

When we have our baby, often we can't help but see parts of ourselves (or of the baby's father) in them. If, however, we do not like these parts, our baby can stir up difficult feelings within us, often without us even being aware of it. This is called 'projection' and can happen with any person we encounter. For example, we may come across somebody who reminds us of a rather strict schoolteacher we had as a child. We 'project' these memories and feelings onto this new person and respond to them as if they are strict and a bit scary, when in fact they may be perfectly nice. However, these findings about the 'in-group'/'out-group' effects of oxytocin pose the question of whether the impact of projecting onto our baby could be made more extreme by the naturally increased presence of oxytocin stimulated within us by childbirth, breast-feeding and physical proximity to our baby. Could this mean that we are more likely to see our baby as 'out-group' when we see things in them that remind us of unpleasant or difficult parts of ourselves?

In addition, research above suggests that oxytocin may bring back memories of our childhood attachment experiences. This can be wonderful if our experiences were positive but can be incredibly difficult if our experiences were anxiety provoking, sad, lonely or frustrating. In the latter case, times of high oxytocin such as childbirth, breast-feeding and physical proximity to our baby may therefore find us suddenly and unexpectedly immersed in feelings that don't really seem to fit with current circumstances. So we might find ourselves having unexplained feelings of sadness, fear, loneliness or anger washing through our bodies when we are with our baby. These are memories or bodily feelings that have become linked to oxytocin when we were young, but which have now been triggered in us once again by these current exceptionally high levels of oxytocin. We can naturally assume that the feelings we are experiencing must be something about our baby or our current life situation when in fact they might be purely feelings triggered by a body memory from the past.

Prolactin

Prolactin is produced when we sleep and it helps our body to repair itself. Prolactin levels increase during pregnancy and cause changes to the mother's brain related to care-giving behaviour. Animal studies have shown that low levels in early pregnancy are associated with increased anxiety and impaired maternal behaviour (such as reduced licking of the fur of their offspring) in the postnatal period.[21]

It is involved in breast-milk production and gives a feeling of calmness and slight fatigue, thought to encourage a relaxed, slow breast-feed. Prolactin is also produced after orgasm and damps down dopamine (which is produced by the drive system), giving a feeling of relaxation and contentment.

Prolactin production increases in fathers and expectant fathers too.[22] It inhibits testosterone in both men and women so reducing sex drive and aggression. However, it is also thought to direct aggression (from both the mother and father) towards any threats to the baby, so it may have a role in increasing protectiveness towards the baby.

Endorphins

Endorphins are considered to be part of the positive emotion system. These give a feeling of euphoria and also happiness and are triggered in both the drive and the soothing system. They are produced when we laugh and when we cry, when a parent and child touch, and during breast-feeding for example. They are also produced in response to the first moments of experiencing pain to help us to bear that pain, but, in contrast, they are also produced when we meditate. Importantly, it now appears that they are also produced in response to emotional pain such as that experienced when we are rejected or ignored by another person.[22] And what is more, those who rate themselves as having higher emotional resilience actually produced more endorphins in response to rejection compared to those who rated themselves as low in emotional resilience, so endorphins seem to provide a buffer against the emotional pain of rejection as well as physical pain.

Cocaine and heroin stimulate the endorphin system and, incredibly, as with these drugs, we can find we get withdrawal symptoms when we are apart from the people or the objects that stimulate our endorphin system. Once a strong opioid bond has been made we may find ourselves becoming agitated, irritable and physically uncomfortable upon separation as the opioid levels drop in the brain, producing a strong urge to return to our partner, baby or home. In a baby, the impact of opioid withdrawal can be alleviated slightly by thumb-sucking or cuddling a comforter such as a teddy or blanket that has also become associated with the feeling of higher opioid levels.

Endorphins therefore help to link us strongly to people (or objects) that make us feel good by rewarding closeness to them with a flush of a positive feeling in our body.

With artificial opioid drugs we become tolerant to them, requiring higher and higher levels to reach the same effect. This tolerance does not occur in bonding, however, because higher levels of oxytocin produced by contact between individuals actually inhibits the development of tolerance so preventing the pleasurable feelings from 'wearing off'. What astonishingly clever and complex bodies we have.

Summary

We are really only just finding out how our brains change during pregnancy and in the weeks and months after having our baby. But in terms of the compassionate mind model it helps us to see that when we become pregnant this amazingly complex pregnancy and mothering machine gets switched on and turned up in us. This causes us to change in ways which we did not choose but which can have a profound effect on our mood, our behaviour, our thinking and so on. It is quite astonishing really.

These changes help us to mother. However, they can also cause unintended consequences such as higher anxiety and a greater focus on threat, which may create real difficulties for those who were already highly threat focused. We also start to realise the many aspects that can be tweaked or thrown off course by external and internal influences, none of which we chose or were our fault but which can have an impact on our mood and how we bond with our baby.

9 Understanding shame

So, we have looked at the evolution of our threat, drive and soothing systems and the role of the soothing system in providing the basis for our evolved capacity for compassion. We have also looked at how the biological changes of pregnancy and new motherhood can impact upon these three systems. However, no doubt as we have travelled through this book so far, it will have been our threat system, particularly in the shape of self-criticism and shame, that has repeatedly tapped us on the shoulder. If we have evolved the capacity for compassion and soothing, and this is considered to be a key factor in the success of the human species, where does the capacity for shame and self-criticism fit in to all of this?

What is shame?

The bodily experience of shame typically comprises a particular pattern of responses: eyes cast down, a loss of muscle tone, a sense of bodily 'collapse', shoulders down and the body curling in on itself. The behavioural urge is to conceal, hide, 'disappear through the floor', to cover one's face, 'to curl up and die'. A number of emotions may be present at the same time, such as a combination of anger, anxiety and disgust. It is often hard to think straight, and the mind may feel confused or overwhelmed.

We can observe similar behaviour in other animals, which gives us a clue as to the possible function of shame. Animals will downcast their eyes, experience loss of muscle tone, and make themselves smaller and lower as an act of submission when faced with a dominant individual. You might notice this if you have a pet dog or cat. The submissive animal is sending out an automatic, highly visible signal that it is not a threat to the dominant animal so no attack is needed. It is a kind of 'I am not going to attack you so please don't attack me!' signal.

We appear to have evolved this same automatic response to signal that we acknowledge we have strayed close to, or stepped over, some social norm. Shame is therefore a protective response in that moment, but it can have damaging long-term consequences because, as we will see, it takes us out of social contact with others, which is of crucial importance to our physical and emotional well-being.

Shame is therefore a threat–protection response, typically involving behaviour indicating submission. We can, however, have different patterns of shame responses; so we may, for example, exhibit a dominant rather than submissive response and express anger outwardly at the other person and try to humiliate them.

When we experience shame, notice how fast our mind reacts to this threat. We can find ourselves being thrown into a particular response, such as submission or aggression, before we have really become aware of what has happened. Our reptilian or old brain reacts first before our neo-cortex or new brain becomes consciously aware of what has happened. So we don't 'choose' a shame response; it happens automatically.

Why does 'shame' exist?

We all have the capacity to feel shame. It is thought that we develop this ability sometime during the second year of life.[1] This is around the time when the brain becomes wired up sufficiently to enable us to have a sense of self, so that when we look in a mirror, for example, we know that this is 'me' rather than just another person.

This is when children become fascinated by the concept of 'mine'; that this toy belongs to me and not that child. For a parent this can be a frustrating period, particularly if there are other children around, but it is also fascinating when we realise the profound developmental shift that this new awareness indicates.

It also requires the ability to understand that other people can look at this 'me' and can have a view about 'me'. If a child sees that they are judged positively they can feel a sense of pride and joy. However, if they are judged negatively they can experience feelings of embarrassment, humiliation and shame. We see just how strong this drive is in children and in adults to be held positively in other people's minds when we consider how important it is for other people to witness the good things that we do. So children will want to show us their 'amazing' new move on the trampoline and will be crestfallen if we miss it or it doesn't 'go right' when we watch. It is as if the good things about ourselves don't mean anything until they are witnessed by another mind.

Some argue, however, that children can experience something that looks like shame much earlier in life. For example, professor of child psychology, Colwyn Trevarthen, observed in children of just six months old their joy in learning a clapping game with an adult and particularly in the experience of anticipating and then seeing that the adult knows what to do and joins in.[2] The joy is in the sharing of this game. When another adult comes who doesn't know the 'rules' of the game the child still initiates the game in joyful anticipation, but when it turns out that the adult does not know what to do, the child displays the downcast look and decrease in body tone that can come with a shame response.

We can experience external shame, which is where our focus is on whether other people will view us as bad, wrong, unattractive, unacceptable or somehow rejectable. We can also have internal shame where we view our selves – our thoughts, behaviour, emotions, body, any aspect of ourselves really – as something that is bad, inadequate or flawed in some way. Internal and external shame can become fused together such that we fear that if these 'shameful' aspects of ourselves were revealed to other people, they wouldn't want to know us. Because shame is experienced as a result of our real or imagined relationship with others, it is sometimes called a social or self-conscious emotion.

Shame is a powerful and aversive experience. It is also considered to be a key factor in many psychological difficulties. So why has such an unpleasant and destructive experience come to be part of our emotional repertoire? We can think about the role of shame through imagining a 'shameless' person – someone who doesn't care what they say or do, who is a bit arrogant, or who is lazy and can't be bothered. How might they behave? How might they be around other people? What kind of emotions might they direct towards themselves and others? How would you feel towards them? The chances are we wouldn't be drawn towards them. In fact we might actively avoid them for fear they might do or say something hurtful or damaging to us, without any care or concern. We might also fear that if we were to feel no shame then we too might become somebody who upsets people or behaves in ways that ultimately mean we would be shunned by those around us.

The hard-wired fear of rejection

We can see that shame is a powerful means of social control, keeping us in check so that we can work together successfully as a group. It is thought that our ability to use the advantages of a social group is what has made humans so successful in evolutionary terms. Shame is a way of keeping in check those aspects that could be particularly damaging to the success of the group. The ultimate shame is to be completely rejected from the group. We can imagine what rejection from the group would have meant during the thousands of years humans lived on the savannah; a high risk of death. This fear of rejection is still hard-wired in us even though we might be able to survive perfectly well without the support of others. This is why just a hint of disapproval in the eyes of another can send panic through us, even if our logical brain tells us that it shouldn't really matter.

> *For thousands of years being rejected from our group represented a major survival risk. Fear of rejection is hard-wired within us.*

A number of experiments looking at social rejection have discovered that this fear of being ostracised or disconnected from others is so strong that we respond to even the slightest indication of rejection. This feeling of rejection occurs even if the person we feel rejected by is someone we don't like.[3]

> *Shame is part of our threat-protection system. It is involved in protecting us from the threat of rejection.*

We don't have to be actively 'pushed out' to feel rejected; we feel a sense of rejection even when we are just not noticed or acknowledged in some way by a stranger in the street.[4] In one experiment, participants were playing a game against a computer.[5] The computer was programmed to say that it no longer wished to include the participant in its game. Even when knowing the computer had been programmed to do this, participants still experienced a physical sense of rejection.

Our brains are set up to assume we are being ostracised even if this is not the case. Imagine for example we have sent a text message or email to somebody. We don't hear back for some time. We might rationalise this at one level, but often it doesn't take long before we wonder if we are being deliberately ignored because we have somehow upset the recipient. This is because our minds are set to be 'better safe than sorry', meaning that we will assume we are being rejected on the basis of very little evidence so that we can set about repairing the situation as quickly as possible. Assuming all is well when it isn't runs the risk of us being cast out of the group without even realising it.

If we have actually been rejected in the past then this bias towards watching for signs of rejection is turned up even further. This is why we can experience panic when our baby cries when we pick them up, when they turn away from us, or when they reach out for someone else. These normal responses in our baby are registered deep in our brains as a signal of rejection and can create strong responses in us of fear, panic, anger and shame. Sadly, I have come across many women who feel rejected by their baby. Realising how our brains are set to be so hypersensitive to rejection is often the first step to being able to remedy what can otherwise become a rapidly strengthening protective strategy on the mother's part of distancing from or clinging to her baby.

When we are rejected or ignored we actually experience it as a physical pain; the same areas of our brain light up as those that register physical pain. We also know that rejection, isolation and loneliness are bad for our physical as well as mental health; it increases our risk of physical illness, reduces recovery rates from physical illnesses and increases our mortality rate.

We are therefore already primed to perceive rejection or disconnection as highly threatening. Shame taps into this fear when we believe there is something within us that, if revealed, will cause us to be rejected by others:

> Shame is an ambivalent emotion which has a double meaning; to be both exposed and concealed. The shamed subject, burning with the sensation of shame, drops her gaze or turns away, and yet she remains exposed. It is the exposure which is shaming; to be witnessed as having done something terrible. Being alone does not erase the experience of shame, since the 'witness' continues to be imagined. (Ahmed, 2004)[6]

This is why we can experience shame even when we are on our own.

Our particular responses are both wired into our human brain, but can also be shaped by the particular experiences we have gone through in life. There can also be gender differences too. So if we generally feel more powerful in our lives we may be more likely to react with anger and to try to humiliate the other person, but if we feel less powerful we may respond submissively.

How shame traps us

The profound problem with shame is that it disconnects us from others. If we believe there is something about us that will be looked upon by others with disapproval or horror then we will try to hide it deep within us. But this leaves us with this sense that we have an uncomfortable secret about ourselves, and that, even when we are in good company, we are not really worthy of being part of that group. We can feel that if others were to get too close to us they might be able to 'look in' and see that horrible part of us. Our fear is that they would recoil with shock, disappointment or disgust, and then not want to know us any more.

> Shame disconnects us. Bringing compassion and understanding to ourselves helps us to work with our struggles rather than shaming ourselves for them and hiding them away. Working with our struggles allows us to connect to others again.

The irony is that we keep these aspects hidden for fear of being abandoned or cast out, but the keeping them in also makes us feel lonely and separate. When we tuck the shame down deep within us we can't see it properly; it lurks within us as a general background feeling of anxiety, murk and blackness. But when we can't see it clearly then we can't remedy it.

To get out of this trap we need to be able to take out and really look at those shameful parts of ourselves; to be able to understand them as being part of the human condition that actually connects us to others rather than disconnects us. We do this by bringing our compassion to these parts. We need our strength to give us the courage to go down into these difficult parts and to be committed to trying to understand and help them as best we can. We need our wisdom to *truly* and *deeply* understand just why we have come to feel or behave as we do, and we need to bring our kindness and our warmth to our suffering about this. If we have harmed somebody (or ourselves) through our actions then we need the strength and courage from our compassion to help us to reach out, to be sorry and say sorry, and to try as best we can to repair this harm.

Shame, guilt and motherhood

Mothers often talk about how feelings of guilt rarely seem far away during pregnancy and motherhood. This is because guilt arises out of the soothing or care-giving/care-receiving system, which of course is the very system that is stimulated when we become pregnant and give birth. Guilt is different from shame in that guilt relates to a specific behaviour or thought that we fear could negatively impact upon the other person. With guilt we put ourselves into the shoes of the other person and can imagine how our behaviour might have caused the other person to feel. Our urge is to repair, say sorry, make it better somehow. Whereas guilt comes from the care-giving system, shame originates in the threat system and is triggered by social threats where we believe we are perceived in critical ways by other people. Guilt is not associated with psychological difficulties, whereas shame is. Guilt is not considered to be problematic (although it can feel like it at the time) because it is associated with noticing a problem and repairing it. Shame, however, is associated with a sense that the problem is a deep, all-pervasive fault within oneself which creates a desire to hide oneself rather than reach out and repair any harm caused. The experience of shame is associated with higher risks of depression and anxiety.

> *Shame makes us hide away what we feel we have done wrong whereas guilt helps us to reach out, say sorry and repair.*

If we can address the shame then we can move from shame to guilt, which can lead to repair and resolution. We can imagine shame as a kind of leaning back or hiding away, whereas guilt is more of a leaning forwards and reaching out.

Guilt is therefore likely to be inextricably linked to motherhood because the care-giving system is so stimulated, thus stimulating our motivation to do the very best we can to help our baby develop and flourish. With it comes a heightened sensitivity to the times when we wished we'd done things better. Guilt alerts us to those times and propels us to try to improve them. Guilt is therefore no bad thing although it can feel horrible. If we can understand guilt in a more positive way it removes the anxiety from it and enables us to move forward with it. Rather than battling against it, we can notice it mindfully and appreciate its presence as a signal of the depth of our caring for our children and a motivation to be as good a mother as we can be in the circumstances.

However, when shame rather than guilt becomes linked to mothering we can really struggle, because at the very time we need the most help, shame can cut us off from that help.

We develop safety strategies for protecting ourselves from shame; for example, by working hard and never making mistakes, being quiet, good, attractive, funny, or poking fun at ourselves before other people do. By the time we reach adulthood we have usually become pretty good at protecting ourselves in this way. However, when we have children, suddenly we are out of control again. Now we have a new little person who doesn't know about our fears and, what is more, has no shame and is totally unselfconscious at first. Our baby has no worries about crying, pooing, being sick and throwing food in public. They will shout in the supermarket, have a tantrum in the waiting room, take toys from other children and cry at the lady with the 'funny face', all without a thought as to how it might affect mum. Suddenly we are exposed to the disapproval of others again. Not only do we fear being judged as 'bad mothers', but as our children can feel like extensions of ourselves, when people see the 'unacceptable' behaviour in our children it can feel as if they are also seeing the unacceptable bit of ourselves.

Having children really does test our self-compassion, but it can also be a real opportunity for an about-turn in how we have viewed ourselves. Sometimes it is the realisation that so-called 'naughty' or shameful behaviour in our baby is actually perfectly normal and understandable that enables us to look at ourselves with fresh eyes. Perhaps we too were just 'being kids' like all the other millions of children in the world rather than behaving in a way that we came to believe was bad, or strange, or different.

'What have you been doing all day?'

We can feel shame when our minds are not understood by another, particularly when we see negative feelings such as disapproval, disappointment or annoyance in the eyes of the other person. A source of shame discussed by many of the mothers I work with is the moment when our partner comes home and sees the mess, a meal yet to be started, and an unhappy wife or partner. Both the mother and her partner might struggle to really understand just what goes on in the day of a mother and try to compare it to the familiar; for example that since the mother is not going to work then it must be like a day off, for example. The image might be of a potential day of coffee, freedom, TV and playing with the baby compared to the image of the partner's day at work of perhaps seriousness, constraint, importance and difficulty.

What makes this particularly hard is that often the mother cannot quite understand what she has done all day either, because there appears to be nothing tangible to show for the immense effort expended. In fact, rather than moving forward through the day, the day seems to have unravelled things further; the house is messier, the washing pile larger, the baby grumpier and ourselves unhappier. Naomi Stadlen discusses this phenomenon in a fascinating book called *What Mothers Do: Especially When It Looks like Nothing*[7]: 'When a mother can't explain her day, she is very unlikely to say to herself: "Maybe the right words are missing." Who has the energy to be insightful at the end of a demanding day? No, a mother who has little to relate usually assumes that this is because there really is very little worth telling' (Stadlen, 2004).

Once we do have words for what we have done, then what we have actually achieved suddenly becomes clear and tangible. We are then able to shift our attention to what we *are* doing rather than what we are not (see Chapter 16 on compassionate attention); for example, keeping our child safe, fed, fed again, fed yet again, warm enough, cold enough, clean, held in mind, noticed, stimulated enough, helped to sleep, and so on and so on . . .

Summary

1.   Shame is a universal human response to social threat. We have the capacity to experience shame from about age two when we can understand that other people have separate minds to us and can therefore have a view about us.

2.   If we see positive emotions about us in the eyes of other people we can feel safe, joyful and proud. If we see negative emotions about us then we can feel unsafe, anxious, angry and ashamed. The ultimate fear is that we will be cast out of our group, which for thousands of years, for humans living on the African savannah, meant one was unlikely to survive.

3.   Shame can have a strong physical effect on the body. We can feel anxious, but find that we suddenly lose energy, so collapsing the body. We might put our head down, want to curl up and feel like we want to 'disappear through the floor'. This is thought to be a submissive response such as we might see in animals that are under threat of attack from a more dominant animal. It is therefore thought to be self-protective in that moment.

4.   Ultimately, though, shame takes us away from social contact and makes us feel like there is something different or wrong about us that can't be revealed to anyone else for fear of rejection. As people are vital to our psychological and physical well-being, shame is ultimately very unhelpful to us.

5.   If we can address the shame, we can move from shame to guilt. Whereas shame compels us to hide our difficulties, meaning we can't really see or resolve them, guilt arises from our care-giving system

and moves us to try and repair, find resolution, and reconnect rather than disconnect.

6. By bringing our understanding, our kindness and warmth, and our acceptance to our shame then we can 'de-shame' shame, and instead of casting ourselves out we can try to connect with ourselves and help ourselves to connect to others and the help they may offer us.

10 Safety strategies and their unintended consequences

Throughout the book we have seen the degree to which we have evolved to stay safe, so much so that watching for and responding to threat overrides just about anything else. This includes staying physically safe, for example avoiding getting run over by a car or becoming ill. It also includes staying socially safe. This is where we are primed through the process of evolution to engage in positive interactions with others, even straight from birth, so that we are held safely in the minds of other people rather than running the risk of being rejected by them. This chapter will look at how our life experiences can interact with our hard-wired threat system, to set up strategies within us as ways of trying to keep us safe from future threats.

> *We develop explicit (conscious) and implicit (unconscious) ways of protecting ourselves. These are our safety strategies.*

In the compassionate mind approach we see four main aspects to how this operates. These four aspects are:

1. Our *life experiences* which have resulted in

2. *fears and concerns* about ourselves and the way other people may treat us.

3. We can carry those fears forward into adulthood but we will also try to protect ourselves from them by developing *safety strategies*.

4. However, these safety strategies can have downsides or *unintended consequences*.

For example, if we have been criticised a lot as children, we may grow up with a fear or concern that we are inferior and not good enough and might worry about other people criticising and rejecting us. We then try to protect ourselves from feeling inferior, or from being criticised, by developing protective strategies. These might be strategies that we deliberately choose such as 'I don't like it when people criticise me so I am going to keep myself to myself in the future', but often they develop without us being totally aware of them. So, for example, we might find ourselves trying to please people all the time, or always keeping people at a distance, without fully realising the fear that drives this behaviour.

It is often only when we cannot use the safety strategy for some reason that we become more aware of the fear that we've been trying to protect ourselves from. So, for example, we might keep people at a distance because we fear we are boring or unlikeable, but we don't quite realise this until somebody we meet at the parent and toddler group invites us round for a coffee, creating panic in us. Or, to try to make sure we are never rejected we may attempt to please others all the time. It is only when we feel torn between two people who both need us at the same time that we come to realise how afraid we are of letting someone down.

The problem is that although these strategies might be able to keep us safe to some extent, often there is a high price to pay in the long run because the safety strategies can have unintended consequences. So we might find that never really letting anyone get too close means we don't get criticised, but we then come to realise that we are actually quite lonely and that when things get difficult there is no one we feel able to call on for help. Or that by trying to please people all the time we never get what we need to be able to function well and to flourish, so we find we get exhausted and resentful. The trouble is then that we can often get angry with ourselves for these unintended consequences. We might criticise ourselves for being 'selfish' at wanting someone to take the baby so we can just read a magazine and replenish for a bit, or we tell ourselves that not having any close friends proves we can't be very likeable.

So, through our attempts to stay safe, we end up struggling in a different way, and then we have a go at ourselves for that too. No wonder we end up feeling so horrible about ourselves. It is because this often happens at a level we aren't fully aware of that we can find it so difficult to see what is happening. We then can't unravel it to see how we might get out of the situation. This chapter is about helping us to be able to see what is happening more clearly so that we can then use our compassionate mind to help us fully understand how it has come about and to try to find a different way of approaching ourselves and our lives that helps us to grow and flourish.

Case Example: Sam and the Quiet Man

Sam (a lady referred to our service), was beautiful, loud, and viva- cious. She moved through life like a speedboat, leaving the people she encountered churned up and bubbling in her wake. She was noticed one way or another, whether for her looks, her jokes, or her complicated demands in shops and restaurants. Her relationships were fast, intense and short-lived. She was frequently subject to envious attacks from other women and acknowledged that on the outside she appeared to have a life of excitement and opportunity. On the inside she felt very differently.

Then she met Shaun. Unlike her other partners who were usually good-looking, outgoing and fast living like Sam, Shaun was a quiet man. He was quite unremarkable in looks and his job, but he had an air of solidity and contentment. Sam was baffled by her attraction to him and was frankly a little embarrassed to be seen with him. But she was drawn to him more and more. However, she would keep walking out of the relationship. He merely waited quietly for her to come back. He loved her deeply, cared for her tenderly and told her repeatedly that he did not want to be with anybody else but her.

Sam found herself pregnant by Shaun after assuming she was infertile. Her panic began to rise. She wasn't quite sure why but hoped it would settle once the baby arrived. Sam moved in with Shaun just two weeks before the baby was born. Far from settling, Sam became more panicked. This became so severe once the baby was born that she found herself unable to sleep night after night. Eventually she was referred by her health visitor to our service.

She came for therapy and started to talk through her life. She explained that her mother was a very beautiful woman, and spent a lot of time on her appearance for the different boyfriends she had. Sam had frequently been forgotten and became thin and malnourished. Sometimes, however, her mother would dress her up and show her off. Sam had felt like a doll, but loved those moments of closeness with her mother and the admiration she got from her mother's friends. She was quiet, vulnerable and pretty. She described being very confused about her feelings regarding being 'shown off'. On the one hand she felt like an object; helpless and powerless. But she also felt powerful; that there was something about her that got her noticed. She left home at sixteen. However, she craved attention 'like a drug'. She described feeling a kind of 'black anxiety' if she walked down a street without turning any heads. She even preferred getting jealous insults from other women to being completely unnoticed. When she really peered into this 'black anxiety', she said, if nobody noticed her then she felt like she was disappearing. Her safety strategies had changed over time, from being quiet and compliant as a child, to being loud, noticeable and sexually provocative as an adult.

However, as one can imagine, there were many unintended consequences to her new safety strategies. She got into fights with women, and although she felt she had the ability to acquire closeness and physical contact with men when she needed it, she believed that men were only with her because she looked good on their arm. She could not find anyone who was able to look beyond her beauty and really 'see her', and, more than that, truly love and care for the person that they could see inside. She felt very lonely and unloved. This was until she met Shaun. He seemed to look right inside her and love her all the more.

When she became pregnant, however, she noticed pangs of jealousy when he felt her tummy. She became angrier and angrier the more excited he got about the baby. She began to believe that he only wanted to be with her because she was the vessel that contained his child. In fury she would leave him, but be drawn back by his concern and care for her.

Her pushing and pulling, which had begun to settle a little before she became pregnant, became much more extreme. When the baby was born Shaun cried with joy. Sam wanted to throw the baby at him and run away. She wanted 'to tear him to pieces' she was so enraged. She told him to choose between her and the baby but he refused. She told him she was going to leave him and take the baby. He took the baby off her as she tried to storm out of the door. He had chosen the baby. She ran out into the night and went to a pub and drunk as much as she could before her quiet man stormed into the pub, his face black with fury, carrying the sleeping baby in a car seat. He took her home. She was shocked to see his face. He had never become angry like this before. He refused to speak to her and she sat in the bedroom shaken, scared and aware that she had nearly lost her quiet man. Her safety strategies were no longer keeping her safe, and her mind became completely frozen with panic. She could not sleep and this is when the health visitor referred her to our service.

We can sense in Sam's story how baffled she was by her feelings and reactions; indeed, she regarded it all as 'a mess'. But actually we can see that it all fits together in a way that makes sense and is understandable; through her experiences as a child she developed fears about herself (these are called 'internal' fears) that she was unimportant, not loved unconditionally but only valued for what she could provide for others, easy to forget, vulnerable, lonely and scared. She also became angry as a child at being used in the way she was but her anger in turn became an internal fear, because if she let out her anger at other people, she feared they would leave her and she would then lose the little bit of attention she did get.

Her fears and concerns about others (external fears) were that people were uncaring, unavailable, powerful, controlling, and only regarded other people as objects for meeting their own needs.

To cope with her fears she developed internal safety strategies for managing her own emotions and feelings about herself. As a child these included criticising herself and cutting off her feelings to try and damp down her anger at others. She became quiet and compliant. As she got older her safety strategy changed to an external one involving just letting out her angry side as much as possible so that she kept people at a distance and controlled the 'rejection' herself. She also tried to make herself noticeable and to get a reaction and physical contact from others to alleviate the feeling of fear and anxiety that accompanied a sense that she didn't really exist.

As well as pushing people away with her anger, her external safety strategies included never letting anyone really get to know her in case they 'saw' that she was actually unlovable and empty beneath the attractive and exciting persona that she presented to the world. So she never let friendships develop and had little more than 'one-night stands' with men. She also spent a lot of time and money on her appearance and when out and about she would engage people in high-intensity interactions such as arguments, flirting, or bringing all sorts of demands into buying goods or a meal.

Her safety strategies gave her a sense that she existed in the world and could pull people to her when she needed them – something that was missing in her childhood – but push them away before they got to know that she was 'boring' and 'empty', as she considered herself. However, these strategies meant that when she did finally meet somebody who deeply loved her, she nearly pushed him away completely because she felt it was just a matter of time before he realised she was nothing special.

She also didn't believe he would have the capacity to love her *and* the baby, so when he started to give attention to the baby she pushed him away first before he could reject her. The unintended consequences were that she felt desperately lonely and, of course, this just confirmed her original fears that people didn't want to be with the 'real' Sam. In the end, she nearly lost the very person and the family she had been yearning to find all these years.

We can see how, looking in from the outside, it would have been easy to blame Sam and for Sam to blame herself, as indeed she did at first. But when we look at the whole picture we see that Sam did not choose these early experiences, and neither did she choose to have a brain that through millions of years of evolution has been set as its first priority to look out for threat and to protect her from it. It has evolved to have a 'better safe than sorry' strategy, so even though there may be many people that she came in contact with who would love her, care for her and protect her, her mind and body has already 'learned' that closeness to people is associated with some feelings of excitement and pleasure, but mainly with feelings of anger, anxiety and disgust. She did not have much of a sense at all that people could bring with them feelings of safeness, soothing and contentment, and the devastation that came with the possibility of letting herself feel this if it was offered, and then having it taken away, just felt too great to bear.

> *Safety strategies can keep us safe in the short term but may have long-term unintended consequences.*
>
> *Bringing compassion and understanding to our innate need to stay safe helps us to find new safety strategies that are more helpful to us as our circumstances change.*

So, just as with a person who loves dogs, where one nip from a dog can make it hard for them to stroke a dog again despite many gentle encounters previously, our minds will make it incredibly hard for us to risk dropping our safety strategies in case we get hurt again. For Sam, as for anybody who had been through the same experiences as Sam, a strong alarm response would have been set off within her body every time she got close to somebody. This was not her fault, nor would it be our fault if it happened to us; it is how our minds have evolved to protect us.

Sam 'tested' Shaun many times and onlookers were surprised that he stayed. However, they are still together six years on and have had two more children together. Our safety strategies are hard to give up, but our brains are malleable and adaptable, and we can gently mould them as we would modelling clay. We can therefore develop new safety strategies that fit better with new environments, particularly if we can take the risk of reaching out to others even when our brain and body shouts at us not to.

Pulling it all together: the four-part formulation

A helpful way of more clearly being able to see the processes that we have been talking about in this chapter is by putting them into a four-part formulation (such as in Table 8.1 below). A formulation is just a way of coming to some kind of understanding of what has led to the current situation. The four columns in the formulation are headed:

1. Our background.

2. Fears.

3. Safety strategies.

4. Unintended consequences.

The 'background' column would include key events that occurred in our lives which proved to be difficult for us. These might include how a particular parent related to us, having an illness or some kind of disability that we had to manage, or being bullied at school. The 'threat or fear' column refers to what it was specifically about the event in the 'background' column that triggered off our threat system. This might perhaps be a fear or worry about other people (external fears); for example, that other people might be critical, unpredictable or unavailable when we need them. Or it could be something we fear about ourselves (internal fears); for example, that I am 'weak and cannot protect myself', 'I have frightening thoughts which people would reject me for if they knew about them', or 'there seems to be something about me that makes me unlovable'. Because we have evolved minds that work to keep us safe, we are driven to try to protect ourselves from our fears occurring again through the development of particular strategies (safety strategies). This is the third column. If we fear that others will hurt or reject us then we might develop an external safety strategy whereby we keep people at a distance. If we fear that we are weak we may keep ourselves safe by avoiding difficult situations in which we might be required to be strong and confident, or we might rely on others to make decisions for us.

These safety strategies can settle into us and stick around for a long time because of our evolved 'better safe than sorry' minds; if a strategy seems to work and keep us safe then we would find it very hard to test out letting the safety strategy go for fear we will get hurt. The problem is that although the strategies might keep us safe in some respects, there may be some downsides or unintended consequences of the strategy. So if we fear we might get hurt, for example, and therefore keep people at a distance to protect ourselves, we then find we are lonely, and in fact feel more separate and unsafe because there is nobody we can call upon if we are really struggling.

We can see in the table that the contents of each column flow from the previous one.

Table 8.1: The four-part formulation

Background	Threat or fear	Safety strategy	Unintended consequences
Mother critical and unloving.	**External:** People can be harsh, unavailable and attacking. **Internal:** There is something bad, unlovable and 'wrong' about me.	**External:** Try and please people so they love me and don't attack. Don't make demands on others in case they get angry or reject me. **Internal:** Keep any angry or horrible feelings suppressed in case the 'bad' bit comes out – criticise self, eat too much, drink alcohol, clean house excessively, exercise too much, 'neutralise' bad thoughts with good ones. Keep self at a distance from others so they don't get to see the horrible bit of me.	Don't get own needs met so get down, angry. Hard to please everybody so feel anxious all the time. Can't ever relax. Get burnt out. People don't do anything for me so still feel unloved. Angry or 'bad' thoughts cannot be suppressed (as they arise normally in all people), therefore I fear I must truly be a horrible person, and I now have the additional problems of overeating, or drinking too much alcohol, or struggling with obsessive-compulsive traits etc. Feel lonely, separate, different. Makes me believe even more that there is something unlovable about me.

We can use this format to give us some insights into ways we have come to cope with life. It can be particularly reassuring to make sense of behaviour that we had previously considered to be frustrating and baffling, for example pushing away the first person in our lives who has really stood by us. What can seem frankly like crazy and nonsensical behaviour suddenly makes clear, understandable and logical sense once we see that we are fundamentally wired up to do whatever we can to stay safe.

It also helps to separate the past from the present. We can see more clearly that we are still responding as if the past were true when in fact the present circumstances might be very different. But we also see that this is not our fault, it is just the way our minds have evolved to protect us, by using 'better safe than sorry' strategies, and focusing us, for example, much more on evidence of threat than on evidence for safeness.

It also helps us to become much clearer about precisely what it is that we want our compassionate mind to help us with. For example, if we've developed a safety strategy of keeping people at arm's length, how might our compassionate mind help us to start allowing people (perhaps including our baby) to get a little closer? If we always tried to please others and put them first, how might our compassionate mind help us to start discovering what *we* enjoy, what *we* need, what is important to *us*, and then help us perhaps to take tiny steps towards bringing these into our lives?

Here are some examples of the formulations of women who have struggled with new motherhood. They help to show how our earlier experiences can interact with becoming pregnant and with new motherhood.

Table 8.2: Examples of using the formulation to make sense of why we may be struggling with new motherhood

Background	Threat or fear	Safety strategy	Unintended consequences
Born into high-achieving family. 'Extreme emotions' such as anger, tearfulness and joy viewed as 'showing off'.	Others are critical.	Be perfect, high achieving, never make a mistake.	Can't tell anyone if finding new motherhood difficult. Feel alone, have no access to help.
	I am only valued when I don't make a mistake and when I do better than others.	Now I have a baby I have to be the perfect mother and never get it wrong.	This is impossible, so stay highly anxious that will fail at any minute.
		Make sure baby is 'perfect' and high achieving too, so that it is loved (and I am loved) – make sure it is well behaved, clever, sociable, crawls first	But as can't control baby this way, feel disappointed with baby and angry with self.
			Feel ashamed that seem unable to cope when usually high achieving.
	My emotions are out of control, and disconnect me from people.	Never reveal emotions. Keep them in through self-criticism.	Feel very tense around baby, which makes baby more tense and unhappy.
	My baby's emotions will reflect badly on me and get us both rejected by our family.	Try to keep baby happy at all times, pre-empt his needs, never take him out in public.	Blame self more for having unsettled, grumpy baby when others seem to be able to parent easily – feel inadequate, separate.
			Impossible to do, so feel a failure.
			Lonely and never see that others struggle too.
			Get panicked and angry with baby if he does show strong emotions. Feel more out of control.

Background	Threat or fear	Safety strategy	Unintended consequences
Lots of losses during childhood – Dad leaving, Grandma becoming ill and dying.	The world is unpredictable. People you love leave you. There is something about me that means people leave me.	Trying to have control over own world – put toys and books in order. Develop compulsive behaviour, e.g. 'If I don't step on cracks in pavement then my mum will be safe.' Try and neutralise 'bad' thoughts or feelings with 'good thoughts and actions'.	When become pregnant and have baby, body, mind and life is suddenly out of control and unpredictable. Hard to keep order and to use strategies that used before, e.g. cleaning, so feel more out of control and highly anxious. Worry will lose baby so highly vigilant to potential threats. Won't let others look after baby so day feels chaotic and obsessive-compulsive behaviour gets really out of control. Unpleasant thoughts and feelings are normal so will keep on arising but the more attention I give them the stronger they become and the worse I feel about myself.
Parents neglectful. Didn't take us into account.	People are uncaring and do not protect me. I am unlovable and unimportant.	Keep people at a distance or just have superficial relationships. Reject people before they reject me.	Secretly hoped baby would give unconditional love and see me as most important person in the world. Find self panicking each time baby looks away or when baby cries. Fear baby doesn't love me. Pull back from baby so don't get hurt. Baby then cries more with me. Feel even more unlovable and alone.

Background	Threat or fear	Safety strategy	Unintended consequences
Mother unwell and I had to look after her from a young age. House had to be kept calm and quiet because noise and upset made her worse. Dad out at work and not really around much.	Others are weak or absent. My own needs are too overwhelming for others.	Keep looking after needs of others so they stay well and don't leave me. Keep on alert for signs of illness. Don't relax or play. Keep own needs suppressed.	When have baby feel overwhelmed by responsibility of keeping them well and happy because brings up body memories of having too much responsibility as child. Feel anxious and angry around baby. Baby gets grumpy and upset making me feel even more panicky. Don't know how to play with baby as never relaxed and played as child. Time with baby is tense, serious and lacking in joy – feel a failure as a mother. Can't ask for help, as others might be overwhelmed by own needs, so struggle on feeling alone, resentful, angry and self-critical.

In Appendix B there is a blank formulation for you to have a go with if you wish. You could also try out formulating your partner or family member, or someone else you know reasonably well. It can be very helpful in coming to understand a little more why someone may have come to relate to themselves and others in the way that they do.

Summary

1. One of our strongest evolved motivations, as with other animals, is to stay safe. When we have experienced repeated or extreme fear or concerns then we develop ways of trying to prevent these fears from occurring again. These are safety strategies.

2. We can develop fears about ourselves (internal fears) such as our emotions, thoughts or behaviour and fears about others (external). Our safety strategies can be internally focused on controlling ourselves or externally focused on our relationships with others.

3. Safety strategies can be maintained for a very long time, even if circumstances change and they are no longer necessary. This is because we are hard-wired with a 'better safe than sorry' mentality.

4. This 'better safe than sorry' hard-wiring can lead us to experience unintended consequences from our safety strategies.

5. We can find ourselves unintentionally enacting our safety strategies with our baby too, e.g. 'don't love him in case I somehow lose him'.

6. Once we can start to see how our past experiences link to our body memories and our explicit fears about ourselves and other people in relation to us, we can start to understand the safety strategies that have become set up within us, how they endure over time, and the unintended consequences they can have.

7. The formulation helps us to see more clearly that we did not choose to have these experiences, this evolved brain, or these safety strategies or their consequences. Instead, we can see how hard this has been for us, which can sometimes evoke sadness for a while.

The formulation contributes to our understanding, and hence our wisdom, which we draw upon when we are developing and using our compassionate mind.

8. Finally, we can start to consider, given what we now know, what would help us move forward from this point and start to shape ourselves into the version of ourselves that we would like to be.

11 'How am I feeling? How are you feeling baby?': Understanding the minds of ourselves and others

As we have seen so far, the compassionate mind approach focuses a great deal on how we feel, and in particular on how we can develop new body memories of being cared for, and of caring for others. However, for many of us our feelings and emotions can be confusing, and understanding them in our body is a real challenge. This can make understanding them in our baby difficult too. This chapter looks at some of the struggles we may have around emotions.

'I have no idea how I feel'

A surprisingly large proportion of the population are unable to identify or name what they are feeling. If they are asked 'what is the matter?' they might have no idea what emotions they are experiencing. One possible cause of this becomes clear when we think about how children learn about their emotions. Children experience the full range of emotions and we only need to watch a toddler to witness the purity of an emotion as it takes hold of his entire body. So, for example, we can imagine how a child would look in the throes of joy, excitement, fear, anger, sadness or disgust. As a child experiences these emotions, they might be reflected back in tone and matching energy levels, and named by those around him; 'What's scared you, Jamie?', 'Oh dear, has that made you sad?', 'Is this exciting, Joe? Are we going to go on the train in a minute?'

Earlier in the book we looked at how there is something very calming about naming our emotions when we are in threat mode. This has been shown on brain scans, which reveal a reduction in activity in the amygdala – the part of the brain particularly concerned with threat emotions – when we give a name to the emotion we are witnessing.

It is almost as if giving a name to an emotion gives it shape and understanding, making it containable: 'So these strange sensations inside me are not so strange actually. They have a name and they are familiar to other people.'

If they are not named, however, they may remain an unclear, puzzling set of sensations within us, rather like listening to an unfamiliar language.

Emotions, of course, have an important role in communicating to ourselves and to those around us. They create a change in attention, thinking, behaviour and so on in ourselves and others. However, what happens if our emotions are ignored or not named for us? Or what if we have to pay close attention to the emotions in other people to predict what they might do next, rather than paying attention to our own emotions? Here we start to see how we lose contact with our own emotions. It is no wonder some of us struggle to know what we are feeling.

The chameleon: 'I don't know who I really am'

Attending only to the emotions of others rather than ourselves can lead to the unintended consequences of trying to please others, but not getting our own needs met. Some people describe how they have no sense of self; they do not know how they feel, what they like or don't like, what they want or don't want. They can have the experience of changing their opinions, values and even their appearance according to the people they are with at that moment.

We all do this to some extent; we adopt different roles with different people; but we still need a core part of ourselves that listens to our needs and guides us according to our values. For example, if we pick up a pair of trousers in a shop, we can decide whether we like or dislike them by taking note of the feelings that arise in us. But if we have never really been encouraged to pay attention to what is happening inside of us, and we don't know what the feeling is called, then we can find this very difficult to do. Imagine, then, being put into a social situation where we have learned to do what it takes to keep the other person happy. If we are asked our opinion, we search in the face of the other person to work out 'what is the right answer'. 'What should I be feeling about this?'

> *We learn a lot about how we are feeling when people name our emotions, particularly when we are young.*

As ever, with time, understanding and, of course, compassion, it is possible to learn what we feel inside. Just as we might learn a foreign language or learn the names of different trees or birdsong, we then find ourselves being able to 'see' the individual word, or tree, or hear the individual bird, whereas before they went unnoticed or registered only on the periphery of our senses. We can start to turn our attention inwards, when we have the sense of safety and space to do so. We can really focus in with an interested awareness rather than judgement, to notice what we find. And we can match it to what is going on externally so that we learn what triggers our emotions: 'When that happened I experienced this sensation inside me.' 'When you frowned at me, it made butterflies in my tummy.' 'When I see the sunshine, I feel as if my chest is big and light like a balloon.'

This is where the practice of mindfulness is so important. It helps us to focus in on the sensations and emotions in our body with an interested awareness and non-judgement.

'My feelings are scary'

We have looked at how we learn about ourselves through our reflection in the faces of those around us. This applies to our emotions too. If we laugh, and our parent laughs joyfully too, we feel good inside. We learn that this emotion makes us feel nice and it makes our parent happy too. However, if we become angry and this is met with anger by our parent, we feel uncomfortable inside. We learn that this is not a good feeling and we are less likely to show it in future. If we are scared by the reaction of the other person, then our anxiety becomes linked to our feelings of anger. If this happens repeatedly then each time we feel angry, we also feel anxious too. Eventually we may find that our anger becomes engulfed by the anxiety and when we might expect to feel angry we find only that we feel anxious instead. (Incidentally, although we are using the example of anger here, this could apply to any emotion, including sadness, and even happiness and joy where these are frowned upon, derided or feared by those around us).

What is more, if our anger does manage to bubble up occasionally we can be really scared by this and develop ways, or safety strategies, to keep it suppressed, such as eating, exercising excessively, drinking alcohol, or being even nicer to others for example.

As well as losing access to important emotions and to the communication that they afford us, we also do not learn the qualities of emotions – that they rise and then fall, that they come and go, that we can feel them, but not necessarily act on them. Instead, we can be left imagining that if we didn't suppress them, they would rise uninhibited and form something perhaps monstrous and destructive.

Even when we feel these scary emotions are suppressed, we can still be left with a sense that there is something unsavoury within us, and if people get too close they may see it and recoil in horror. These perfectly normal and important emotions then become a source of shame.

Any of our emotions can make us feel anxious, depending on our association to them learned through our life. Anger, however, can feel like a particularly difficult emotion when we have a baby because it can make us want to shout, fight and attack. As we have seen, our threat emotions begin automatically so it can be alarming to feel ourselves beginning to draw ourselves up into a dominant, angry stance in relation to our tiny, helpless baby in moments of sheer anger and frustration. The problem is there are many triggers for our anger with a new baby; from lack of sleep, inability to finish a job that would make us feel slightly more in control, inability to finish a thought in our head without interruption, trying to get out of the house to an appointment when the baby needs feeding or changing again . . . But anger is particularly scary if this has been squashed down in us as a child. Then we have not learned that even anger comes and goes, that we can listen to it but not necessarily act on it, and that we can moderate our reaction; so we might curse under our breath or walk away rather than hit out. Instead, we might imagine that if we let it out it would just carry on growing into something huge and destructive like the Incredible Hulk.

If we don't like an emotion in ourselves then we may really struggle when our child starts to express that emotion. We might think 'Now it is in my baby too and, what is more, my baby is showing this shameful or scary emotion in public. Will they think that my baby is made up of my horribleness?' We can feel that not only are we shameful, but our child is too. So to protect ourselves from this threat of rejection by other people we might adopt the safety strategies of keeping our self and our child away from other people, and distancing our self from our child at home, or get angry with our child when they are angry; to try to stop them exhibiting emotions that we fear will cause their, and our, rejection by others. These safety strategies are driven by fear and the desire to protect both ourselves and our child from rejection, but they have the unintended consequences of causing isolation and loneliness, removing us from sources of help, from being able to see other children and from understanding how anger is normal.

As ever, we can use our compassion to get us out of the trap that our shame can draw us into. First, we can understand that we are born with the ability to have the full range of emotions, and that these have been carefully selected through millions of years of evolution to exist within us because they help us.

Second, we can look into our past and see how our emotions were regarded and managed by those around us. Were we allowed to express our emotions? Were they named and responded to in a validating, accepting and understanding way, or were they met with disapproval, horror, anger or fear? How did we learn to manage our emotions so that they did not evoke this reaction in those people whom we relied on to look after us? We can see that we didn't choose these ways of keeping ourselves safe, in fact they often began to be shaped before we even had the words to describe what was happening. These safety strategies can have down sides or unintended consequences that are unfortunate and not chosen by us either.

> *Emotions can become linked, or conditioned, to other emotions. So sadness can be linked to anxiety, for example, or it could be linked to feeling safe and soothed depending on our experiences.*
>
> *We can learn to link the feelings produced by our compassionate mind (safeness, strength and soothing) to emotions that have previously scared us.*

Third, we can start to think with our compassionate mind about what will help us to move on, grow and develop from here. This might include spending time coming truly to understand the importance to us of all of our emotions, noticing the role they have for our baby, and then slowly, step by step, allowing these emotions back into our lives. This is a de-sensitisation approach, just like we might use with anything that we are scared of but really need to overcome in order to live fulfilling lives, such as going out of the house when we feel scared of meeting people, or getting in the car and driving again after a car accident. By looking at and exploring these feared emotions with an interested awareness and compassion, they start to lose their fear and shame and therefore we are enabled to connect again with those around us.

Importantly, too, we also develop a different relationship with the emotions of our baby. Compared to when we are in threat mind, which focuses our attention on ourselves as 'under attack', when we are in our compassionate mind we can look outwards with a broad open mind. This enables us to look into the mind of our baby with an interested awareness concerning what their emotions might be communicating to us. Our motivation is to try to help them as best we can. Our strength and wisdom helps us to stay with our baby and to try to help them even when they are really distressed.

'When I am upset I can't think clearly about you or me': mentalisation

Mentalisation is the ability to understand our own minds and the minds of another person, for example the mind of our baby. It comes from our understanding that other people, including our baby, have separate minds from our own. It is what enables us to consider that our baby might be hungry when we are full, or cold in their buggy when we are hot from pushing the buggy uphill, or that our baby can be wary of someone that we really like. A struggle to be able to mentalise can lead us to assume that whatever is in our minds must be in the minds of others too. This can lead us to believe that other people hold the same beliefs, motivations or feelings as us. So, for example, if we believe that we are unlikeable we may assume that our baby doesn't like us too.

Our ability to mentalise, however, is affected by different factors.[1] It can be impaired by conditions such as autism and Asperger's syndrome. It is also thought that our ability to be able to mentalise well may be connected to the security of our attachment as a child. This in turn is also connected to the ability of our care-givers to mentalise well. For example, mothers with insecure attachment strategies were more likely to respond with sadness when their child was sad, whereas mothers with secure attachment strategies were more likely to respond to their child's sadness with concern. This is one way in which it is thought that secure or insecure attachment can get transmitted from generation to generation.

A care-giver who can look with curiosity into the mind of a child and put themselves 'in the child's shoes' is more able to respond quickly and accurately to the child. If a child protests at a noisy toy being rattled close to their face but the mother just keeps smiling, rattling it and carrying on talking to her friend, the baby develops no understanding of its mental state; they might have an uncomfortable feeling in their body which causes them to cry out or push the toy away but no words are given to explain the sensations, the toy doesn't get taken away and the mother doesn't show any sense of understanding the emotion and then responding to it. The baby is just left with feelings of frustration and helplessness. However, a mother who hears and sees the distress might respond 'Is that rattle getting annoying? Okay, how about holding Bear instead? He isn't noisy and he is lovely and soft.' Here the baby's discomfort has been noticed quickly, it has been understood, it has been given a name ('annoyed'), and it has been responded to (by stopping the rattling) so the child learns that they have the ability to control their environment and change it from being unsafe to safe. The child also learns about their own mind; that it is understandable and safe. They learn to become safe in their own mind and in the mind of their mother.

What helps us to mentalise? Safeness and soothing

In addition, when we feel safe and soothed we can look out from ourselves and take in information in new and creative ways. We can observe with curiosity the emotions and behaviour of other people and learn about *their* minds. Where a care-giver has very good mentalising abilities, a child can learn that even difficult emotions in their mother, such as witnessing her sadness, frustration or anxiety, does not have to be anxiety-provoking for themselves. If this mother can be upset, or cross, or scared but at the same time make it clear to her child that these emotions are about her and not about her child, then her child learns that such emotions do not have to be contagious or worrying. She can both be upset but calming to her child, even if this has to be slightly after the event in the form of reparation and apology, for example 'It's okay Joe, mummy is just a little bit sad at the moment. I will be okay in a minute', or 'Sorry Joe that I got cross with you then. I feel very tired and crotchety. It isn't your fault love.' Even if children are too young to understand the words, their amygdala can pick up the soothing voice tone and facial expression and be calmed by this.

> *When we feel safe and soothed we become better able to put*
> *ourselves in the shoes of others (and ourselves).*

Our ability to mentalise is also affected by how safe or unsafe we feel, so sometimes we can be better at thinking about the mind of somebody else (or our own mind) than at other times. When our threat system is activated then it can become harder to mentalise. In other words it becomes harder to really understand how the other person is feeling or what they might be thinking. A key point here is that although the ability to mentalise well is linked to feeling safe, this sense of safeness can be different for each of us. Our ability to mentalise is not fixed. It can vary from moment to moment, in fact, according to how threatened or safe we feel, as we saw above. And what is safe to one may in fact feel unsafe to another. So a positive, reliable relationship to somebody who is used to being repeatedly let down may actually feel unsafe, because they believe it is only a matter of time before this good thing will end. Happiness for another may feel unsafe, because this is when dad or mum would get angry.

Therefore if the cry of our baby triggers our threat system (for example, by tapping into a belief that crying signals inadequacy on our part, or by pulling up emotional memories where crying has become associated with overwhelming sadness, grief, fear or aloneness) then we may find it extremely difficult to move away from our sense of threat and into the mind of the baby. This is not our fault, it is precisely how our minds are designed to behave under threat; to become narrowed in focus, to assume the worst ('better safe than sorry'), and to focus on getting ourselves safe. But the unintended consequence is that we are then much more likely to struggle to respond accurately to the baby's distress when we are distressed. This leads to the situation familiar to most mothers where the distress of the baby and the mother feed each other and it escalates, leaving both feeling wretched.

On the other hand we might feel safe when a baby cries because we might have had many experiences of dealing with consoling crying children, and our childhood experiences of crying have created emotional memories linking crying to solutions and finding safety, so crying does not alarm us. We therefore have a 'felt' confidence that we can sort out the distress in our baby. But for others, as above, crying can provoke a sense of feeling unsafe.

Emotional contagion: when I feel what you feel

One of the reasons that safeness helps us to mentalise is thought to be due to the production of oxytocin when we experience a feeling of safety. It seems that when we produce oxytocin we are better able to separate out the feelings of others from our own feelings. When oxytocin is not produced then we can experience 'emotional contagion' where the emotions in somebody else just 'wash through us'. It can feel like their feelings are our feelings. This is what happens to babies where the crying of one baby sets off crying in other babies. Of course we do naturally feel what others feel. This is 'sympathy'. But when we feel safe and can produce oxytocin then we can still experience the feelings of another person; but we also have a sense that it comes from them and not us. This means we might be less likely just to react automatically. Instead we have a little space to work out what might help the other person if they are feeling this way. This might be different from what might help us in that situation.

When we feel a safeness around particular emotions we are then more able to mirror back to the child that we understand their distress but that we can cope with it, and that it is manageable and not distressing to us. The child learns that their own emotions may feel uncomfortable but they are not scary to others and therefore they don't feel scary to them. In turn, as the child grows up, they are less likely to be scared by the emotions of others so they are therefore much more able to mentalise and so look with an interested awareness into the mind of another and respond more appropriately.

'When it gets too much, I can't think properly'

There was an illuminating experiment using rats in a cage. It went something like this: each time a picture of a blue circle was shown they were given some food when they pressed a lever. Each time a red square was shown, they were given an electric shock. The rats could enter and leave the cage at will. The rats actually coped well with this because it was clear what they needed to do to keep safe. Gradually the red square and blue circle were then merged to form a purple ellipse. The rats no longer had a clear strategy and their behaviour became more uncertain and disorganised. This happens to us humans too; when strategies start to conflict and there is no longer a clear way of staying safe, we start to experience very high levels of anxiety and confused behaviour. Our mind can feel like it has become overloaded and frankly a little crazy.

We can see this in a more extreme way in children who are hurt emotionally or physically by their care-giver. When they are hurt, their attachment system is automatically fired up and they seek safety from their attachment figure. However, if that is also the person who hurts them, then they need to pull away and protect themselves. Mary Main, an academic researcher into attachment, called this 'fear without solution'.[2] These safety strategies are in direct conflict with each other and become broken down or disorganised. The resulting 'best' safety strategies in the circumstance give rise to apparently strange and disorganised behaviour such as falling to the floor, approaching a care-giver with one's head averted, or a blank or glazed expression.

As adults we may notice that situations in which we feel trapped create a sense of high anxiety but also a blanking out, as if our mind has 'blown a fuse'. This can be particularly hard when we feel this in response to our baby. An example of this is where a mother doesn't feel she has the ability to calm her baby. Her baby cries so she is pulled to hold and soothe her baby, but her fear is that she doesn't have the skills to calm him and that he will in fact get more distressed and angry in her presence. She may become overwhelmed and her mind become blank or dazed. The unintended consequence is that the baby becomes more distressed, making her feel more helpless and inadequate, and ultimately the baby is indeed harder to calm.

When we are under threat, our mind shifts automatically from using the frontal part of the brain (as well as other parts of the brain), which allows us to think in a broad way about the situation, to using the old brain and its very primitive, narrow-focused defence systems of fight, flight, freeze and faint. This is because taking the time to think it all through could prove highly dangerous; the brain drives us to act first and think later in what it perceives to be dangerous situations. This also shows just why it is so hard to bring in our compassionate mind to situations like this, because it uses more of the frontal part of our brain, the very part that gets shut down, as well as our old brain (attachment system). As the brain reverts to simple strategies when under threat, we need to rehearse the compassionate mind steps over and over again so that we automatically use the strategy when feeling overwhelmed.

So when we find ourselves 'locked up', feeling stirred up, confused, and struggling to know what to do, particularly when we are trying to look after a baby, this is not a failing on our part, it is the normal way that our brain responds to conflicting threats, particularly if this has been our childhood experience too. We need to bring compassion to the difficult situation we find ourselves in, particularly when we are struggling to parent. We also need to appreciate just how hard it is to move into our compassionate mind in those moments of threat, which is why the building up and practising of the compassionate mind exercises that we come to later in the book is so crucial; they will then start to be incorporated into our way of responding.

> *Our minds struggle to think clearly when we have conflicting emotions.*
>
> *Spending a moment bringing mindfulness and compassion to feeling overwhelmed can help us to feel calm enough to begin to think more clearly.*

What can be particularly difficult here is that if we have had childhood experiences that meant that we have learned not to trust the very person who is meant to care for us, we can then find it very hard to trust anybody at all, *and that might even include ourselves*. When we practise compassion towards ourselves we can notice the feelings that come up in our body and the thoughts that pop into our mind. If we notice some resistance or anxiety then it can be helpful to check back to our own experiences with people we relied on to care for us. This may give us clues to any associations our body has learned in relation to being looked after. These can get triggered off again even when we try to care for ourselves. The key thing here is to separate out your care-givers' difficulties from your motivation or intention towards yourself. We can make the understandable but tragic mistake of assuming that because they didn't treat us well, there must have been some flaw in us. And this can *feel* like it is true. To become the best of ourselves we need to be a steadfast, reliable, understanding and caring attachment figure to ourselves, even when other people couldn't be – a far from easy thing to do, but something we can move towards with practise.

Our babies need time to catch up when we change

An important point to note here is that, just as we developed safety strategies as babies to help us get the best available care from our parents, so our babies develop safety strategies to get the best available care from us. As we recover from postnatal depression, or try out new strategies with our baby such as holding them when they are distressed rather than leaving them to cry or letting them be soothed by somebody else, our babies will at first be a little surprised by this turn of events.

Do not worry if your baby does indeed need a little time to get used to your new behaviour such as being held by you, or having you looking into their face rather than avoiding their eyes. They will need a little time to catch up, but catch up they will, particularly if they receive this new behaviour consistently so that they come to learn that it is here to stay.

The message here is that at the moment you take the biggest risk, for example by holding your baby to see if you can calm them rather than leaving them to cry, they may in fact become more distressed initially because it disrupts their safety strategies. You will really need your compassionate mind with you here to help you hang on in there. The best smell in the world, the best voice in the world, the best skin in the world to our baby is our own, whether we like this or not, or believe this or not. Our baby is pulled to us, and it will not be long before our baby associates all these aspects of us with feeling calmed and soothed. Just give your baby a little time to catch up!

Summary

1. Some safety strategies can affect how we relate to our own emotions; for example, if we learn that it is best to focus on others' emotions rather than our own, the unintended consequence is that we do not know how we feel, or if we do feel something we don't know what it is, or what it will do to us or others.

2. If on the other hand we learn that some emotions within us cause anger or anxiety in others then we can become very scared about particular emotions and try to keep them suppressed. As our emotions guide us, the unintended consequences are that we lose the information they are trying to convey to us. For example, if we learn to suppress our anger then we may find it hard to stop people 'walking all over us'.

3. When we struggle with our own emotions we can sometimes struggle with those in our baby too. So we might find we struggle to know how our baby is feeling or we may find a particular emotion in our baby is much harder to manage.

4. If two or more emotions have been conditioned to each other then we can find ourselves suddenly experiencing a whole set of emotions all at once. Sometimes they conflict; for example, we might feel anger which propels us forward to attack, but then also anxiety which sends us into retreat. This can be overwhelming and as our brain struggles to cope with conflict it can go into a state of confusion as if it has 'blown a fuse'. We find it hard to think clearly or behave in a clear manner. This is how our brain is hard-wired and it is not our fault.

5. By looking at our own emotions with our 'compassionate mind', i.e. by trying to bring our wisdom, warmth, strength and awareness to them, we feel safer. We become better able to notice them, understand the information they are giving us, and then respond from our compassionate mind rather than our narrow-focused threat mind.

STAGE TWO

Developing
our compassionate mind

12 The nature of compassion: What makes up a 'compassionate mind'?

When we are suffering, we wish that the suffering would go away and that we could feel better. This in itself is self-compassion. However, imagine you go the dentist with a very painful toothache. You discover the tooth is rotten and infected. It is so painful that you ask the dentist not to touch it but just to take the pain away. You are given a powerful painkiller but the dentist leaves the tooth untouched. Is this a truly compassionate act on the part of the dentist and ourselves? Or again, a child is unwell; they may need a procedure to make them better which hurts and scares them. Our compassion helps us to help them have the procedure that they need to be able to get better rather than merely to take away the pain and fear in that moment (though we can try to do this, too, as best we can). In these two examples the compassionate thing to do is not just to try to dull the pain but actually to engage with the causes of the pain. It is very easy for people to misunderstand compassion and to think it's about softness, weakness, just being kind or even a bit of an indulgence – sometimes even confused with pity. But in fact one of the most important qualities of compassion is how it builds courage; the courage to be able to do sometimes difficult things to help ourselves or others.

There are various definitions of compassion that all, more or less, focus on how we engage and deal with suffering in ourselves and others. One definition of compassion is: *a sensitivity to suffering in our self and others, and the motivation to alleviate and prevent it.*

However, it is not just about dealing with suffering, but also about helping ourselves and others truly to grow and flourish, which of course can also have an impact on how we manage suffering. So too with our children; we may wish we could just keep them tucked up safe next to us, free from harm and suffering, but ultimately this would not help them to grow and flourish. We also teach them skills and help them to develop confidence in themselves by allowing them to 'stretch out their wings' step by step, with ourselves providing a source of safeness and encouragement.

> *Compassion is about the willingness to turn towards rather than away from suffering.*

Returning to the definition of compassion that we are using here (*'a sensitivity to suffering in our self and others, and the motivation to alleviate and prevent it'*), we see that there are two key aspects to compassion. The first is 'sensitivity to suffering in our self and others'. This is the willingness to turn towards suffering and genuinely try to tune into it and understand its causes. The second is the motivation and desire to try to acquire the wisdom and skills we need in order to be helpful in alleviating and preventing it. Because suffering is unpleasant and sometimes seemingly unbearable we can be drawn to trying to make it better, in ourselves and others, before we really understand what has caused it. In the dentist example, the real cause of the suffering was a problem with the tooth, not the pain. The first aspect of compassion ('sensitivity to suffering in ourselves and others') enables us to look properly into the cause of the toothache. We may also have the motivation or desire for the toothache to be sorted out; however, we are unlikely to have the skills ourselves to remedy this, so we seek out somebody who can, and this is the second aspect of compassion – attempting to alleviate the suffering wisely.

Here are two other examples of the two psychologies. You see somebody fall into a fast-flowing river and jump in to save them. That is the first aspect of compassion (sensitivity to suffering) but then you realise you can't swim! So the intention is good but there isn't the wisdom and skill behind it to know what to do. Or imagine you wanted to be a doctor in order to prevent and alleviate suffering in others. That is your compassionate intention, but then you have to study for many years to acquire the skills to know what to do. Intention alone is not enough. And it is the same with ourselves. Having the desire to address suffering in ourselves and others is the first step but then we have to set about developing skills to do so. These skills include developing ways of thinking, feeling, acting, imagining and attending, which help us to relate to ourselves and others in a compassionate way.

> *Compassion is also concerned with flourishing and growth.*

Compassion to the 'dark side'

It's helpful to realise that we need compassion for *the difficult things*, not just the easy things. So, for example, it's relatively easy to have compassion for people we like but more difficult for people we don't, particularly our enemies. We are more likely to feel compassion for people we see as like us with our values – be they religious, political, or concerning how to bring up children – than for people who are different. And it's the same in relation to ourselves. It might be relatively easy to show compassion to ourselves for things we find physically painful, for example, but much harder for things we find emotionally painful or even shameful.

Some people think that to develop compassion means they must not be angry any more, never have difficult thoughts or urges, no longer experience panic attacks or have an urge to run away. Even the Dalai Lama gets angry! That is not what compassion is. Compassion is not getting rid of feelings like this; it is understanding that because we are human, we all have these difficult aspects to ourselves and it is therefore how we learn to deal with them in a compassionate way.

The question is, then, how we develop compassion for our anger, for our anxiety, our sadness, our jealousy, our difficult thoughts, our urges; how we develop compassion and understanding for those overwhelming feelings of just wanting to run away – rather than being scared, or ashamed or self-critical of them. The reason compassion is important here is because what we are dealing with are our common human experiences – especially given our difficult brain. So compassion is for the hard things as well as the easy things – and that is why it is about courage.

A Buddhist view of compassion uses the metaphor of a lotus flower growing in the mud to represent these skills of engaging with our suffering and of trying to alleviate it. To grow, the lotus flower seed needs first to settle in the mud. The mud represents the dark, painful and difficult parts of ourselves that we take great pains to hide from others (and often from ourselves too); the envy, the anger, the 'bad' thoughts and impulses, the shame. The mud is our suffering. Although instinctively we want to be rid of the mud, in fact the lotus flower has to be embedded in the mud in order to grow and flourish. So in other words we need to have our suffering in order for our compassion, or lotus flower, to be able to grow. To really understand our suffering in order to be able to make it better we need to be able to delve into the mud. This is why we say that a key part of compassion is strength and courage because these attributes are required to enable us to go into these difficult places.

The case of Lisa and her 'charmed life'

Lisa is a lady that, from the outside at least, many might want to be. She is attractive, bubbling with energy and excitement, able to get just about any job she wants, and seemingly unafraid of anything. She was referred to our service after having her first baby with a possible diagnosis of mania. She explained that despite appearing to have a charmed life, in fact she never felt settled. She was constantly searching for the thing that would make her feel 'just right'; perhaps a new job, new partner, new country, a baby.

It transpired that beneath all this she actually felt incredibly sad, fearful and desperately lonely. She also realised that she was envious of others who seemed to have achieved this perfect life and was secretly pleased when they failed. This made her despise herself. She *was spending almost every minute of each day trying to move away from this state of loneliness, disappointment, sadness and anger.*

By never really 'looking' at or engaging with the suffering, it became terrifying. She described these feelings of loneliness, disappointment, sadness and anger as being like a dark lagoon that she was constantly in danger of slipping into. Over time she did, however, tentatively start to turn her attention to the 'lagoon'. It was as if she first sat by the lagoon, then dipped a hand in, then really looked into its depths. She started to realise that it did contain deep sadness and pain but it didn't swallow her up. She could go into it, swim about a little, and get out of it. It wasn't all of her; it just occupied a part of her. In fact she discovered it was a great deal smaller and shallower than she imagined and she could even see the bottom. She also realised that it wasn't her fault that it was there, but it was nevertheless part of her and she needed to hold that in mind when looking after herself and moving forward in life. So this lagoon was actually her emotional memories of pain and sadness from earlier times but which were still being triggered off in the present, causing her anxiety and confusion. By swimming around 'in them' she could see what they were more clearly, and identify that these emotional memories are part of her but come from the past rather than the present.

In the end, once she 'knew' the lagoon properly she was no longer fearful of it, or preoccupied by it. She could look up and out at the rest of the landscape. Moreover, she felt safe enough to be able to move out and away from the lagoon and explore the wider landscape. For the first time she described feeling free.

Lisa's experience demonstrates the two parts of compassion; first, moving down into the 'mud' to engage with the suffering and seeing the basis of it, which are often emotional memories and past hurts. Second, when we begin to see into the causes and nature of our suffering, we can then set about alleviating the suffering, using wisdom, understanding and strength to take the necessary steps to becoming more at peace and to help ourselves grow and flourish.

Lisa's experience of being able to 'swim around' in the 'lagoon' of her sadness highlights how for the second aspect of compassion, our wisdom would be that we might need to learn to swim first. We can learn these skills of being able to move around in, and get in and out of, our difficult emotions just as we can learn to swim. And as with learning to swim, we start off where it feels safe, and where we can get in and out easily, for example the shallow end of the lagoon, rather than where it is difficult, such as jumping straight off a cliff into the deep part of the lagoon. Figure 8.1 below shows the two psychologies of compassion; **engagement with** (the inner circle), and **alleviation of** suffering (outer circle), and the skills and attributes that we can learn to help us with these.

Figure 8.1: The six attributes and six skills of compassion

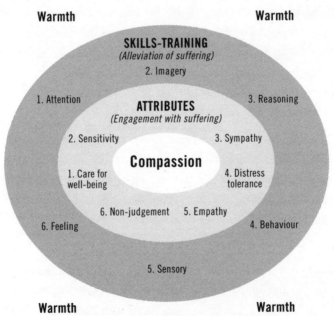

From Gilbert, *The Compassionate Mind* (2009), reprinted with permission from Constable & Robinson Ltd.

> *The six **attributes** of compassion give us the qualities that enable us to turn towards, bear and understand our suffering.*
>
> *The six **skills** of compassion enable us to alleviate suffering by stimulating compassion towards ourselves in different ways.*

The second circle entitled 'Attributes' can be thought of as the stance we take when approaching the distressing, frightening or dark, 'muddy' side of ourselves. Once we begin to understand this part of ourselves we use the aspects in the outer circle, entitled 'Skills', to then skilfully alleviate the suffering of the struggling part. Here we deliberately shift our position in relation to ourselves so that we are thinking, behaving, imagining, attending, feeling, and using our senses in a way that stimulates compassion towards ourselves. We will look at these skills and attributes in more detail; really understanding these aspects can help us if we find self-compassion difficult because we can identify which particular skills or attributes we are finding particularly hard. Once we have identified and worked with these blocks then we find that self-compassion starts to flow.

Six attributes of a compassionate mind (engagement with suffering)

Case example: Molly and Baby Maya

Molly came to our service antenatally with a fear of childbirth. She was terrified of uncertainty and needed life to be predictable with no surprises. Understandably, the prospect of childbirth filled her with fear. The more anxious she got, the more she tried to get control, but now she was in unchartered territory as she had no experience of pregnancy in herself or others, so she was having to rely on other people. Her anxiety and panic would often trigger anger when she felt blocked or not understood by other people. Her anger frightened other people and they backed off, leaving her feeling even more alone and out of control.

Sadly, the birth of her daughter was difficult and she was separated from her for a while. Molly was physically unwell and needed a blood transfusion. It took her a long while to physically recover. Breast-feeding was difficult, which unfortunately isn't uncommon after such a delivery, but her increasingly agitated requests for help in trying to breast-feed were seen as evidence of 'her mental illness' and she felt people didn't take her seriously and subsequently shut off from her. Again she felt scared and alone. She was critical of herself and felt she had let down baby Maya. She didn't feel she could 'deliver her right or feed her right', and, more than that, she didn't feel she was able to fight for Maya and get her the help she needed to give her what she saw as 'the best start in life'.

At first Molly struggled to bond with Maya but over time she started to experience a greater and greater sense of love for her.

We can think about the attributes and skills of compassion in relation to Molly's journey through the difficult early months of having Maya. Looking first at the attributes of compassion in Figure 8.1, we start at 'nine o'clock' on the middle circle and move clockwise. So we start with a motivation to 'care for well-being'.

1. Motivation and willingness to care for well-being

The journey of compassion begins with some kind of motivation and willingness to start the journey – to begin to think about and be open to considering the difficulties we might be having. Imagine how we would hold ourselves, move and behave if we developed a desire, a motivation, a willingness to **really care for the well-being** of that struggling or difficult part of ourselves. Rather than wishing to turn away from it, or pity it, or protect ourselves from it, we commit ourselves to turning towards it and trying to understand what it needs, and to then help it as best we can.

Molly initially came to our service in a panic, completely focused on how to get the help she needed to stay safe in terms of having control over delivery of her baby. She was highly motivated to 'care for her well-being'. But once this threat was over she was able to step back a little and become more reflective and saw that this was not just a one-off problem that she needed to overcome but a recurring story through her life that created a great deal of pain and suffering for her. She decided that she would like some psychological sessions to try to understand this and to see if there was a different way through.

BABY NOTES

What really helped Molly to notice and tune up these attributes of compassion, was when baby Maya arrived. She found it easier to see these attributes in how she was relating to Maya, which helped her to consider how she might relate them to herself. Despite not feeling particularly connected to Maya in the early weeks, she was very motivated to give Maya the best care she could. There appeared to be a cyclical effect between Maya and Molly; as Molly started to turn towards herself a little more, she started to develop more warmth and love towards Maya. As she saw how she was with Maya this helped her to reflect on just what would help her.

2. Sensitivity

Once we are motivated then we begin to *pay attention*. That means we have *sensitivity* to our pain and struggle. So it helps us start to look with open attention at the emotions arising within us. This can be difficult to do, particularly if our childhood experiences meant that we spent more time having to attend to the emotions of others, with little attention paid to ourselves. Sometimes where people have been critical or hostile towards our feelings we learn to be ashamed of them and to hide them away, or we can fear that if we pay attention to our feelings we will be scared or overwhelmed by what we find or 'let out' – so there can be many blocks at this stage. The key is to take a step at a time, like learning to swim without a need to jump in the deep end.

For Molly she found herself rapidly experiencing and responding to anger. She was in threat and not surprisingly she responded entirely from her threat system. We spent some time using mindfulness (see Chapter 13 for further details about mindfulness) to help her slow down and attend in more detail to the different emotions arising in her. She became aware that rather than just feeling angry; her anger in fact came after fear.

BABY NOTES

Molly was very sensitive to Maya's physical and emotional state and was very motivated to understand the meaning of her different cries. This very detailed sensitivity to Maya seemed to help Molly identify the subtleties of her own distress.

3. Sympathy

'Knowing' what we see when we look at ourselves with sensitivity is facilitated by the attribute of **sympathy**. This is the ability to be moved by the distress of others, or of ourselves. It is automatic and rapid. Sympathy is thought to be connected to the firing of what have been called mirror neurones. These 'mirror' in our brains what we see happening to somebody else. For example, if we see somebody bang their toe on a table leg, then the part of *our* brain that registers pain in our toe is activated. We literally 'know' what it felt like and can wince along with them. However, it can be hard then to separate their feelings from our own. It can seem that their feelings have washed over us too. If they feel overwhelmed and helpless then we can feel overwhelmed and helpless too.

As soon as Molly became aware of the fearful part of herself she became moved and had a real urge to care for and protect herself.

As Molly recovered from the delivery of Maya and also started to get some more sleep she seemed more able to open herself up to Maya's distress and let herself really feel it in herself.

4. Distress tolerance

If we really allow ourselves to be moved by distress, how do we manage that distress? What we feel from our sympathetic reaction to ourselves or others can sometimes feel hard to bear and this would make it difficult for us to really turn towards distress. We then need the next attribute of *distress tolerance* to help us be able to bear the distress that we are now feeling. We learn distress tolerance through our experiences of knowing in ourselves, or seeing in others, that the feelings will end, that all emotions, pleasant or unpleasant, wax and wane and eventually pass.

We also learn that emotions do not destroy us or send us mad, although it can feel at times that they might. This can be difficult for us if we have had few experiences of having our distress soothed by others. If we have been left alone in great distress for long periods of time, for example, particularly when we were young, our distress can become linked to additional feelings of terror, abandonment and feeling overwhelmed. We can come to believe at some level that distress is enormous, unending and inconsolable because of our early experiences, and as such requires something drastic to block it out or manage it, such as alcohol, overeating, medication, drugs or self-harm.

When we consider these early experiences, what ends this experience of fear for a baby? It is just to be picked up and held. Nothing extreme, or enormous or drastic, just being safe in someone's arms. Even if in reality we cannot or would not like to access physical comfort when we are in distress, just this knowledge that our distress is 'soothable' can be enough to help us bear it.

For Molly, distress tolerance was quite difficult. She found that if she felt pan-
icky and she didn't feel there was a way out then she moved rapidly into anger,
which could be aggressive and frightening to other people. The more people shut
down or turned away from her to protect themselves, the angrier she got. She
identified that she wanted to be able to take note of these feelings and the warning
they gave her but to be able to settle herself enough to be able to react in a more
moderated way.

Baby notes

Once again Maya proved to be the best teacher to Molly, particularly during the early weeks after the birth. Molly felt tired, physically unwell,
scared and confused, and she could feel her anger and frustration rising
as she struggled to get Maya to sleep, feed, settle and so on. However,
she was certain of one thing, and that was that she did not want to harm
Maya. This meant that Molly did whatever she could to be able to bear
her anxiety and anger around Maya, including waking her husband up
in the early hours of the morning and handing over Maya so she could
walk away and calm down. Through this, Molly learned that she had a
considerable capacity to manage both her own distress and that of Maya;
something that she would not have previously believed was an attribute
that she possessed.

5. Empathy

So the attributes of compassion towards ourselves or others starts with
a willingness to engage with the struggle, to be able to be sensitive to
noticing when we or others are struggling, to feel moved or have a sympathetic reaction to the struggle, and to be able to bear the distress that it
may trigger in us. Then we need to be able truly to understand the unique
origins of the struggle and therefore just what the particular needs might
be. This is where our **empathy** comes into play.

Empathy and sympathy can often be confused. Whereas sympathy
is being able to feel the suffering of others, empathy is being able to

understand what that person might need, which might be very different from what *we* might need in that situation. For example, a young child, Billy, who sees another child, Jane, in tears might go and get his own mother to comfort Jane. However, an older child who has a better-developed capacity for empathy would know to get Jane's mother instead.

Empathy involves a wise understanding of the causes of the pain. Unlike sympathy it is not automatic, but instead comes from the effortful willingness to 'stand in someone else's shoes' and have a curiosity and wonderment about the origins of their distress. As we learn about ourselves we become better able to have real empathy for our own distress rather than simply being engulfed by it. So, rather than being washed over by great sadness, for example, which can feel overwhelming and alarming, we are able to say 'I feel incredibly sad, but when I think about my experiences this is understandable.' It allows a sense of containment as if it is a part of us rather than the whole, and gives a feeling of slight separation from it as if we are standing next to, rather than being completely filled up by, it.

For Molly, she gained a great deal from understanding why she experienced such strong feelings of panic in certain situations. She related this back to feeling different from others at school and being bullied for this. She was rarely helped by her teachers; in fact some made it worse and she felt very alone and vulnerable. Molly clearly got a lot of relief from developing this understanding and it helped her to shift from a self-critical to a much more compassionate way of viewing herself. It also helped her to begin to contemplate the impact her anger may have on others, which then reinforced her motivation to try to communicate her anxiety in ways that could be received by others so that they would be more inclined to help her, rather than pull away.

Baby notes

Molly really struggled in the early weeks to understand Maya and she was often in a high state of anxiety when Maya got upset. However, as Maya's cries started to differentiate into different cries for different feelings, and when she started to smile and show a wider variety of emotions, Molly felt she was getting to know Maya. She found it easier to say, 'Maya enjoys . . .' or 'Maya really doesn't like it when . . .' She could identify what Maya might need and also see that another baby might need something different in Maya's situation.

6. Non-judgement

When we are looking at this shadow part of ourselves, **non-judgement** is the ability to just notice it, exactly as it is, without condemning it. It allows us to observe aspects of ourselves and others with clear and open curiosity so we can see it just as it is without having to push it or pull it into something different. It enables us to have a much more accurate insight into those parts of us that we ordinarily try to keep hidden from ourselves or others. By taking this stance of non-judgement we allow ourselves to take these aspects out into the light so we can look with clarity. Non-judgement is a key component of mindfulness; being able to notice our emotions, our physical sensations, our thoughts and so on with an acceptance rather than condemning or judging ourselves for having them. It doesn't mean a kind of resignation or inaction though. So we might accept that we have angry thoughts and urges but decide that anger isn't perhaps the best frame of mind to act from.

Molly initially viewed herself as 'a little crazy' with a mind that she thought was different from everybody else's. However, she came to see that this 'craziness' was in fact a consequence of a crazy mind that we all share, combined with her own unique set of experiences. Her reactions came to make sense to her and she was able to soften towards herself. She also found she was able to take herself out into the world more because she no longer felt so different.

BABY NOTES

Molly found it much easier to accept Maya than herself. She could see quite clearly that although sometimes she would rather Maya was a little less grumpy, or less wide awake in the middle of the night, she could understand it without condemning her for it. Being able to step back and see this for Maya made it easier for her to begin to step back and see this for herself too.

Six skills of a compassionate mind (alleviation of suffering)

As we will see, the skills and attributes of compassion (the outer and the inner circles of Figure 8.1) are interlinked; each of the attributes supports the development of the other attributes, which in turn enable a compassionate mind-set to develop. Once we see clearly the nature of the suffering in ourselves and others, we are much better able to consider what skills we might need to alleviate it. As we develop the skills to alleviate it, these skills also help to build further the attributes of motivation to care for well-being, sensitivity to distress, sympathy, distress tolerance, empathy and non-judgement. So there is no real 'right' place to start; instead, we will be constantly moving around and between the skills and attributes, with each building on the others.

1. Compassionate attention

Whereas sensitivity to distress (in 'attributes') is attention to what we or others are struggling with, compassionate attention is focusing on what is helpful to alleviate the distress and to prevent it in the future. For example, if we develop a particular familiar type of headache, noticing this and perhaps looking a little deeper into just what we are feeling is the attribute of 'distress sensitivity', whereas turning our attention to what might help is compassionate attention. So this might include recalling what has helped before when we had this particular headache. We will look in more detail at the nature and practice of compassionate attention in Chapter 16.

For Molly, when she was struggling she would remember how much had 'gone wrong' already in Maya's short life. This often overwhelmed her and made her feel down. When she moved her attention to thinking about what might help her, she was able to bring kindness and encouragement towards herself and to turn her attention to what had gone well with Maya. This would often have a 'snowball effect' where her attention broadened out to other positives such as how much easier things are now than they were, how surprisingly well she coped with all of this, and how helpful she has been to a friend who is struggling.

BABY **NOTES**

When Maya became upset, Molly noticed this but then moved her attention to what might help Maya, such as giving her something else to look at, or picking her up and cuddling her.

2. Compassionate imagery

Using our imagination is a very powerful and fast way of stimulating our minds and creating different feelings and responses within us. For example, if somebody asked us to imagine the worst place to find ourselves on holiday, we might picture a stony beach with lots of litter and a half-built hotel. It would make us feel a particular way inside, such as angry or disgusted. However, if we were to imagine our perfect holiday destination, then we might picture a white sandy beach, with a clear warm sea and somebody bringing us delicious drinks and food. This image might make us smile and feel relaxed and at peace.

We don't have to have 'good' imaginations or be able to imagine something as a clear picture; generally our imagination just gives us a vague sense of an image or just a feeling.

We can use imagery to stimulate particular emotional and physiological systems in our brain and body that foster the emergence of our compassionate mind. It can also be a way of tapping into compassionate behaviour and compassionate thinking by imagining what a compassionate person or the compassionate part of ourselves might think and do.

Molly initially found it easiest to imagine herself as compassionate when she thought about herself looking after her dog, and then, as her love for Maya grew, she focused on compassion for Maya. She struggled for a while to bring compassion to herself but she found that if she got herself into a compassionate mind-set for her dog or for Maya then it was easier to bring it to herself.

3. Compassionate thinking (reasoning)

Here we can consider what our compassionate part might think or say to ourselves when we are in distress, or to someone else who is struggling, or what a compassionate person might think about or say to us when we are struggling. Our threat system catches hold of our thinking very easily and we can quickly find ourselves worrying and ruminating, so we have to work with effort and intention to switch to considering what our compassionate self might think or say about our worrying and ruminating. Again, focusing on our warm voice tone and facial expression can really help in switching to compassionate thinking.

Molly found it helpful to test out her compassionate thinking and reasoning by checking whether that was something she would really say to someone she deeply cared about. She also carefully listened when she said things back to herself and she was able to feel whether it was said in a genuinely helpful 'heartfelt' manner or whether an edge of criticism or anger had crept in.

Baby notes

Molly would check out the things she said to herself with how she would like to talk to Maya if Maya were struggling in the same way later in life.

4. Compassionate behaviour

If we consider compassionate figures in history, or in films or books, what behaviour do we see that marks them out to us as compassionate? It could range from tiny mannerisms of warmth and gentleness shown towards others, to acts of generosity, strength and courage. When we are relating to the struggling part of ourselves with compassion, how do we behave towards that part? What might we do to help it right in the moment it is struggling? For example, compassionate behaviour might be just sitting with the struggling part and really listening to what it is finding so hard or painful. What could we do to help it in the short term such as in the next hour or day? Compassionate behaviour might perhaps be phoning somebody just to connect back in to others, or going out for a walk with the baby even if it's raining. And we can also think about what we can do to help in the long term, such as making a commitment to practising compassionate mind exercises for five minutes each evening, or sorting out childcare so that we can go to an exercise class or evening class each week.

Compassionate behaviour often requires courage and strength. If, for example, we are worried about taking our older child to school, we may believe that compassionate behaviour is getting somebody else to take them so we can stay safely at home. In fact compassionate behaviour is acting in a way that will really help us to grow, develop and prosper in the long run, which might be to take the courageous step of taking our child ourselves. It may be compassionate to hunker down for a short while, or to take some time out, but our compassionate mind will know when it is time to start reconnecting back into the world again. Compassionate behaviour is therefore not necessarily about being 'nice'. So, a compassionate sports coach may see the potential in a child and get them to try again and again until they succeed when the child would rather give up at the first problem and never do the sport again. A compassionate parent may let their child have a small bar of chocolate but refuse to let them have more.

For Molly it took a great deal of effort to get to sessions but she felt they were helpful and she began to believe that she was worthy of help. Her compassionate behaviour included getting herself to sessions even when she had hardly slept. She also realised she needed help from other people and called upon her mum, and her husband; something that she initially struggled a great deal to do.

BABY NOTES

Particularly in the early days, so much of what kept Molly going was her real motivation to care for Maya even when she was exhausted. Her care for Maya was one compassionate act after another, be it feeding her, changing her, or cuddling her again and again when she woke in the night. She did this even in the early days when she did not feel very connected to Maya, demonstrating that we can behave in a compassionate way even if we don't necessarily have compassionate feelings. In fact often we need to engage in the behaviour first and the feelings eventually follow.

5. Compassionate sensory focusing

This is where we focus on the sensory qualities of compassion, such as how we breathe, how our body feels, how we hold ourselves (our posture), the expression on our face, our tone of voice and how we move.

Molly began to notice how differently her body felt, how she spoke, how she breathed when she was anxious or angry, versus when she was in a more compassionate mind-set.

BABY NOTES

Molly discovered that Maya gave her immediate 'feedback' on her body posture, breathing voice tone and facial expression because she would pick up very quickly when Molly was worried or angry and would become agitated and fretful. It was fascinating to see that as soon as Molly began to do a compassionate exercise in the session, Maya would become calmer, more settled, in a state of quiet wakefulness. Regarded as a 'colicky baby', interestingly Maya often let out wind or did a poo as her body relaxed during times when Molly practised her compassionate mind exercises in the sessions!

6. Compassionate feelings

These are feelings such as kindness, warmth, friendliness, and a kind of openness and confidence that arise in us when we are relating to other people or to ourselves with compassion. Whereas the attributes of sympathy enables us to feel the pain of our suffering and the suffering in others, the skills of compassion bring positive feelings of kindness, friendliness, a 'heartfelt wish' that we or others could be happy, and a feeling of joy when we imagine the suffering has been alleviated. A focus on imagining a kind, warm voice tone and facial expression are important in helping to generate these feelings.

Creating patterns of compassion within ourselves

As we move through our day, our week, or through the years, we move in and out of different roles in relation to ourselves and others. The role that we are in at a particular moment can govern what we focus on, how we think, how we behave, what we feel and what we imagine, so many of us can find that we are quite different when we are a mother compared to when we are a wife, a working woman, a daughter, gently flirting with someone, or going out with friends, for example. Paul Gilbert calls this a 'Social Mentality'[1] because the roles come into play when we are relating, or imagining relating, to other people. We give out different signals to others according to the mentality we are in, which trigger a response in the other person. We also respond to the particular mentality of another person. So we will respond to them differently if they are a doctor caring for us in hospital compared to if they came to us for help. We can imagine being like actors going through many character changes in a day, even swapping clothes to get into role as we go (how many of us change our clothes to change how we want to feel, think and behave? For example, 'power dressing' if we need to feel more in control, or putting on our 'lounging about at home' clothes to relax. Imagine swapping them around!) This is not to say that we are acting or pretending, it is that we are constantly shifting and adjusting our genuine responses, emotions, thoughts, body posture, attention and behaviour according to how we are relating and responding to others, as are they to us.

*If we don't feel we can be compassionate towards ourselves or others, we can begin by acting **'as if'** we were. Just like an actor getting into role.*

If we start with the intention to be self-compassionate, the feelings will eventually follow.

We have a vast number of neurons in our brain, which are all interconnected, creating a web or network. They fire together in configurations like weather patterns in the brain. Particular patterns may come up repeatedly, but no one pattern will arise exactly as before because the myriad of influences will be slightly different each time. As we move into different social roles these 'weather patterns' will change accordingly. In the compassionate mind approach, we are trying to move into the caregiving or compassionate social mentality, or 'weather pattern'. As we move ourselves into this role our thoughts, feelings, behaviour, attention and so on all take on the quality of compassion. It is like gently changing the weather from stormy or rainy, to a warm, spring day.

The aim of this approach is for us to learn to spend more and more time in the compassionate social mentality so it starts to become our 'trait' or usual way of relating to ourselves and others. Even if we do not initially feel we can be this person, we can start to act 'as if' we were, perhaps just for a minute or so to start with. We can begin to play around with the idea of *'If I were* to handle that problem as a compassionate person, what would I say? What would I do? How would I feel? What would I focus on?'

In developing self-compassion we need to be able to give care, but also to receive it, in relation both to others and ourselves. Care giving and care receiving are in fact two different social mentalities. Think about how you would think, behave, hold your body, attend and feel when you are caring for or helping somebody compared to when you are being cared for or helped. You might notice real differences. You might also notice that one feels easier than the other. As we need to be comfortable in both mentalities we need to work with both. But, as ever with the Compassionate Mind approach, we begin with the easiest first and work up to the harder one.

A compassion face-lift!

A lovely way of thinking about which person we would like to become was brought to me by a lady attending our service. She had noticed that as people get older their faces 'set' into the expressions they spend most of their time exhibiting. She had seen an old lady whose wrinkles were set into a gentle smile with crinkles around her eyes. My client said that she realised that she wanted her face to 'set' like that too as she got older. She wanted to be more like this old lady. So she endeavoured to spend as much time as she could acting as she thought this lady might, including bringing expressions of kindness and warmth to her face. It doesn't get rid of the wrinkles though!

How compassion shapes our threat, drive and soothing systems

At any particular moment our mind will be forming a particular pattern in relation to the 'three circles' or emotion systems of threat, drive and soothing. We can imagine how the pattern might change throughout our day (or night) even from moment to moment. So the pattern might be different when we are trying to get the baby ready to leave the house, compared to when we pop our head round the door and check on the sleeping baby. In Figure 8.2 we can see how the pattern of the three circles might look when we are in our compassionate self.

Figure 8.2: The compassion process

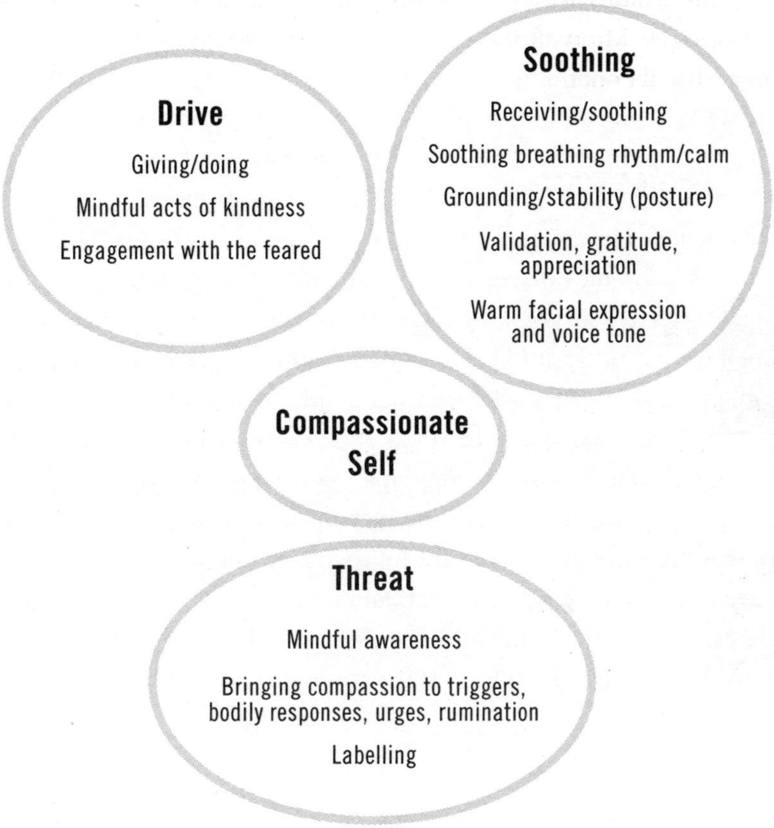

Drive

Giving/doing

Mindful acts of kindness

Engagement with the feared

Soothing

Receiving/soothing

Soothing breathing rhythm/calm

Grounding/stability (posture)

Validation, gratitude,
appreciation

Warm facial expression
and voice tone

**Compassionate
Self**

Threat

Mindful awareness

Bringing compassion to triggers,
bodily responses, urges, rumination

Labelling

Reproduced with kind permission Paul Gilbert

Being compassionate doesn't mean we never feel angry.

*It means that we are better able to understand the source of our
anger and deal with it in a calmer, more skilful way.*

As we can see, compassion doesn't mean we don't feel any threat emotions such as anger or anxiety. It may be that we are trying to work with
these from our compassionate self. Or it may be that actually these threat

emotions are driving our compassionate self. So a firefighter that runs back into a fire to rescue a child is acting from their compassionate self, but their anxiety may be high, as will be their drive system. They may be trying to use the soothing system as well to remain as calm and as focused as possible. Compassion can also be driven by anger as a consequence of injustice or unfairness. So, we might be angry that another child has just hurt our child and this stimulates our threat system and prepares us to take action. However, rather than just respond with anger (where the soothing system may be completely switched off and our drive system is propelling us towards making the child and their parent scared and apologetic), we might want to try to bring in our compassionate mind. Here we might deal with the situation with perhaps more wisdom and skill than the purely angry part of our self would allow. Although we may still feel angry, we might use our soothing system to calm and steady us so that we can think more broadly and respond in a slower, more considered way. Our drive system may be less fired up than before and the focus may change from wanting revenge or submission to getting more information perhaps, or to watching the child's mother to see if maybe she is struggling, or even to helping our child to learn how to manage difficult situations like this.

The benefits of compassion

It has long been believed that humans have evolved for conflict and fighting; that the most successful groups were those that were the most aggressive. However, there is a growing body of evidence that suggests that in fact natural selection favours not the most aggressive, but the most cooperative, helpful, altruistic and compassionate. Humans are so successful as a species because we have adapted to be able to live in such diverse terrains and climates. This adaptability is thought to have been possible because of the highly sophisticated social interactions between humans, which mean we can work together as a group to achieve more than we could as individuals.

It would appear that we only engage in physical or verbal attacks when threatened [2]. In fact it seems that we have evolved to live primarily in a resting state (the soothing system) where we can conserve energy and digest food, think, learn, and integrate new information. It is also the state linked to being social, where we seek out affection, companionship and a sense of belonging. We are at our healthiest both physically and psychologically when we are in this state. Conversely, there is now evidence that people who feel the most *dis*connected from others, such as those who are lonely, may be as at risk of ill health as smokers and people who are obese.[3]

Some of the benefits of growing our compassionate mind:

- Helps us to engage with and bear emotional pain.

- Can help to calm our anger and anxiety.

- Builds emotional resilience: our ability to get through difficult times and to pick ourselves up when knocked down.

- Helps to keep us physically well: it brings us back to a resting state which conserves energy, reduces inflammation and illness, and enhances our immune system.

- Reduces the risk of depression and anxiety.

- Increases our ability to connect to others including bonding with our children.

Basically, we are designed to love and be loved and when this is the case we function at our best, both emotionally and physically.

For a wonderful summary of the benefits we gain from fostering the soothing or affiliation system, see David Hamilton's book *Why Kindness is Good for You* (2010).[4]

Summary

1. One of the definitions of compassion is 'a sensitivity to suffering of ourselves and others, and a motivation or desire to alleviate or prevent it'. This shows the two different psychologies of compassion;

first, to be willing to turn towards and pay attention to the suffering (engagement with suffering), and second, to want to try to make it better (alleviation of suffering).

2.   In Buddhism there is the analogy of the lotus in the mud. The mud is the suffering, or the difficult 'muddy' parts of ourselves. The lotus flower is compassion. For compassion to grow, the 'seed' has to drop into the 'mud' of our suffering. So without suffering there can be no compassion.

3.   The compassionate mind approach focuses on six attributes needed to be able to turn towards suffering:

   i.   A motivation to want to care for and help ourselves and others.

   ii.   A sensitivity to suffering.

   iii.   Feeling moved by our distress (sympathy).

   iv.   Being able to bear that distress (distress tolerance).

   v.   Ability to understand just why we are struggling and what might help (empathy).

   vi.   Being able to understand the suffering without judging it (non-judgement).

4.   We try to alleviate suffering by bringing our compassionate 'self' to it. We can 'switch on' and grow our compassionate 'self' by using different skills. These skills include:

   i.   Compassionate attention, where we focus our attention like a spotlight on anything that stimulates our soothing system.

   ii.   Compassionate imagery, which is imagining an ideal being or person relating to us with compassion, or imagining ourselves being our 'best' compassionate self and relating to somebody else.

   iii.   Compassionate thinking or reasoning, where we might think what we would say to somebody we really cared or about, or what they might say to us.

iv. Compassionate behaviour, which is any action that helps to prevent suffering or make it better, no matter how big or small.

v.   Compassionate sensory focusing, where we focus on the sensory qualities of compassion, such as how we breathe, how our body feels, how we hold ourselves (our posture), the expression on our face, our tone of voice and how we move.

vi. Compassionate feelings, which include warmth and kindness, strength and courage.

5. We take on different social roles in life depending on who we are with and what we are aiming to do. This is called a 'social mentality'. These organise many different aspects of our mind and body into particular patterns, like weather patterns. With the compassionate mind approach we are trying to organise our mind into the patterns of care giving and care receiving. For example, the focus of our attention will be different when we are looking after someone compared to if we were competing with them. Our thinking, behaviour and feelings will be different too.

6. We are tuning up our care-giving mentality when we practise being our best compassionate self. We are tuning up our care-receiving mentality when we are practising our compassionate image, or when we are accepting help from others.

7. When we are in our soothing system we can be very creative. Our attention is not taken up by threat or by the need to acquire or achieve (drive). When we feel safe our mind is very open and can put together ideas and thoughts in very creative ways. This is why the soothing system is the best system for coming up with solutions or ways through the difficulties of life.

8. Rather than being designed primarily for aggression, as was once thought, it seems that the success of humans may be down to our motivation to care for others and to be cared for. We are at our best in terms of psychological and physical well-being, and at our most

creative and productive when we are operating within our soothing system as much as possible.

9. We live in a very 'drive'-orientated society. Often, when we are in threat, we move straight from threat to drive. In fact we will manage threat better if we go via the soothing system and compassion first before we go to drive. We are aiming to develop our compassionate self as a primary guide through life.

13 Preparing the compassionate mind: mindful awareness

Can I really change my brain?

John Bowlby, in his book *A Secure Base: Clinical Applications of Attachment Theory* (1988)[1], reminds us that we change throughout our life. We never stop changing. This means that at any point in our lives we have the potential to be affected by adversity, but we also have the potential to be affected by positive influences too. In other words, it is never too late for us to change.

It used to be thought that once our brains have passed through the time of massive development which occurs between birth and about three years of age, they become 'set' and subsequent changes are small and difficult to make. In fact we now know that through something called 'neuroplasticity', our brains have the potential to develop until the very ends of our lives. If you have tried to learn a new skill recently, you may have noticed that it can take longer to learn as an adult than when you were a child, which can be pretty frustrating, but learn it you can. What is more, each experience of learning can be seen on brain scans as a thickening of the corresponding area of the brain. The brain is just like a muscle in our legs and arms. If we work it, it grows, or in the phrase used earlier in the book: *'neurons that fire together, wire together'*.

If this is the case, considering the physical and mental activities that we engage in each day, which parts of our brains are getting the best workout? Inadvertently, it is often the parts that we perhaps don't want to grow – such as those relating to anger or anxiety – that are actually getting a great deal of workout, thus increasing their strength. If we consider how much we worry and ruminate, or how much our anger is simmering throughout the day, then this part is being repeatedly exercised and is therefore getting stronger and stronger.

An eye-opening way of considering this is to consider the proposition that a genius, typically, is somebody who has put in more than ten thousand hours of practice in a specific area.[2] How many hours of practice have we already put in to our threat system? We probably reached ten thousand hours many years ago!

Compassionate motivation

As we have seen, our threat system will roll along unchecked and it can be very difficult to tone it down. This is not our fault; it is the way our mind has evolved to give us a rapid system for keeping ourselves safe. We could therefore let our mind carry on this way. However, we now also know that a powerful system for regulating our threat system is our soothing system. How about we put ten thousand hours of practice into growing that? Perhaps this seems a little daunting. We are our life's work, however, so we have a long time to practise. Also, every second we practise fires our neurons in a particular pattern which gets built upon and strengthened every time we practise a little more. We can think about the person we want to become, and then take tiny steps along that journey. A journey, after all, just comprises lots of single steps.

Cultivating the garden of our mind

Just as with a garden, we can leave our minds to 'grow' untamed, or we can decide to cultivate it in a particular way. So what is our motivation? What part of our self do we want to develop? How do we want to cultivate the garden of our mind?

In the compassionate mind approach we are, of course, aiming to cultivate our compassionate mind, so we are setting about to shape our mind in a particular way. Our motivation is to develop the wisdom and the skills needed to turn towards, and to help alleviate and prevent, the suffering of ourselves and others.

Our wisdom comes from understanding that we are shaped by forces we did not choose and which are not our fault, such as evolution and our early experiences. The person we are might not be the person we would have chosen to be. However, we can also learn to shape our experiences, and deliberately train up and develop the person we would like to be.

Motivation is the key starting point because it organises the mind in particular ways (see Chapter 13). For example, when we want to compete, this organises our thinking, our behaviour and our attention around success, losing, and beating others. If our motivation is compassion, this organises our mind in a different way so that our thinking, attention and behaviour is focused on giving and receiving care and helping ourselves and others to grow and flourish.

As with a garden, developing our compassionate mind might need a lot of work at the beginning, but once it starts to take shape it becomes much easier to maintain.

Two wolves

The following is a lovely little story which beautifully and simply illustrates the change that we are trying to create. It is a Native American Indian story about a grandpa walking along with his grandson:

> Grandpa: There are two wolves inside of me. One is anger and the other is compassion.

> Grandson: Which wolf will win, Grandpa?

> Grandpa: The wolf that I feed.

> *We can choose to shape our mind by repeatedly shifting our attention from aspects which stimulate threat to those which stimulate compassion.*

We can make a decision about which wolf we are trying to feed. What is more, we don't have to fight or suppress the parts we don't want. We merely 'feed' them as little as possible. When we ruminate or grumble to ourselves, or criticise ourselves, we can remind ourselves which wolf we are inadvertently feeding. Then we can try to switch our energies to the wolf we do wish to feed: compassion.

There is a rapidly growing body of research demonstrating how deliberately stimulating the part of the brain concerned with different aspects of compassion is actually thickening and growing that part. What is more, it also shows that changes can be seen on brain scans after just a half an hour of daily practice over a few weeks in people who haven't engaged in these types of practice before. And for those who practised for more time each day, the gains were greater than those who practised less.[3] In other words, we don't have to meditate for five hours a day to grow our soothing system; just a few minutes will help. But the more we do, the greater the changes we will experience.

Keeping going – 'growing a tulip'

Author and clinical psychologist Christopher Germer gives a lovely illustration of the process of growing our compassion. He likened the process to growing a tulip;[4] we first make the decision that we would like to grow a tulip. This is the very first step: motivation, or making the commitment to growing our self-compassion. We then prepare the soil by weeding it, digging it over and perhaps putting in some compost. Then we plant the tulip bulb deep in the soil. We 'water' and 'feed' it with our mindfulness and compassion exercises. Day after day we do this and keep checking the soil but nothing seems to be happening. We might get fed up and feel like giving up. But one day, we notice the tiny point of a green shoot emerging from the soil. Without our realising it, the tulip had been growing after all.

This is often the pattern with compassion exercises: we come to realise that all our practice has been quietly but steadily making changes in our brain; for example, when we feel a tiny spark of warmth towards ourselves, or to our baby, or don't get quite so knocked as we usually would by criticism. No practice is ever wasted.

Beginning to practise

We are going to go step by step through the exercises. Each one is a stand-alone practice but later a number of them will be used together to form the basis for other exercises. The exercises have been divided into those that prepare the mind and body to create a sense of settling and stilling (Chapters 13 and 14), and those that are designed to then create the particular pattern of compassion in the mind and body (Chapters 15 and 16). In reality, as we will see, these cannot really be separated in such a clear way, as the preparation exercises can in themselves stimulate the compassionate mind. We can think of the process as like going across a series of stepping stones from the threat or self-critical mind to the compassionate mind. Each exercise is a stepping stone.

In learning the exercises it is worth spending some time on each, for example trying them for a few minutes a day for a week. This helps us to understand the point and the process of the exercise, and to see that the experience can vary and will never be precisely the same each time. This also makes sure that we don't discard an exercise the first time we try it because it doesn't 'work' or isn't for us. Often the most challenging exercises are challenging precisely because they are the ones we most need. They can turn out to be the most beneficial of the exercises to us, so we need to give them time.

> *The hardest practice can turn out to be the most beneficial practice.*

Time to practise

The majority of people who begin mindfulness and compassion exercises can realise that days or weeks go by without doing any practice at all. When we are trying to develop particular brain systems by exercising them ('neurons that fire together, wires together'), then, as with exercising our body, we need to find a way to enable ourselves to do this practice. Of course, the people that most need the exercises are those whose time is filled with doing and worrying. And when we consider putting a baby into the equation, we see what a great challenge this is, particularly as a baby often means that there may be no predictable time or space to practise or perhaps hardly any space at all. This in itself needs our compassion; a recognition that, with a baby, a precious moment of time to be still and to settle can be so difficult to come by.

So how do we manage this? First, we need to have the motivation to do it, so we need to keep bringing ourselves back to just why this is important to us. Then we need a way of remembering. Third, we need the time to do it. It can help to identify some time when it may be possible to practise and then to set up some reminders at this time. We may initially want to pick times that are easiest, such as when the baby has gone to sleep for the night or in the car if the baby naps after a drive (when you have parked up, rather than driving!) As the exercises become more familiar we might want to choose moments when, typically, we find moving into our compassionate mind trickier; for example, when we find ourselves feeling anxious, worried, frustrated or angry. So we might want to put a sticky note, sticker, symbol or picture next to the bed for when we wake up, next to the front door, the telephone, or on the door to the baby's room, somewhere in the kitchen, on the handle of the baby's buggy, or on the dashboard of the car; anywhere where we want a reminder to try to move into our compassionate mind as best we can. If you have a mobile phone then the picture or background could reflect your compassionate mind because we might look at that picture many times a day. There may also be ways to set up reminders on your phone. Many mobile phone apps are now available to set up reminders and also provide meditation and breathing exercises and even courses that take you through exercises each day.

Ways of practising

There are two ways of practising. One is a more formal practice, and the other is a more naturalistic practice in which we engage in moments of mindfulness and compassion as we go through the day. It is helpful to try to fit in some formal practice because this really enables us to get to know the practice and to get to know our minds, but ultimately we want to be able to use these practices as we move throughout the day, so practising 'as we go' is also important. With formal practices, even one minute is important, but the longer the better. If you aim for just one or two minutes then you are more likely to have a go, and you may find the one minute has been able to turn into five, ten, or perhaps even twenty.

Where to practise

The answer to this really is 'anywhere' because the aim is to be able to use the compassionate mind approach whenever you need it and you never know when that might be. However, for formal practices you might want to identify a space where you can create conditions which help you to settle and be still. Consider all your senses: what you see, hear, smell, touch and taste. You might want to clear a corner and choose what you want there.

- Thinking about the sense of **sight**; you might want to create a particular kind of light perhaps by bringing in a lamp. You might want a picture or an object that creates a sense of peace and warmth in you.

- With regard to the sense of **touch**, you might want a cushion or particular chair to sit on and perhaps a soft blanket to keep you warm if you are doing this in the early hours of the morning or at night. Some people enjoy holding something like a smooth stone, which can provide a focus for attention.

- **Smell** is important too and eventually through association can form an anchor or trigger so that you can use it when you are struggling to help you move more rapidly into a more settled and compassionate state. So find a smell that you would want to put in this place, perhaps on some dried flowers, on the radiator or an oil burner to be released by the heat, or on a tissue, or a scarf that you can drape round yourself.

- Consider **sounds** too. You might want to find some meditation-type background music (see the website coherence.com), or you may prefer quietness so that you can hear the birds or sounds from outside, such as the rain or the wind, or the steady rumbling of the traffic.

- With regard to **taste,** you may want to create a sense of freshness in your mouth by drinking some water before you begin.

> *Although a formal 'sitting' practice is helpful, we are aiming to be able to use our compassionate mind anytime, anywhere.*

Make this a space that you look forward to being in.

You might also want to make it a space that you can come into easily with the baby so that you can eventually do some of the practices while you feed the baby, for example, while the baby is asleep or even when the baby is upset.

However, it is important that not having the 'right space' doesn't become a block to practice. Really, we can practise anywhere in any moment; we can create these external qualities within our own mind. It is just that having such an external space can make it easier to create this space within ourselves, and the very process of setting it up helps to stimulate that part of the mind.

Mindful awareness

We are now quite familiar with the speed at which the threat system takes hold of us. Before we know it, our heart is pounding, we are feeling scared or angry, and our minds are full of angry or anxious thoughts. We can become completely caught up in these thoughts or feelings. It is almost like we have been suddenly pulled into a raging river. We are swept downstream and it can feel impossible to pull ourselves out. However, there is a way, and what is more, it is a skill, which means it can be learned. This is the skill of mindfulness, which we touched upon earlier in the book. It is the ability to observe our inner experiences without judging them or trying to change them in any way.

There is a Buddhist expression, '*Mind like the sky*'. This is mindfulness. With mindfulness we are trying to move into a conscious awareness of our mind and body as if we are the blue sky and we are watching the clouds move across. The clouds might be things going on inside us, such as our thoughts, our emotions or our body sensations. They might also be things going on outside us, such as sounds, smells, textures or colours, or the interactions between ourselves and others. Rather than being carried along and reacting to these stimuli, we simply observe them, notice them, without judging them or trying to change them in any way.

Another analogy is imagining setting up a deckchair at the side of the road and just watching the cars passing by. We are aiming not to get too caught up in judging the cars, or trying to ignore the ones we don't like, or pulling over the ones we do like. Nor do we get in one and get carried away. We merely sit and observe.

When we do this we learn all sorts of important information about our mind. We might notice that everything comes and goes, that no one thing is identical to another, that nothing stays the same. We might notice that sitting in the deckchair or being the blue sky is calming but once we get caught in our emotions, for example, or our thoughts, we can become stirred up by them. We might notice that we have many thoughts; that many of our thoughts are about the past or the future rather than right now; that the majority of our thoughts and feelings are threat related; that we try to resist some thoughts and feelings, but hold on to others; that mindfulness is hard to do!

Mindfulness can seem like such a simple practice but, as we shall see, if you try for example just to observe your out-breath from beginning to end, you may find you don't even reach the end of one breath before you are caught up in thinking that you must put milk on the shopping list. It is a skill, however, that gets easier with practice. It is also a crucial skill because it enables us to be able to notice what is happening in our minds, to step back slightly from rather than being entangled in it, and to then choose how we want to shape it, which in the compassionate mind approach is into a pattern of compassion.

We might ask how mindfulness can possibly help when what we want is to *not* feel anxious or angry or self-critical rather than simply to observe these feelings without judgement. The way that mindfulness can help us is demonstrated very powerfully by looking at the premise behind a treatment for recurrent severe depression which is getting excellent results. It is called Mindfulness-Based Cognitive Therapy (MBCT) and has been developed by Mark Williams, John Teasdale, Zindel Segal and Jon Kabat-Zinn (detailed in their 2007 book *The Mindful Way Through Depression: Freeing Yourself from Chronic Unhappiness*).[5] MBCT came about after the authors of the book set out to try to find a way of helping people who had experienced recurrent major depression from relapsing into future episodes of depression. It was derived from Mindfulness-Based Stress Reduction (MBSR), developed by Jon Kabat-Zinn[6] for dealing with anxiety and chronic pain.

> *Mindfulness helps us to let thoughts and feelings pass, without us fuelling them with additional panic, frustration and self-criticism.*

With regard to chronic pain, Jon Kabat-Zinn noted that not only do we endure the pain itself but we then worry, ruminate, and feel frustrated and resentful about the pain, which then tenses us up more and increases the chronic pain. It turns out that a similar process occurs with depression. Once we have had an episode of depression we are then more likely to have another one. Each time we experience depression the chances of recurrence increase. So even if antidepressants work to stop the depressive episode, they do not seem to prevent recurrence. MBCT came about from a quest to see if there was a way of intercepting these episodes in order to slow down or prevent recurrence.

This is what came to be understood about recurrent depression: if we have had an episode of depression, this affects many systems within us. We feel differently in our body, we don't have much motivation, our thinking is affected, our attention is focused on the negative, we tend to remember only self-critical or upsetting memories, we imagine worst-case scenarios.

Once we have recovered from an episode, what happens if we wake up one day feeling a little sad or fed up? We are constantly moving through different feelings and emotions throughout the day, but once we have had depression, feeling 'fed up' takes on a particular potency. 'Fed up' now has all sorts of associations; it may bring back body memories of fear, or sinking down. We may suddenly recall the feelings of desperation or hopelessness. We may start having thoughts of 'Oh no, it is going to happen again! I can't cope if it does.' Or, 'Stop, I don't want this!' It is as if all of these terrifying aspects have become added to what was to be a fairly fleeting feeling of 'fed up'. Each of these aspects further stirs up the threat system, which has gone from being gently poked by 'feeling fed up' to being fully awake and on red alert. We have moved from a moment of 'fed up' to minutes of panic and fear. The ball has begun to roll and it is hard to stop it. The longer we worry the more convinced we become that this could be a new episode of depression. Fed-up moments can turn into a fed-up hour, to an awful day, to a bad week, to a new episode of depression. The premise behind Mindfulness-Based Cognitive Therapy is that if we can allow the 'fed up' moment to come and then go, without trying to suppress it or panic about it, then it may never turn into another episode. And research has proved that this works. Those who have learned the skills of mindfulness are significantly less likely to experience further depression even if they have had many previous episodes. In fact research trials have found that MBCT can halve the risk of relapse in those who have had three or more episodes of depression.[7] It is now being found to be effective even for intervening in a full-blown episode.[8]

There is a vast body of evidence demonstrating the effectiveness of mindfulness for a whole host of difficulties including managing chronic and incurable physical health problems. It is therefore a skill very much worth cultivating.

The compassionate mind approach rests upon the skills of mindfulness. It enables us to turn our attention 'inwards', thereby tuning up our sensitivity to what is happening within us. It also reveals important information about the characteristics of our inner world, for example that thoughts, emotions and body sensations wax and wane, rise and fall, come and go, that we are not our thoughts or emotions, and that letting them come and go can significantly reduce our suffering. As we learn to notice our suffering, then we can look in, not just with awareness, but with a determination to alleviate it, so we bring our compassion mind to it. We will therefore spend some time learning this skill of mindfulness.

An empty mind?

One of the assumptions associated with mindfulness or meditation-type exercises is that we are striving for a clear, empty mind. The first part to notice here is the 'striving'. If we are not aware of our mind-set then 'doing' mindfulness or 'doing' compassion becomes just another focus for our threat and drive systems and our attention has then moved to the drives to achieve and avoid failure with respect to mindfulness practice itself.

Rather than being an effortful 'achieving' or 'striving', it is a shift in the focus of our attention; a step back from the 'doing' and moving instead into 'being'. In the 'being' mode we can observe the 'doing' rather than being caught up in it. We can notice if we are slipping into trying hard to get it right by becoming aware of our body and our breathing. A way of checking which mode we are in is to see whether the face is frowning or relaxed, whether the teeth are clenched or relaxed, whether the shoulders are raised or lowered and back, whether the upper arms and hands, and tops of the legs, are tensed or relaxed. If we are in 'doing mode' we notice that our body is tensed up ready for the 'doing', like a dog that has got its lead ready to go for a walk. When we notice this we can bring our mindful awareness to it and then see if we can allow ourselves to let go of this tension, because no 'doing' is necessary at the moment.

The second part of the assumption is that we are aiming for a clear, empty mind. This experiment helps us to become aware of the nature of our mind.

Experiment: Awareness of the restless mind

Sit upright with your feet on the floor and your hands resting in your lap so you are comfortable but alert. With your eyes open, let your mind rest in the present moment. Become aware of your surroundings; the sounds around you, what you can see, an awareness of the feel of the floor beneath your feet and the chair beneath you. See if you can notice any smells. Sit for a few minutes in this mindful awareness.

You might notice that, before long, rather than attending to what you can sense in your surroundings, you are caught up in thoughts. When this happens gently bring your mind back to sensing your surroundings once again.

So just how still and settled is our mind even when we are doing nothing but just being aware of our surroundings? It can be quite astonishing to see how quickly our mind gets taken over by thoughts, and we can travel quite a long way caught up in the 'story' or dialogue of our thoughts before we become aware of where we have gone.

And what was the nature of our thoughts? Usually we get caught up in thinking about the past or the future rather than the present moment, and often the thoughts are threat focused. So we worry or get frustrated about what has happened, or what might happen, or what we haven't done but need to do. We might ruminate about arguments and worry about our relationships with people.

What we see in this exercise is the interplay between our old and new brain; our old brain that focuses on threat and safeness, getting food, reproduction and social relationships, and our new brain that plans, imagines, thinks and ruminates and generally keeps 'stoking' and stirring up the worries and concerns of the old brain. This is precisely what we see when we spend a moment looking in and observing our mind; a restless, ruminative mind concentrating primarily on worrying about the past and the future with a particular concern about our relationships with other people. This is the natural state of our mind; restlessness and a tendency towards threat focusing. This is not our fault; it is just how our minds have evolved.

So what precisely is mindfulness?

Jon Kabat-Zinn, in his book *Wherever You Go, There You Are*[9], describes mindfulness as deliberately paying attention to what is happening to us right now, and paying attention in a way which is non-judgemental. It can be paying attention to anything; for example our thoughts, feelings, urges in the body, bodily sensations, what we see, hear, touch, taste and smell.

This definition has three components. It is something we do *intentionally* in contrast to the unintentional loops we slip into when we get caught up in our thoughts. Second, it involves focusing on what is happening in the *present moment* rather than drifting into thinking about the past or the future. And third, it means *allowing what we find to exist without judging it, condemning it or wishing it was something other than it is*. So if we imagine for a moment experiencing a sensation of sadness. When we are mindful of sadness, we are deliberately turning our attention to just the sensation of feeling sad, without trying to get rid of it, or berating ourselves for feeling it, or panicking about feeling it. If we have had an experience of sadness which spiralled into depression then we might find that as we mindfully observe the experience of sadness, we notice that a thought has popped up, for example 'Oh no, what if this is the start of depression?' But rather than getting carried away with these thoughts and sensations we might respond with an interested awareness: 'Ah, there it is. When I have this particular feeling, these particular thoughts tend to pop up.' Now we have moved into observing rather than inadvertently fuelling the depressive response.

Once we have developed the ability to be mindful, we can consider just how we would like to respond to what we are noticing occurring. This is where compassion comes in; not only can we respond to what we observe with an interested awareness, we can also bring to it our real intention to try to help ourselves to alleviate whatever causes us pain and struggle. As we have seen, when we bring our care-giving and care-receiving mentality to bear in the form of compassion, then our mind and body responds to this automatically and the original threat may even subside because our body calms and settles more. So when we mindfully notice the sensation of sadness we can then bring our compassionate mind to this. This might be an attitude of validation, understanding, containment and warmth; a kind of 'Ah, here is sadness. It does feel painful and that can be hard to bear, but it is possible to bear and it will pass', said with a warm, kind face and voice.

Mindfulness and compassion

First, we are mindfully noticing the pattern of thoughts, feelings, urges and emotions that are occurring within us.

Second, we are deciding on the particular pattern that we would like to create; in this case, the pattern of our compassionate mind.

So, now that we have created the intention towards which we wish to direct our attention, let's look at an important effect of attention which will help us in both our mindfulness and our compassion practices.

Directing our attention

When we are mind*less* it feels like we are being controlled by our mind and body, helplessly caught up in wherever our thoughts and feelings send us. It is as if we have fallen into a fast-moving river and are being pulled along helplessly. What happens, then, if we take charge of where our attention lands? Instead of being swept along in the river, we climb out and sit on the bank, watching the thoughts, sensations, feelings and urges passing by.

You may remember this from earlier in the book. If we imagine our attention as like a spotlight or torchlight, we can try an experiment that demonstrates the nature of attention.

Experiment: Spotlight of attention

Sit upright in an alert position with your feet flat on the floor and close your eyes. Now imagine that your attention is like a spotlight. First, direct it to your left big toe. You may notice sensations within the toe, or where it makes contact with your sock or footwear. You may notice a sensation of your toe being in contact with the floor. Now move your attention to your right big toe. Next move your attention to your lips. Then rub the tip of your forefinger and thumb together and notice the sensations.

What happened to your left big toe when you moved your attention to your right big toe, and when you moved your attention from your right big toe to your lips and then your finger and thumb? You might have noticed that whatever you focused your attention on completely filled up your awareness. So, just like a spotlight, your attention illuminates whatever it focuses on but leaves everything else in the shade. This is the nature of attention. We can try the same exercise by attending to sounds, or smells, or what we can see or taste; the unattended-to sensation just seems to disappear, and the attended-to sensation appears to become much stronger. For example, we might suddenly become aware of the sound of a ticking clock in the room, but if we then shift our attention to the sound of a bird outside, we no longer notice the tick of the clock.

What is more, we can deliberately take hold of the torchlight of attention and move it around. So we can *choose* where to focus our attention in this present moment. We might adjust the spotlight to narrow beam and focus on something very specific like our left big toe, or we could widen the beam and allow our attention to take in our whole body, for example.

The other aspect of attention demonstrated by this experiment is that whatever our attention focuses on stimulates our mind in different ways. So, focusing on the ticking of the clock could be irritating while listening to the birds brings a feeling of calm. This is the same when we focus on emotions, feelings and memories. For a few minutes, then, bring to mind a memory of a time of real happiness, perhaps of sharing a funny moment or a smile with somebody. Notice how it feels in your body. Notice your face and how it might have softened and perhaps formed a smile. What your attention is now illuminating is affecting you physiologically in powerful ways. Now bring to mind a time when you felt a little cross or frustrated. What happens in your body now? What has happened to your face? The chances are the happy memory has faded into the background and this memory now fills up your mind. Not only that but it has changed the physiology of your body so that you are experiencing very different sensations and urges.

When we realise not only that can we choose to move our attention but also that what we focus it on can affect us in very different ways then we can start to choose to shift our attention to something that may be more helpful to us, such as our compassionate mind. We will return to this in the chapter on compassionate attention.

Our attention is designed to get hijacked by the threat system, and when it does threat becomes the sole focus of our attention, any positive thoughts, feelings or memories disappearing out of our awareness. And, given that 'what fires together wires together', this further strengthens our threat mind. However, now that we know we can shift the focus of attention, once we notice what is happening (using the skills of mindfulness) we can choose to shift our attention to whatever stimulates our compassionate mind, such as times when we really helped somebody, or overcame something that was difficult. This will then fill our attention, the threat will fade into the background, and we have moved to firing and wiring – and therefore strengthening – our compassionate mind.

The simple little experiment of shifting our focus from our toes to our lips demonstrates three aspects of the nature of our attention that can really make a difference to us:

1. That attention is like a spotlight which brings to the foreground and illuminates whatever it focuses on.

2. That attention is moveable. Although it can be taken over unintentionally by our threat and drive systems, we can also intentionally direct it.

3. That whatever we focus our attention on creates very powerful physiological affects within us, and as soon as we shift attention the physiological effects change immediately too. So, when we focus on compassion, warmth and kindness, we feel very differently from when we focus on unhappiness, worry or frustration.

To summarise, when we are experiencing difficult feelings, thoughts or emotions, mindfulness can help us to stay with them rather than avoid them, but it also allows us to step back and observe them rather than being caught up in them. Just this process of stepping back can affect us physiologically because there is a sense of calmness and containment when we step into this observing or 'aware' mind.

Once we have moved to observing the threat mind rather than being caught up in it, through this process of mindful awareness we can then decide whether the most helpful thing for us in that moment is to stay with this focus on observing the threat mind, or to shift our awareness to something else, intentionally choosing to create a different pattern in our mind, such as the compassionate mind.

An important point here is that this ability to shift attention is not about 'just think happy thoughts, and don't think unhappy thoughts'; it is about being able to bring a balance to our mind, and with it a wisdom and understanding of how our minds work, which enables us to find ways of really helping when we, or others, are struggling.

Settling the mind and body

As we have seen, our mind often has control over the spotlight of attention, and moves it rapidly for us, creating all sorts of feelings and reactions within us. We can feel very stirred up inside. When we are trying to take hold of the spotlight of attention and focus it on just one thing, it can help if we settle our mind, allowing it to become more still. It is like wading around in a pond in our wellington boots. This stirs up the mud and we can't see anything. Once we stand still, the mud slowly and gently settles to the bottom and the water becomes clear. We can use our breath to help us to settle and still our mind and body so that we can see more clearly. As our breath is always with us, learning helpful ways to use our breath means we always have with us a powerful means of regulating our body and mind, and there is no risk we might leave it behind somewhere.

This concept of just standing still and patiently waiting rather than wading around in the muddy pond is one we bring to mindfulness practice. When we find we are trying too hard, getting frustrated because we can't find what we are supposed to find, clenching our teeth and frowning, we know that we have started wading about again in the 'search for mindfulness'. This is a sign that we need to stop, turn our attention back to the breath, and let ourselves settle into watching the pool become clear again.

Core mindfulness exercises

Exercise: Mindfulness to the breath

As the breath is always with us, it can become an anchor to help still our restless mind. It helps us to be in the present moment. Sit upright, with your feet flat on the floor, in an alert, dignified posture with your shoulders dropped and open. It is easier to focus on your breath if you close your eyes, but if you prefer just let your eyes gaze in an unfocused manner on a point in front of you.

Bring your attention to where you notice your breath, for example the tip of your nose, or the rise and fall of your chest, or by placing your hands on your stomach, fingertip to fingertip, and feeling the rhythm of your fingers moving apart and coming together again. Just turn your attention to your breath and see if you can follow it from the start of the in-breath to the end of the out-breath. You are not trying to change your breathing in any way. You are just noticing it exactly as it is without judging it.

You will find that you may not even get to the end of one breath before your mind has been captured by your thoughts. This is normal. Just notice this with an interested awareness and warmth, and then gently guide your mind back to your breath, just like you might gently shepherd an overexcited puppy or toddler. You will need to do this repeatedly because the mind is so restless, but each time you notice your mind has wandered, this is a moment of mindfulness. So the more times you notice your wandering mind and return it to the breath, the more you are exercising and strengthening the mechanisms within the brain concerned with the ability to be mindful.

What you might notice is that although you are not aiming to change the breath, just the process of focusing on it in this non-judgemental way can actually be calming and you may find your breath naturally lengthening. This isn't, however, the aim of the exercise. The aim is just to practise directing our attention in a particular way. If we start seeking calm through this exercise then this is akin to beginning to wander about in the muddy pond again, this time looking for calm; we just stir up the mind again by bringing in irritation, frustration and perhaps some self-criticism too. Then focusing on the breath becomes harder. When this happens, as it probably will (because our drive and threat mind are rarely far away) allow yourself to notice the searching, notice the irritation and the frustration, perhaps even just naming them as such (for example, 'this is irritation', 'this is frustration') and then just turn your attention back to noticing the breath in a gentle, curious, non-judgemental manner. You are in effect standing still again in the muddy pond just watching the silt settle back down again with a warm, interested, non-judgemental mind.

Exercise: Mindfulness to sounds

Close your eyes and let sounds drift into your ears, just like your ears are satellite dishes simply picking up sounds. Don't interpret the sounds, label them or judge them. Just allow them to flow in. If you find yourself reacting to the sounds, just notice your reactions with an interested awareness and then return your attention to whatever you can hear.

Exercise: Mindfulness to the senses

We often eat or drink without paying much attention at all to the taste. This exercise is often done with a raisin but you can try it with any food. We will use the example here of mindfulness to chocolate, because it is a delicious treat, yet we often only enjoy the first mouthful and pay very little attention to the rest.

- Feel the weight of the chocolate in your hand.

- If it is wrapped, feel the texture of the wrapping by gently and slowly running your finger over it.

- Look at the way the light falls on the wrapper. Notice the patterns and colours on the wrapper.

- Very slowly, unwrap the chocolate with an awareness of the feel and sound of the wrapper as it tears or opens.

- Become aware of the smell released as you open the wrapper.

- Notice the sight of the chocolate; the variations in colour, patterns, texture.

- Slowly break off a square, noting the feel of the chocolate between your fingers, and the sensation and sound of the chocolate breaking.

- Just hold the chocolate for a moment, noticing how it feels as it melts slightly from the warmth of your fingers.

- Now slowly lift the chocolate to your nose and inhale the smell of the chocolate, just noticing without making any judgements.

- Slowly take a bite of the chocolate, attending to the feel of the bite and the moment when you first become aware of the taste.

- Let the chocolate rest in your mouth, noting the sensations.

- Notice any increase in saliva and the sensations of swallowing.

- Notice any sensations in your mouth once you have swallowed the chocolate.

Mindfulness to the body

This is one of the key mindfulness practices[10] because so much is learned from it. Sadly many women have difficult relationships with their body and this can be particularly so after having a baby when the body may have acquired an appearance it never had before. It may be tender after birth, there may be strange new sensations, and it is in a process of rapid transition following birth. The body also holds memories for us. We may rather not think about our body so this exercise may be hard. If so, start by initially focusing just on one area of the body that doesn't stir you up too much, such as the fingers or soles of the feet or top of the head.

The reason this exercise is important is because the body is where we experience our emotions, and also our body memories. If we are always turning away from our body we lose the information that helps to make sense of our reactions and experiences. When we can turn instead towards our body we learn that emotions and bodily experiences never stay the same, but wax and wane, come and go. We also become aware of the degree to which our thoughts interact with our body, for example that worrying about pain can increase the degree of pain. Particularly when we have difficult experiences with our body, such as pain, uncomfortable memories or harsh judgements, we become aware of the possibility of bringing a curious and compassionate awareness to even the most difficult of these experiences, which can be generalised to many other experiences outside of this exercise.

Exercise: Mindfulness to the body

- Lie down or sit comfortably in an alert but relaxed position.

- Take a few slow breaths to settle your mind.

- Starting from your feet, just bring your attention to the soles of your feet (this has been shown in itself to be calming when you feel anxious or angry).

- Just notice any sensations without making any judgements.
- As your mind drifts, gently bring it back to the object of your attention. Spend a few minutes focusing on each part.
- Now focus on the top of your feet.
- Your ankles.
- Lower legs.
- Upper legs.
- Pelvis.
- Bottom.
- Stomach (you may notice judgements or memories entering your awareness as you attend to particular parts of your body. Just notice these with a fleeting curiosity, perhaps labelling them as 'judging', 'criticising', 'worrying', and then return your attention to just allowing that part of your body to fill up your awareness for that moment).
- Chest.
- Back.
- Shoulders.
- Arms.
- Fingers.
- Neck.
- Throat.
- Mouth.
- Inside the mouth.
- Nose.
- Eyes.
- Back of the head.
- Top of the head.

Bringing gratitude and compassion to the body

In this exercise we are turning our attention to the body in a mindful way as in the exercise, but this time our intention is to purposefully turn up and intensify the patterns created by bringing gratitude and compassion to the parts of our body, and the emotions, memories and sensations, that are generated when we shine the spotlight of attention on them.

If you think you may fall asleep or struggle with drowsiness then sit up, with an alert dignified posture, rather than lying down. (If you are really sleepy, you may decide that the most compassionate thing to do is to have a nap, if possible, and try this another time). The aim of the exercise is to bring an alert awareness to the body rather than relaxation or falling asleep, although relaxation may be a by-product of the exercise.

Exercise: Bringing gratitude and compassion to the body

Close your eyes and bring your awareness to the rhythm of rising and falling in your stomach and chest created by your breathing. Become aware of your whole body for a moment, and then bring your attention to where it makes contact with the floor, seat or bed. Now imagine that your attention is filled with real warmth and kindness. You may even have the sense that it is a warm colour, mist or light. Now, focusing on your toes, imagine that with each out-breath your warmth is pouring into your toes and then filling up your feet. Imagine the warmth wrapping around them. Bring a sense of gratitude to your toes and feet, for all the work they do without us really noticing them.

Now bring this warmth to your lower legs, your knees, the tops of your legs and your buttocks, breathing your gratitude, warmth and kindness into and around each part. If you notice any tension or discomfort, let your awareness settle around it like the warmth of a hot water bottle. See if you can allow a softening around the edges of the discomfort.

Then bring your awareness to your pelvis and stomach, breathing into each part the warm light or colour of your gratitude and tenderness for each part, remembering how each has tried to serve you as best it can, of the hard work it has gone through, and the healing it might need. It can help to place your hand gently on each part and feel your warmth and tenderness pass from your hand into that part of your body. Keep it there for as long as you wish.

When you are ready, move to your lower and upper back; areas that work so hard for us, particularly during pregnancy, and often suffer a great deal as a result. Then move your warmth, gratitude and tenderness to your chest and your heart area, to your breasts and the complicated changes these have undergone as they do the best they can in regulating, starting and stopping milk production.

Now bring your warm awareness to your shoulders, the tops of your arms, your elbows, lower arms, wrists. Bring gratitude to all that these parts do for you, including their ability to grow in strength to meet the needs of carrying a heavier and heavier baby. Then breathe gratitude and warmth into the palms of your hands and your fingers.

Next bring your awareness to the back of your neck, the top of your head and then your face and jaw. Allow your face to soften around the jaw, tongue, forehead and eyes. Feel the temperature of the air on your face.

Now bring your awareness to your whole body, breathing your warmth, gratitude and tenderness around the whole of it.

Bring your awareness back to your breath for a moment, then gently start to move your toes and fingers, then gently stretch your whole body. If you are lying down, roll to one side and push yourself up gently and slowly into a sitting position. Then, when you are ready, slowly stand up.

Mindfulness to emotions

An analogy sometimes used for this exercise is imagining an old Chinese man sitting cross-legged on his meditation cushion in his garden. He is smoking his pipe and sitting in quiet contemplation. A bird lands on his shoulder. He notices it and then brings his attention back to his pipe. Some children come and play in the garden. They shout and laugh and play their games. He just remains sitting quietly. He sits in the rain and sun and wind.

Our emotions can be viewed as the children, the animals and the weather, while our stance in relation to this is represented by the man smoking his pipe. We try not to judge our emotions or get too caught up in responding to them. We just notice them as they pass through us. We are not our emotions. They are just temporary 'visitors to the garden'.

The old man is not trying to grasp hold of and keep the pleasant emotions, nor push away the unpleasant emotions; he lets all of them come and go. This is difficult to do, because our emotions are designed to stir us to action. With practice, however, we can learn a little separation between becoming aware of, and reacting to, our emotions. This then allows us a space to be able to move into a different mind-set, so we can respond more wisely and skilfully rather than in a purely reactive, and perhaps unskilful and unwise, way.

We can also be mindful to the characteristics of emotions; how they appear, build, reach a peak, then fade away. All emotions, pleasant or unpleasant, come and go, rise and fall. We can learn to 'surf' emotions. Imagine watching seagulls bobbing about on the sea. As a wave comes they rise up with the wave and then follow the wave back down again. They have no resistance to the wave, they just go with the rising and falling. This is the relationship we are cultivating to our emotions in mindfulness; allowing them to come, build to a peak and then fade away again.

Exercise: Mindfulness to emotions

- We are going to start by sitting with an alert, dignified posture, with our feet flat and grounded on the floor. Close or half close your eyes. Let your breathing settle. Now we are going to bring our attention to however we are feeling right now by scanning our body, including our chest, stomach, face, arms, legs and hands and noticing the particular patterns of sensations that each emotion brings. Without trying to change them in any way, we just observe the sensations.

- We can also experiment with deliberately bringing different emotions to mind to see how they play out in our body. First, we can bring to mind a time when we felt a little anxious. How does that feel in the body? What sensations in the body tell us that we are feeling a little anxious? Perhaps a tension in the arms and the upper legs, a quickening of the heart rate, an increase in our rate of breathing, a slight clamminess to our skin.

- Then bring a pleasant memory to mind and notice how that feels in the body. There may be a sense of warmth and tingling in the chest, a relaxing of tension in the muscles, a smile on our face, a feeling of the body opening up rather than contracting.

So we are learning to observe the different emotions as different patterns of physical sensations which wash through our body, build, peak and then fade like a wave.

Mindfulness to thoughts

Our thoughts are very potent triggers for our emotions and behaviour. If we imagine being ignored in the street by somebody we know, we may think, 'She's forgotten her glasses again.' This might make us chuckle and then call out affectionately to her. Or we might think, 'I wonder what I've done to make her ignore me?' We feel very differently and we may put our head down and want to get home as quickly as we can. Our thoughts sweep us along from one to another, to another, as if we have fallen in a river. However, just like sounds or physical sensations, we can also observe our thoughts as just mental activity that forms and then disappears again in the mind. This is a very powerful practice to do because it allows us to unhook ourselves from our thoughts so that we are not caught up in reacting to them. This is, however, very difficult to do because we have become so identified with our thoughts that it can be hard to stand back from them. It can take a lot of practice and it is very easy to find we have slipped from the bank of the river, observing our thoughts appear and disappear like eddies and swirls of water, to falling in and getting swept along again. However, the practice has such great benefits that it is worth staying with it and coming back to it repeatedly.

Exercise: Mindfulness to thoughts

- Sit with an alert, dignified but relaxed posture. Close or half close your eyes.

- Let your attention settle on your breath.

- Imagine you are sat by a stream or standing on a bridge watching the stream flowing past.

- Notice the trees, the feel of the air, any sounds, any smells.

- Turn your attention to the many thoughts that arise and then disappear in your mind.

- Imagining 'catching' each thought and then notice it appearing on a leaf, which you watch bobbing and twirling down the stream.

- Imagine the next thought appearing on another leaf, which gently floats down the stream.

> - If you think you have no thoughts, become aware that this is in itself a thought, which then floats down the stream on a leaf.
> - Alternatively, you might imagine watching the eddies and swirls of the stream and then imagine the eddies forming each thought, which takes shape for a moment and then disappears again.

This exercise gives us a little separation from our thoughts. They become less potent and emotive. We also become aware of how many pass through our mind, and that each one can pull our body to respond quite strongly to it. If we let go of them then they just carry on passing along without pulling us this way and that.

Another way of thinking about thoughts is to imagine our mind as a clear blue sky like we did previously. Thoughts are the clouds that float across the sky. Some are light and wispy, others are grey and large, and others might be black and thunderous. But all of them are just passing across the clear blue sky of our mind.

A rather lovely way of considering thoughts is imagining them as being written on water with a stick. They form and then immediately dissipate.

Mindfulness 'on the go'

Exercise: Eating like a baby

When you are about to eat or drink something, imagine that you are coming to this as a baby who has never seen or tasted this before. See if you can get into that state of wonder and curiosity. Unlike a baby you also have the ability to be aware of your wonder and curiosity and to notice your reactions, thoughts and feelings. When we introduce new foods to our baby we can bring our mindful awareness to our baby's awareness, and just observe how our baby uses every sense to explore this food.

Exercise: Mindfulness to the washing up

This is a good way to build a mindfulness practice without having to set aside specific time. If you dislike or resent doing the washing up, you never know, it may even turn something unpleasant into something you look forward to! Choose a washing-up liquid that makes you feel calmed and soothed when you smell it or look at its colour.

- Start by taking a few long, slow breaths.

- As you run the water, just observe the patterns of the water in the bowl.

- Squeeze some washing-up liquid in the bowl and just notice the stream of liquid.

- Notice the effect of the washing-up liquid mixing with the water.

- Really look at the bubbles forming.

- Inhale the smell and notice how it makes you feel inside.

- Listen to the sound of the water filling the bowl.

- Notice any taste in your mouth.

- Gently lower your hands into the water and become aware of the feel of the warm water covering your hands.

- Notice the feel of the plate or cup against your hand and the cloth in the other hand.

- Wash each item, mindfully observing each one becoming clean.

- Notice the water and bubbles sliding down as you put the item on the draining board.

We can try this with any activity we are engaged in so that we are fully present in it, for example cleaning our teeth, making a cup of tea, changing the baby, taking the washing out of the washing machine and so on.

Exercise: Mindful walking with the pushchair

This is a good exercise to do, particularly when it is hard to find the time to practise mindfulness.

- Take a few long, slow breaths.
- Feel your hands against the handle and the feel of resistance in your arms as you push.
- Notice the sensations of your feet making contact with the ground and then lifting and leaving the ground.
- Bring your attention to the feelings in your lower and then upper legs as they move.
- Now move the spotlight of your attention to your senses.
- Notice what you see around you – try narrowing your attention to perhaps a flower or leaf, and then widen it to take in all that you can see.
- Now focus on what you can hear. Let the sounds just drift into your ears without effort.
- Turn your attention to smells and then to tastes.
- Bring this mindful attention to your baby, just taking in what you see, what you feel, without any judgement.

Summary

To be able to move into our compassionate mind, we must first be aware when we are not in it. This is not easy because the design of our mind means that we easily fall into the grip of our threat mind. Mindfulness is a skill which, through practice, enables us to notice when we are in our threat mind so that we can make a choice about how we relate to this mind and whether or not we want to shift our attention to our compassionate mind.

14 Preparing the compassionate mind: Activating the soothing system

Moving from our threat mind to our compassionate mind: the five stepping stones

By now you will probably have noticed just how easy it is to find ourselves in our threat system. We don't need to practise this at all. It can, however, take conscious effort to move from our threat mind into our compassionate mind. We do this by 'bridging across' from the threat to the soothing system. These are a set of techniques that help take us from one physiological state to another, like a bridge or a set of stepping stones. We use five core techniques to do this:

1. Strong, confident body posture.
2. Long, slow out-breath.
3. Mindfulness – non-judgemental awareness. These three techniques can be remembered with the phrase ('*body like a mountain, breath like the wind, mind like the sky*').
4. Kind, warm facial expression.
5. Kind, warm voice.

The first three techniques – body posture, breath, and mindfulness – help the body and mind to become more grounded, settled and clearer, enabling us to become aware of what is happening within us. They also move us from the sympathetic nervous system, which is involved in the activation and energy of the drive system and the flight/fright response of the threat system, to the parasympathetic nervous system, which is involved with calming the heart rate, rest, recuperation and a physiological sense of safety.

The techniques place us in an optimal state for being able to stimulate our compassionate mind. We then begin really turning up our compassion system by bringing a warm, friendly expression to our face and imagining hearing a warm, friendly voice speaking to us. Part of our parasympathetic nervous system connects muscles involved in smiling (particularly those around the eyes), and the middle ear, to our heart and to our inner organs above our diaphragm. When we smile and use a friendly voice, or detect these in others, we feel a sense of 'warmth' and safety in our body and our heart rate is calmed.

This particular physiological system is sometimes referred to as 'the social engagement system'[1] and it shows the extent to which we have developed to be highly social animals. We will be using this knowledge about the power of a kind face and voice in regulating us physiologically in many of the compassionate mind exercises.

By using these five techniques we give ourselves the best chance of bringing a compassionate response to ourselves and others.

1. Embodiment: changing your body posture to change your mind

How we hold ourselves affects how we feel, think and our physiology. We know this intuitively. Imagine you have got to make a difficult phone call, perhaps to sort out an incorrect bill. Would you make the phone call lying on the sofa, sitting on a chair or standing up? Even though the person at the other end can't see you, we know that we feel and therefore come across differently according to our posture.

> *Changing our body posture changes how we feel.*

Research has found that by standing or sitting in a more upright, confident posture we have more energy and are less likely to feel depressed.

This body posture also raises our levels of testosterone and lowers our levels of cortisol so we feel more confident and calmer[2, 3]. When we slump or collapse our body, drop our head, curl up, and cross our arms or legs, we are adopting a 'submissive' posture. We see this with animals. We are therefore sending a message to our brain that because we have adopted a submissive posture we must therefore be at risk of potential attack from a dominant person, even if this isn't the case at all. Our body then feels under threat and our thoughts and behaviour become threat focused too. Conversely, by sitting or standing in a confident but relaxed way, we signal to our brain that there is no threat and that we are safe. Our body correspondingly relaxes and our thoughts become more optimistic.

When we start any of the exercises we are moving our body into a posture that engages the physiological systems most likely to help us feel compassion towards ourselves and others. As compassion requires strength and courage, the posture is one of strength, courage and confidence but also of openness and receptiveness. So, even if we don't feel this way, or believe these are qualities we have, we can change our body posture to increase the chances of feeling a little more this way.

We also need to hold in mind how, for some of us, a confident posture might have been met with threat when we were children, so a more collapsed, head down and 'folded in' body posture would have been protective. As with all the exercises, then, we need to take this slowly and gently, holding in sight our intention and the person we want to become, but also respecting the strategies our body has developed, often without us being consciously aware of this, to keep us as safe as possible in times of threat. So we can slowly and gently move our body into a more confident, open posture, but keeping it within a position that feels safe rather than overwhelming. We can then experiment with taking this slightly more confident and open posture into our engagement with the world around us and see what happens. Once we discover, first, that it doesn't make us less safe, and second, that actually it might bring us benefits in how we relate to others and in how others relate to us, we will feel encouraged to keep going with these changes.

So how do we work out the posture for our compassionate self? The following can be a helpful experiment to try:

Experiment: Finding a compassionate posture

Imagine standing up with your feet together. This will work better if you actually do this, because you can feel the position in your body. Now imagine somebody gently pushing you. You are likely to wobble and lose your balance if you are pushed while standing this way. Now change your stance so that you might sway a little but won't fall over if pushed gently again. Notice how you are instinctively holding yourself now; you are likely to have your feet about a hip-width apart with knees slightly bent, shoulders dropped and open, with your head upright, eyes facing forward and the weight going down through your head, neck, down your spine and down through your legs into the floor. Your feet feel as if they are anchored into the floor like the roots of a tree anchored into the ground.

Now, while keeping this strong confident posture (sometimes called a 'dignified' posture), sit down with your bottom at the back of the seat and the base of your spine resting against the back of the chair. Check that your shoulders are dropped and open and that your spine is upright but not too tense. Your eyes are facing forwards rather than downwards or upwards, and the weight of your head is supported by your upright spine. Rest your hands on your lap. You can place them palms upwards if you wish. Try experimenting with laying your right upturned hand in your left upturned hand with your thumbs gently touching. Soften your jaw and face. You might notice a sense of heaviness, solidity and stillness as you sit in this posture.

This posture is the one we will use to begin all of the compassionate mind exercises. It is important for compassionate mind exercises, particularly if we worry about feeling vulnerable or where we have a tendency to 'float off' and lose ourselves when we close our eyes. It also helps us to feel in our bodies that compassion is not 'soft and fluffy' but rather a position of strong, dignified, quietly confident courageousness. We may not feel that we possess these qualities but our determination is to begin to try and grow a little more of this within ourselves so that we can help ourselves (and others) through difficult times.

The 'method-acting' techniques used by actors to help them act a character different from themselves can be a really helpful technique, particularly if it is hard to imagine just what being compassionate 'looks like'. Actors research their character in great detail, right down to the voice, the facial expression, the clothes they wear, how they hold their body, how they move, how they interact with others. They then act 'as if' they are that person, even if they are ordinarily very different from the person they are playing. This is what we are doing here: acting 'as if' we are compassionate, even if we do not yet feel this way. There is an expression 'fake it until you make it', or, more accurately, 'fake it until you become it'. This is the premise behind what we are doing here.

Now, once we are sat with this upright, 'dignified' posture with our feet firmly grounded on the floor, we are going to shift our attention to a particular type of breathing called 'soothing breathing rhythm':[4]

2. Soothing breathing rhythm

Soothing breathing rhythm has many functions but primarily it provides a support on which the other exercises rest. It is like a strong pair of arms which both hold us and help us through difficult times. It is a powerful practice in its own right, particularly when we are feeling 'stirred up' and need to calm down or think more clearly, or when we need to get through something that is difficult. And, of course, our breath is always with us so if we can learn how to recruit it to help us, we have a powerful way of helping ourselves that is with us all the time.

Exercise: Soothing breathing rhythm

Once we have sat ourselves in a strong, grounded, dignified position (see last exercise), with our feet planted firmly on the floor a hip-width apart, hands resting on our knees, upturned if we wish, and head upright and facing forward, we gently close our eyes. Remembering our attention as a torchlight, we just shine the light onto our breath. Just notice the sensations on breathing in, the slight pause in our breath, and then the sensations of breathing out. Notice with an interested awareness and warmth, just as if you are watching a sleeping baby, or a little sleeping animal. As your mind wanders, as it naturally will many times, just gently bring it back to noticing your breath. This is mindfulness to the breath as we practised in Chapter 13. Try following three in- and out-breaths.

Now, rather than just watching our breath mindfully, we are going to deliberately change the rhythm of our breathing to a particularly soothing rhythm. We are going to turn our attention to creating a rhythm between the in- and the out-breath.

When we are in our threat system our breathing can become quick and shallow. The focus is on the in-breath, which helps prepare our body for action. Think about what happens when we have just got through some difficulty; we often give a 'sigh of relief'. This long, slow out-breath is the opposite system to the fight or flight system; it is the parasympathetic 'rest and digest system' connected to the soothing system. A long, slow out-breath therefore calms, settles and grounds us and can help us to remain this way through difficult situations.

Imagine a child's drawing of a wave of water with the 'up' and the 'down' the same height. Now imagine an animation of a ball rolling up and down, following the line drawing of the wave. We are going to follow this with our breath, so we are matching our in-breath to our out-breath. We are trying to reach a rhythm of a count of between four and five as we breathe in and then the same as we breathe out. It can be easier to start with breathing in and out to a count of two. Then, over time, increase this to a count of three, then four, then five if this is comfortable for you.

Stephen Elliott has investigated the physiology of breathing and has identified what he has termed 'coherent breathing'. He explains this further on his website, coherence.com. Coherent breathing is where the body is working at its most efficient; when we breathe at five breaths per minute with both the in- and the out-breath equal in length. When you are able to find this rhythm you might notice a deep feeling of calm and tranquillity.

An important book that explains the science behind finding the optimum soothing, breathing rhythm is *The Healing Power of the Breath: Simple Techniques to Reduce Stress and Anxiety, Enhance Concentration, and Balance Your Emotions* by Richard P. Brown and Patricia Gerbarg.[5] It also contains a CD which takes you through the process of learning coherent breathing.

If you find the counting tricky then just focus on lengthening the out-breath for now. A helpful way of thinking about this is to imagine you have a full glass of milkshake. Your task is to make bubbles in it by blowing through a straw. If you blow too fast then the milkshake leaps out of the glass. If you blow too gently then no bubbles appear. The aim, therefore, is to find a gentle, long out-breath.

> *Lengthening our out-breath calms us.*

As your out-breath lengthens you might notice that your body starts to feel a little heavier and more grounded and settled. After a short while you may also notice that your body has begun to find its own soothing rhythm.

Although breathing in this way may sound easy, many people find it tricky at first. We can bring a great deal of effort and self-criticism to it, in terms of trying to get it 'right', which moves us into the opposite state to the calming, grounded one we are aiming for. Our breathing then changes to being quick again, which can make us feel dizzy or light-headed. The breathing we are aiming for is very gentle and slow, rather than deep in-breaths and big out-breaths. The out-breath is as gentle as this: imagine there is a candle in front of you and your aim is to create the gentlest flicker for as long as possible with each out-breath.

It can help to place your hands on your stomach with your fingertips touching. Then shift your attention for a while from your breath to your hands moving apart and then closer together with each breath, just feeling the gentle rhythm of your breath in your body. If this still feels difficult, shift your attention to the soles of your feet in contact with the floor, and your body in contact with the chair. Concentrate on the feeling of the solidity of the floor and the chair supporting you. Keep returning to your breath when you can, because being able to master the ability to create this inner sense of feeling settled, still and calm by using your breath is a very powerful technique to have with you at all times.

3. Mindfulness: attention without judgement

This is the state of awareness that we have practised previously in the book.

Exercise: Mindfulness to the breath

Sitting in our dignified, upright position with our feet flat and grounded on the floor, eyes shut or half focused on a point a few feet in front of us, move into the observing part of your mind, as if you are taking a step back from the activity of your mind and are watching rather than being caught up in it. Using the metaphor of the mind being like the sky, we are trying to move into the 'blue sky' part from where we can observe our thoughts and sensations as if they are clouds that pass by, rather than being carried away with the clouds. We are aiming just to observe our breath moving in and out of our body with a kind, gentle, non-judgemental mind. As an anchor for our attention we might focus on the tip of our nose, or our hands on our stomach just gently rising and falling. As our mind gets caught up in thoughts, which it inevitably will, we gently shepherd our mind back to our breath.

---

4. Kind, warm facial expression

Here, we are intentionally switching on what is sometimes referred to as the 'social engagement system' (see above). This is our highly evolved system for detecting and rapidly responding to safety or threat in the face and voice of others. When we detect genuine regard or kindness in others this has a rapid physiological effect on our body by calming our heart rate. And as we saw with the 'meal/brain exercise' in Chapter 6 (Figure 6.2), our mind doesn't distinguish whether something is outside of us (for example, a real meal) or inside of us (a meal we imagine), so when we direct a kind voice and facial expression towards ourselves this has the same effect as if somebody else has regarded us in this way.

Experiment: Neutral face, kind face

Sitting in our grounded, stable position with feet a hip-width apart, shoulders dropped and back, take three long slow breaths. Then have a go at this experiment. First, bring a neutral expression to your face. Notice what this feels like in your body. Then bring a gentle, warm friendly expression, perhaps by bringing to mind a memory of a time, or perhaps a film or television programme, that made you feel this warm friendliness. Notice how this feels in your body. Then return to a neutral facial expression and notice how this feels in your body.

We are hard-wired to feel safe and calm when we detect a genuine smile, particularly one that crinkles the corners of the eyes, even when we smile at ourselves. This may feel odd but try to practise with this gentle smile. Just bringing a smile to our face enables us to better manage stressful situations, even if we don't actually feel happy.[6] Again, then, we are practising 'fake it until you make it' or, more to the point, 'fake it until you become it'.

In experiments, often we perceive neutral faces as critical or hostile. We will therefore respond to our own neutral face as if we are being critical towards ourselves. Kind, warm, smiling faces, however, have a rapid and dramatic positive effect within us, regardless of whether it is someone else, or ourselves, smiling at us.

We may find this exercise difficult if we have had experiences of trusting someone whom we thought was genuinely kind and they then betrayed our trust. Our minds can then register smiles as threatening, whether they are the smiles of others or own smile towards ourselves. The first step in overcoming this is being aware of the association between a smile and feeling uncomfortable, and then bringing kindness and acceptance to ourselves, recognising that this is not our fault. Then, because being able to take in the kindness of ourselves and others is so important, both psychologically and physically, we can set about using our compassionate self or compassionate image (see Chapter 15) to desensitise us to the fear of smiles. We do this by intentionally bringing our attention to kind smiles (our own or others) and bringing our compassion to any fear that arises. Over time this then creates new associations of warmth and kindness rather than fear or anger when we experience a smile.

5. Kind, warm voice

The social engagement system (part of the parasympathetic nervous system) connects not just the facial muscles, but also the middle ear to the heart. When we detect the higher pitches of a positive human voice this slows down our heart rate and we feel calmer. Again, as for the face, our minds detect both external voices, and the voice in our own mind. We can experiment with this as we did above.

Experiment: Neutral voice, kind voice

With an alert dignified posture, feet flat on the floor, breathing gently and slowly, and a mindful awareness, we are going to say 'hello . . .' followed by our name, in a neutral voice, and notice how this feels in our body. Then we are going to say 'hello . . .' and our name with a tone of real warmth and kindness, and notice how that feels in our body.

In later exercises we will be using our compassionate self to give us words of understanding and encouragement. The tone of voice that we use towards ourselves can make the difference from hearing the words as just meaningless platitudes that 'wash over us' to hearing them as genuinely heartfelt words that can create an emotional experience within us. It is this emotional experience that starts to build up memories within us of being held positively and with warmth, even if this is by our own mind. These emotional memories and experiences create a real sense of safety within us. They are the basis for the development of compassion towards ourselves and others, and for receiving it in turn. Just this tiny change of 'warming up' the tone of voice we use to ourselves is far more powerful than we might ever have imagined.

We now have the five preparatory exercises that help to bridge or step us across from our threat system into our soothing/affiliative system. We will now look at exercises that really build the particular pattern within us that forms the basis of our compassionate mind. We are aiming to build the compassionate self as our self-identity. So, rather than being motivated to relate to ourselves and others from a critical mind, or a competitive mind, we are aiming instead to build a mind that relates to ourselves and others with compassion; with a desire to help, support, encourage, take joy in the well-being of ourselves and others. These next exercises are focused on helping to build this compassionate self-identity.

15 Strengthening the compassionate mind: Compassionate imagery

Earlier in the book we looked at the two psychologies of compassion. The first aspect of compassion is concerned with the willingness and ability to turn towards the suffering of our self and others. This is why mindfulness practices are so important, because they help us to turn towards our suffering and to be able to hold it in awareness in a manner of warm acceptance. They form the foundation for the development of compassion. However, it is no good just diving into something difficult without the skills to help ourselves get through it. We may, for example, have the motivation to jump into a stormy sea to save somebody, but this is not helpful if we do not have the skill of swimming, or of swimming with the strength necessary to save them. The second aspect of compassion is therefore about developing the skills we need to help ourselves when we are struggling, and then to be able to use these skills with others too.

When we are going into something difficult and perhaps anxiety-provoking or frightening, we have greater courage if we have somebody to help guide and support us. The difficult thing might be something outside us, for example dealing with a tricky situation, or something within, such as trying to help ourselves with difficult feelings, thoughts, images or memories. We are trying to build up a part of ourselves that has the strength, understanding, wisdom and willingness to come with us into these difficult places, and which will guide, encourage and help us through them. This is the compassionate self.

The compassionate self draws on our positive emotion systems of both drive and soothing/affiliation. So, when we have been stirred up by our threat mind, we can draw on our soothing/affiliation system to calm, ground and settle ourselves sufficiently to enable us to move into a state of more open attention, empathy, and kindness to both ourselves and others. The drive system helps us to maintain our motivation and determination to keep working in a way that is most helpful. It helps us to hold in mind the relief, joy and pleasure we feel when we can alleviate suffering in ourselves and others.

> *Just as we would when learning any new skill, we build our compassionate mind step by step, moving from easier to more challenging practices.*

The qualities of our compassionate self or compassionate mind are skills that we can build, just like building up strength in our muscles through physiotherapy or exercising in the gym. As we build our capacity for compassion, we can face more difficult situations. But, just as we wouldn't try to run a marathon if we had only taken up running the week before, so it is with our compassionate mind; we need to build it little by little, step by step and start off by bringing it to aspects of our lives that are reasonably easy and not too overwhelming. And, just as with our muscles, we need to keep exercising our compassionate mind to increase its capacity to help us, so that we can draw upon it more and more through our lives. The more we do this, the more it changes from something we have to put effort into remembering to use whenever we have been taken over by our threat mind, into becoming the way we are more likely to approach life in the first place. The threat mind, of course, will never disappear because we have evolved to have this as a highly developed part of us to protect us, and we are not trying to get rid of it. Instead, we are trying to learn to sit as much as possible in our compassionate mind, to use that as our authority or guide through life, even in terms of helping us when our threat mind has popped up.

These exercises have been arranged from the least challenging to the more difficult to help with this step-by-step building of our compassionate mind. However, because our minds have been shaped in different ways by our genes and experiences, we might find that we need to practise the exercises in a different order. Try each exercise and stay with those you find easiest for a while before moving on to something you find a little harder. The hardest are likely to be those that you will gain the most benefit from in the long run so rather than discarding them, keep revisiting them. Each time you revisit them, your compassionate mind will have developed a little more from the other exercises, so you will be revisiting them with greater wisdom each time.

The three flows of compassion

We can direct compassion:

1.   To others.

2.   To ourselves.

3.   We can also be open to receiving and being helped by compassion from others.

We can put these three flows of compassion into a 'ladder' or hierarchy from easiest to hardest. So, for example, we may feel willing and able to engage with the suffering of other people but struggle to receive it, or we might find it easier to receive compassion from others, but really struggle in being compassionate to ourselves. The exercises in this chapter aim to develop our capacity for all three flows of compassion. So, again, bear in mind the order of exercises that is most helpful for you, noticing with an interested awareness which you find more difficult. Sometimes it can surprise us and perhaps challenge our view of who we thought we were. So we even need our self-compassion when engaging with our compassionate mind exercises. This is why we take it slowly, step by step, but keeping in mind the intention to continually revisit those we find the hardest, because those are the ones that are likely to have been missing in our lives and so have the potential to make the biggest difference.

Do I need a good imagination for these exercises?

Following the premise already mentioned above – that we can stimulate particular physiological responses just by imagining them – many of the exercises that follow use the power of our imagination. Many people don't have clear images or pictures, and worry that they don't have any imagination. However, if we try to imagine a bike, or last night's dinner, then usually something pops into our mind. If we try to imagine a pink bike with yellow spots then again a fleeting image or the fragment of an image might pop in. Even if we don't get a picture, we can just focus on the feelings that arise, because it is the feelings that we are really try-ing to stimulate. So, for example, one lady could not generate any visual images at all, and found this frustrating at first. But then she realised that if she thought about being next to a warm fire on a cold day, wrapped in a soft blanket, she felt a real sense of warmth and calm within herself, even though she had no pictures in her mind at all.

Creating a safe place in our mind

We will start with a practice called 'safe place', which helps us to begin to create a sense of safeness within our own mind. Just like a child who needs a safe base to allow them to explore, we need to be able to create a sense of safeness within our own mind so that we can then move out and explore different parts of our mind, but then come back to this place of safety.

The exercise comes with many names, including 'joyful place', 'wel-coming place' and 'compassionate place'. Here we will call it by its traditional name of 'safe place', but experiment with using this notion of 'safe' because for some the mention of 'safe' automatically brings with it a focus on whether or not it is actually safe and the focus then shifts from safety to threat. If this happens then note the intrusion and bring your mind back to focusing on what it *feels* like when it *is* safe.

Exercise: Safe place

- Sit with your strong, upright posture with your feet firmly on the ground, a hip-width apart, and your shoulders open and dropped. Close your eyes and begin your soothing breathing rhythm. Notice this with a mind that is warm and accepting. Bring a warm friendly expression to your face, and say 'hello' to yourself with real warmth and friendliness.

- Then imagine that you find yourself in a fantasy place where you feel completely at peace. It may have elements of real places but it is ideal for you in every way so you can give your imagination free rein. It is a place where you are free to be you, however it is you need to be at the moment. Just being in the place feels like you can really breathe out and become calm and comfortable.

- Now, using all your senses, make this place as vivid as you can (if you struggle to see anything clearly just enjoy a sense of peace and calm in your body). Focus first on what you see in this place. Notice whether you are inside or outside, what time of day or night it seems to be and what season you are in. Become aware of how this affects the colours and sense of light and shade.

- Turn your attention to the sounds; perhaps birdsong, the rustle of a breeze in the leaves, the crackle of wood in the fire if you are inside next to the fire for example. Listen for the louder or closer sounds. Then turn your attention to any fainter sounds, such as the babbling of water flowing over stones in a stream or, if you wish to have an animal present, perhaps the animal's gentle breathing as it sleeps next to you. Whatever you see and hear brings a real sense of comfort, peace and calmness.

- Now, focusing on touch, move your attention to the feel of the air on your skin, whether or not you feel air movement, perhaps the gentle warmth of the sun or a log fire warming your body. Notice what you can reach out and touch that might give a feeling of softness or comfort. You might notice a real sense of the solidity of the ground beneath you.

- Notice smells, both stronger and more subtle.

- Turn your attention to any tastes in your mouth.

- Become aware of just how it feels in your body to be in this place. Let it soak into you. You might have a real sense that this place belongs just to you and that you are somehow deeply connected to it. You may have a feeling that this place welcomes you; that it takes real joy in you being there. Notice how it feels to be held in this way in this place.

- Notice whether you are alone or whether you have people or animals with you. Remember it is just as you need it to be. Sometimes you may be alone, other times there may be people with you or there may just be a sense of a warm presence there with you, perhaps in the distance or close by. You might become aware of a real sense of joy being in this place.

- When you are ready, give this place a name or a phrase, or imagine taking a snapshot of it which you tuck away so that you can come back to it whenever you want to; this place is only a word, a thought, an image away (and you don't need to pack or have a passport to go there!).

'Safe place' with your baby

This place is constructed using the same process as the 'safe place' exercise above, but here imagine a fantasy place where you go with your baby. It may be the same place as above but you may find it helpful to have one place that is just for you, and a different place for you and your baby. When you are first beginning these exercises you may not want to include your baby to start with. You may therefore prefer just to read this exercise through for now and then return to it in the future.

Exercise: 'Safe place' with your baby

As before, get yourself into your strong posture, engage in your soothing breathing rhythm, get into your 'blue sky' awareness, bring your kind face and voice to mind, and then imagine a place where you and your baby feel comfortable, safe, peaceful and joyful. Use all of your senses to construct this place; what you see, hear, feel with your skin and fingers, what you can smell and taste.

Your baby might be asleep there with you or might be playing joyfully or contentedly, either with you or with something or someone else while you look on. Imagine whatever is most helpful to you.

If you struggle with being with your baby, bring this place to mind as way to help you. It is just as you need it to be. If your baby cries or becomes frustrated, this place helps you deal with that, perhaps bringing a sense of calmness and safeness to you and your baby, or enabling you to have the space and safety you need to find your way, in your own time, to helping your baby without pressure or judgement from others. There is a real sense that this place is with you, giving you just what you need to work your way through the situation with your baby. Imagine that this place takes real joy in having you both there, in helping you both. Notice what it feels like for you just being in this place of total acceptance, peace, safety and commitment to you and your baby.

For the following exercises you may wish to experiment with imagining being in your safe place when you do them. Alternatively, the safe place exercise can be a wonderful place to return to after doing these exercises.

Compassionate colour

Here we are moving from experiencing safeness and having a feeling of being welcomed and connected, to beginning to experience the qualities of compassion flowing into us. The image does not have a human face, so this exercise can be an easier way of starting off with experiencing compassion flowing in, without the associations of a human face, which can make it harder for some of us. Even though the colour is non-human we are going to imagine it has the qualities of compassion: wisdom, strength, warmth and kindness, and a real intention to help us.

Exercise: Compassionate colour

Start with five preparatory 'stepping stones' as always: your alert dignified posture, soothing breathing rhythm, mindful awareness (the expression 'body like a mountain, breath like the wind, mind like the sky' can make this easier to remember), kind face and kind voice. Now imagine a colour that you associate with real kindness and warmth. Imagine it surrounds you as a mist or light. Notice how it feels to be surrounded, held and supported by it in this way.

Now imagine that the colour, light or mist flows into you through the top of your head or through your heart, and slowly spreads all through your body right to the tips of your fingers and toes. As it spreads through you, it fills you up with its qualities of wisdom, strength, kindness and warmth. Notice its intention to help and support you. If you find any blocks or resistances to this arise, just notice them with a kind smile and bring your attention back to the sense of this kind, warm colour filling your body. Remind yourself that the intention of the exercise is simply to stimulate particular parts of the mind concerned with the qualities of compassion.

When you are ready to finish, bring your attention to your breathing, your awareness of your feet on the floor and your hands in your lap, then gently open your eyes. See if you can still hold on to this sense of your compassionate colour being with you, supporting you.

Exercise: Compassionate colour flowing out

The compassionate colour exercise can be a helpful way to begin to imagine compassion flowing out of us to others. Repeat the compassionate colour exercise as above but once you feel filled with the colour, imagining sending this out of yourself to other people. Imagine it as an endless supply of compassionate colour that flows in through the top of your head, or through your heart, fills you up and then flows out of your skin, hands or heart towards other people. Imagine the colour, light or mist surrounding them and then filling them up with kindness, warmth, strength and wisdom and an intention to help and support them. Start with people you find this easy with, or with an animal or pet; you might imagine doing this from a distance at first and then being able to become a closer presence. Then you can try with neutral people and eventually those that you struggle with. You can try this with your baby too. If blocks and fears arise then refocus on the intention to send this colour out to them.

Compassionate self

We have looked previously in the book at how the person we are now is just one version of ourselves. If we had been kidnapped at birth and brought up in a vastly different family and environment, we would now think, feel and behave in a different way. We also move in and out of different 'parts' of ourselves throughout the day. As we do, each 'part' has a particular impact on many systems within us. So, when we are in our angry part, for example, we think, feel and behave differently to when we are in our anxious part, or our driven part, or our loving part, or our joyful part. We can see that some parts can seem to take us over without much effort, such as the angry or the anxious part, but that it can feel an effort bringing other parts to the fore. We can, however, decide which part we wish to cultivate a little more (as in the 'Two Wolves' story earlier in the book; which wolf do we want to feed?) because the part we stimulate is the part we wire up. This can depend on the values we hold dear to us. With the compassionate mind approach we are aiming to cultivate the part of us that can be strong, wise, supportive, kind and warm in the face of difficulties. Even if we do not feel we are this person, we can decide that we wish to become a little more like this and then practise thinking, feeling and behaving *as if* we were becoming a more compassionate person. So we can consider *what it would be like if we were to have these qualities of compassion.* The key message here is that we can purposefully grow the part of us that we want to become.

Exercise: Imagining becoming your compassionate self

- Moving across the five 'stepping stones', start with your posture – hold yourself or 'embody' the position of a compassionate person, sitting in a strong, grounded, confident, dignified position with your feet firmly planted on the floor, a hip-width apart, your head upright, your shoulders relaxed.

- Close your eyes and begin your soothing breathing rhythm. Notice the rhythm of your breath moving into your body, a pause and then the long, slow out-breath. Gently allow the in- and out-breaths to lengthen. As they do so, you might notice a sense of slowing, stability and increased stillness in your body.

- Watch your breath from your position of your 'blue sky' aware-ness where you are observing your breath with non-judgemental, gentle awareness.

- Focus on your facial expression. Allow your jaw to relax, and let your face break into a gentle, friendly smile. Compare it to a neu-tral face.

- Hear your warm kind voice saying 'hello' to you. Compare it to your neutral voice.

- Now begin to imagine that you have the quality of wisdom. This includes understanding that:

    i.   We have just appeared in the flow of life with a brain and a set of genes which we didn't choose, and a sense of self shaped particularly by our early experiences which we didn't choose either. These can contribute to our suffering and our struggles in a way that we didn't wish for, didn't choose and is not our fault. It is a wisdom that does not blame, but just understands this situation with a deep kindness and wish to help.

    ii. Become aware of the wisdom that has arisen in you from insights you may have gained from each stage of this book (you may wish to flick through the book to remind yourself of the different aspects); for example, that we have a brain and body evolved to change when we become pregnant and have a baby; that these changes can interact with our early experiences in unforeseen ways, and this is not our fault; that modern ways of birthing combined with evolved changes in the structure of our body sometimes helps, but sometimes hinders pregnancy and labour; that we have evolved to require support in order to best bring up a baby but in many places society has changed in such a way that support is no longer easily available; and that these things are not our fault yet can have a considerable impact on our experiences of mothering a new infant.

    iii. Second, become aware that although we have a mind that tries to 'fix' us into a solid sense of who we are, in fact our thoughts, feelings, behaviour, etc. constantly change. We constantly move in and out of different parts of ourselves, which each create very different states within us. This is the nature of impermanence; that both the good and the bad, the unpleasant and the pleasant, will come and go, wax and wane.

    iv. Third, recognise that we can often be overtaken by parts of ourselves that we do not wish to be, but we can also choose to feed and grow a particular part of ourselves.

v.   Fourth, understand that we will make mistakes, but rather than condemning or shaming ourselves for them, which makes us try to hide these parts, we can turn towards them with kindness and an interested awareness, with a genuine wish to learn from them, repair where necessary, and turn once again to growing ourselves.

- We now imagine ourselves with the qualities of strength, authority and inner confidence. This allows this part to take charge and to hold or contain other parts which try to surface. It gives us the ability to turn to face towards that which troubles us.

- We now focus on our compassionate motivation; the desire or wish truly to help ourselves understand our suffering and alleviate it as much as we can. We can imagine it as the direction we turn to face and the place we wish to move to. So, although we can see with our wisdom that we did not choose to struggle in this way, our motivation or commitment is to help ourselves learn, grow and change so that we become better able to manage the difficulties that life throws at us.

- This is all felt with an emotional tone of kindness and warmth. We can imagine it as a limitless warm light or mist that surrounds us and then fills us up and expands us; as filling us up until it starts to gently flow out of us; as endless and boundless.

- Now imagine moving and walking as this compassionate person. See in your mind's eye how you would relate to people who you encounter as you walk. Notice your facial expression and your voice tone if you speak to them, your wisdom and understanding of the difficulties they will inevitably have, the heartfelt wish that they be well, that they be free from suffering, that they be happy and at peace.

Focusing the compassionate self

Now we are going to practise focusing the compassionate self, either on others, or on all or part of ourselves. As with learning any skill, we work with the easiest rather than most challenging first. This might be a different order from that listed below so if you find one practice too difficult initially, find an easier one and then come back to the more difficult one later.

Exercise: Bringing compassion to someone you care about

Bring to mind an image of somebody or something you really care about (it could be an adult, child, baby, or perhaps a pet or an animal for example). Now focus your compassionate feelings on them. In your mind's eye say to them, 'May you be well (say their name). May you be happy (say their name). May you be free from suffering (say their name). May you be at peace (say their name)' Don't worry about remembering the words; you might choose different phrases. It is the feeling and heartfelt wish for them that is important.

Exercise: Bringing compassion to ourselves

Imagine looking down from above, watching yourself as you do this exercise. Bring your compassionate mind to your ordinary self going about your day, with your troubles and worries. But rather than getting caught up in the feelings and worries that you witness, focus on your intention to watch and be with your struggling self from a position of warmth, kindness, wise understanding, strength and a heartfelt wish to help yourself as best you can. Notice what your heartfelt wishes might be (expressed on your out-breath); perhaps that you be well, that you be free from suffering, that you be happy and at peace.

It is normal to experience some kind of resistance to bringing compassion to ourselves; perhaps feeling we do not deserve it or that we might become weak, or overwhelmed with sadness. Turn your compassionate mind to these parts if they do arise (see below), ensuring that you are still in your strong, dignified grounded posture, with your soothing breathing rhythm, 'mind like the sky' and kind, warm, face and voice as you do this. Then let those parts go and refocus on the whole of yourself that you see going about your day below you.

When you have finished, bring your attention back to your body and its points of groundedness; focusing on your breath and then where you feel contact with the floor and the seat beneath you. Then gently open your eyes and stretch a little.

Compassionate image

Here we are providing our mind with the experience of being cared for, of having compassion flowing into us, of being supported and encouraged just by using our own imagination. Just like when we imagined a nice meal or holiday, we can imagine being in the presence of a compassionate 'other' and our minds will respond to this even though they are not really there. We can use our imagination to create the sense of being with a person, or in fact anything that has a mind which is encouraging, supportive, strong and accepting. Examples used by people include a wise old tree, a compassionate light, a wise old animal and an angel with huge wings. The image you create is ideal for you in every way, and has the qualities of wisdom, strength (in terms of confidence and authority), a motivation and commitment to your well-being, and real warmth and kindness. It might be male or female, neither, or a mixture of both. Imagine how old it is, the experiences it may have had, how it has acquired such wisdom. Notice the expression on its face if you can imagine a face. Imagine how its voice might sound if it spoke.

Exercise: Compassionate image

Now sit in your strong, grounded posture and engage in your soothing breathing rhythm so that you are embodying the being you are trying to imagine. Bring to mind your warm voice and facial expression. Then bring to mind an awareness or sense of being in the presence of your compassionate image. It can help to imagine it appearing in your safe place. Notice how you need it to relate to you. It might just be a comforting presence some distance from you, or it may stand by you or sit with you perhaps. Notice what it feels like in your body to be with this presence, feeling completely safe and cared for, knowing that it is here with a deep commitment to help you. If you struggle to feel safe then imagine what it would feel like if you did feel safe.

If you struggle to accept its compassion, perhaps not trusting it or feeling undeserving of it, then notice how your compassionate image understands and helps you with these struggles. You may feel sadness. Again your compassionate image understands this and just stays with you with warmth and understanding as your sadness passes, no matter how long this takes.

Imagine your compassionate image saying the following phrases to you in a warm, kind, heartfelt manner:

May you be free from suffering (say your name in your mind).

May you be find peace (say your name in your mind).

May you be happy (say your name in your mind).

Although you are receiving compassion from this image, it has been generated from within you, so you are in effect both giving and receiving compassion. It is a way of developing an inner guide that you can consult when you are struggling.

Summary

When we wish to move from threat mind to a compassionate mind we can help this process in a number of ways. We have looked at five in detail; changing our posture, our breathing, the focus of our attention, our facial expression and our voice tone. These steps help to prepare our mind and body to be in the most receptive state for our compassionate mind exercises. It is rather like 'warming up' our muscles and mentally preparing our mind before we exercise in the gym or go running.

The compassionate mind exercises focused on particular qualities which, when combined, can help us to think, feel and behave in a compassionate way; these include wisdom, strength of character, and motivation to help ourselves and others to be free from suffering and to flourish. We can use our imaginations to imagine ourselves as compassionate, or to imagine a compassionate presence helping and supporting us.

16 Strengthening the compassionate mind: Using compassionate attention and behaviour

We investigated the nature of attention earlier in the book where we imagined our attention as like a torchlight or spotlight which we shone on our left toe, then our right toe, then our lips, then finger and thumb. We noticed that we could move our attention at will, that whatever we shone our attention on filled up the field of our awareness and everything else seemed to disappear into the shadows. And whatever filled up our attention had the potential to stimulate us physiologically in particular ways, so we might feel differently when we focus on birdsong as opposed to traffic noise, for example, or on happy memories as opposed to unpleasant memories.

As we go through the exercises in the book we will notice that the threat system is designed to pull our attention to it, and it is an effort to move our attention away from it. It is almost like a magnet. This is why cultivating the compassionate mind takes training so that we learn to take hold of the spotlight of our attention again and again, and shine it on that which stimulates our soothing and affiliative system. This might be a memory of when we felt real care towards somebody or when we experienced warmth and care from someone else. Or it might be just attending to kind faces in the supermarket or in magazines, or going outside and listening to the birds, or experiencing the calmness of watching the clouds.

If we think about the 'three circles', the same principle applies; when worry, fear or anger take hold of us they fill up our attention. Everything else seems to disappear. If we can take hold of the spotlight of our attention and instead shine it on our soothing system, then our soothing system will fill up our attention and our threat system will fade into the background. And, of course, whatever we are focusing on will stimulate our mind and body in particular ways. As we have seen, if we focus our attention on a memory of a holiday that went wrong, or somebody who has upset us, our thoughts, feelings, hormones in our body, emotions, images and motivation get stirred up in a particular way. But if we focus our attention on a memory of a holiday that we enjoyed, or a person who was really kind to us, then our thoughts, feelings, hormones, emotions, images, motivation and so on get stirred up in a very different way. This is why our attention is so important; just the process of noticing and shifting attention can have a profound effect on us at so many levels, and, what is more, of course, it wires up our brain in particular ways.

We can test out this impact of simply shifting our attention when, for example, we are pushing the buggy in the rain. We could focus on feeling wet and cold, on thoughts of what a pain it is because we can't carry an umbrella and we have to struggle with the rain cover on the buggy, or we could shift our attention to the way the rain hangs on the leaves and branches of the trees, how it cleans everything and brings a smell and a sense of freshness, or the way it makes us feel alive and connected to the world around us.

Clearly, if the threat system has been triggered, that will take priority, so if a cyclist came up behind us ringing his bell we would forget the wonder of the raindrops in an instant. However, most of the time when we are in our threat system we are taken up with worrying about the past or the future rather than focusing on that particular moment. If we can focus on the present moment, the vast majority of the time all is okay. In fact many moments are more than just free from threat; they are positively pleasurable, such as sitting comfortably in a chair, or having a warm shower, or drinking a cup of tea. But because we are so filled up with worrying about the past and the future we miss them.

If we can learn, first, to pause for a moment and become aware of our mind, and then decide what we actually wish to put in this present moment, then we have an exceedingly powerful way of dramatically changing our mood and our brain. We start to see that we can choose what to fill up the present with. We might choose to worry, for example, or if we are trying to grow our compassionate mind, we will be trying to shine the spotlight of our attention on anything that will grow it. This can be anything at all. It might be memories of times we helped somebody, or kind faces we see in the street, images of our compassionate person, or senses – smells, pictures, sounds, tastes etc. – that stimulate feelings of warmth and safeness within us.

Here are a series of exercises for focusing our attention on different aspects that can stimulate our compassionate mind. These are just a fraction of the many possibilities that we might encounter each day. But once we start to practise shifting our attention then we naturally start to look at our world a little differently. We suddenly start to 'see' the possibilities for stimulating our compassionate mind whereas before there seemed to be perhaps none at all.

Exercises: Compassionate attention . . .

(With all of these exercises begin with the five stepping stones of body posture, breathing, mindfulness, warm face and warm voice).

. . . to memories

- Times with my baby when it felt comfortable, less difficult, better than usual, a tiny sense of feeling okay, gentle, warm or peaceful. These could be fleeting. But really focus in on them in detail, as if you are looking at them under a microscope; how did you feel in your body? How do you imagine your baby felt? What was the expression on your baby's face? Bring lots of detail to this. Where were you both? What time of day or night was it? What was the temperature like? And so on. This makes it a strong memory rather than a fleeting memory. We tend to ignore these memories and instead ruminate over and over again on upsetting memories. As 'what fires together wires together', with compassionate attention we are strengthening the memories that build our soothing system.

- Times when I coped better than I thought I would.

- Times I felt scared but did it anyway.

- Moments of peace.

- Times when I helped somebody.

- Moments when I felt real kindness towards somebody.

- Times when somebody smiled with real kindness at me.

- Times when I helped somebody to feel safe.

- Times when I stayed with somebody who was struggling.

... to gratitude

A gratitude diary has been found to be a powerful way to increase mood through shifting attention so that 'we become what we think about'.[1] It is more effective if we begin with a clear intention to spend more time focusing on what we are thankful for. The idea is to write down three things each day that we are grateful for without repeating any that we've written before. Just write a sentence: for example, 'being able to appreciate the colour of the flowers', 'the man who let me go in front of him in the queue because my baby was crying', 'having a warm duvet'. Writing down gratitude to people is particularly powerful.

Try doing this every day for at least a week so that you notice the interesting process that often occurs; at first it might feel like another chore to do this, then you start feeling delight when you notice something during the day that you can write down in your diary that evening, then you start to deliberately look out for anything that you feel grateful for. Your attention has now shifted from focusing on threat, to focusing on soothing and pleasure. And of course 'what fires together wires together', so you are now literally strengthening your soothing system.

If you wish to carry it on subsequently, once a week is enough. Some people have put the diary up on the wall and other members of the family add to it too. Children particularly seem to really enjoy this. And there is nothing quite like finding that something you did or said has been put up there by another member of your family. Some families have said that it has had such a big impact on their children that they have taken down reward charts and replaced them with a family gratitude diary instead. The aim is to keep it genuine and heartfelt rather than slip into subtle attacks ('I am grateful to you for you putting your shoes away for a change!') or to try to shape behaviour. There should be no strings attached to the comments, just a reporting of your genuine gratitude.

... to parts of our baby

The nature of threat is that it focuses our attention on the threat and on ourselves as under threat. It is necessarily a narrow focus. As we switch from threat-focused to compassion-focused attention, we might notice that our attention broadens. If we bring this compassionate attention to our baby we can now take in the whole of our baby rather than focusing more narrowly on the parts that bother us. Now we might notice, with a gentle curiosity, that different aspects of our baby evoke slightly different emotions and bodily responses within us. We don't need to judge these responses, just notice them. We can scan our baby, from their hair, to their ears, their eyes, nose, mouth, neck, to their hands, arms, fingers, toes, knees and so on. We can look at how their skin differs in texture and colour. We can also bring our attention to their different 'selves' or states of being; asleep, drowsy, grumpy, scared, excited, alert, tired, 'talkative', contented and so on, noticing with an interested awareness the feelings and body impulses these evoke in us.

... to times when it is easier

Our threat mind will naturally focus us in on the particularly difficult times but will barely attend to times when things are a little better. This is a normal characteristic of human minds but is not very conducive to well-being. We are learning to redress this balance by building the ability to attend to and really take in times when life is a little more positive, or at least a little less negative. Our compassionate mind is able to take in the whole picture without judgement and with kindness and acceptance. It can allow us to see the times when the anger, anxiety or indifference perhaps feel a little softer or when there is a slight feeling of warmth or tenderness. These times might occur when we watch our baby sleeping and see the tiny breaths or the fluttery smiles and frowns that appear and disappear on their face. It might be when we are feeding our baby or just holding them and talking to them. It might be when we are watching them watching the world while pushing them in their buggy.

As the threat mind is designed to focus us on and therefore highlight the difficult, ignoring anything else, our baby, and our relationship with them, can become a single, narrow experience; 'stressful, a nightmare, difficult'. In contrast, our compassionate mind allows us to see how our relationship and our time together subtly shift and change constantly. We see that it isn't just one experience but many experiences, and moreover, these come and they go, they come again and they go again.

This means that we need to hold less tightly or defend less vigorously particular experiences, becoming aware that we can bear the difficult and can have faith that the good will come along again.

This takes deliberate practice initially because our minds are so good at just sliding past or ignoring completely any moments that are good or not as bad. It can help to put up reminders on sticky notes or on your phone to 'take in this good moment' and then allow your attention to focus on what is good in that moment, or what is not as bad as it usually is. Your mind might naturally drift to the negative, as it is wont to do, but just gently bring it back to what is good in that moment. Try to let it soak into you for a few seconds so that you turn a fleeting moment into something you are fully aware of. A wonderful book which focuses on this concept and practice is Rick Hanson's *Hardwiring Happiness: The Practical Science of Reshaping your Brain – and your Life*.[2]

... to using all of our senses with our baby

Our baby will be guided by their different senses and the physical feelings in their body. As adults we can become so caught up in our thoughts that we tune out of our senses and our body. In this section we are turning our attention to tuning back into our senses. We can focus on one sense at a time, just noticing what arises with a compassionate mind. We might start with our vision and look at different aspects of our baby without judging but with wonderment and acceptance, just as if we are looking through a child's eyes at a flower. Try not to label or think too much but just allow what you see to flow into you. You might try photographing your baby or even drawing or doing a painting of them. Look at them from near and from far away.

You might then use your sense of touch; perhaps stroking their hand, just becoming aware of the feel of their fingers holding tightly to your finger, feeling their skin, then perhaps gently stroking their hair. You might try massaging their hand with some baby massage oil, paying attention to the feel of their skin against yours. You might hold them while they are asleep and become aware of the feel of their warmth and weight against your body.

Smell is an important but often neglected aspect of bonding. It is known to be critical for bonding in animals and we are realising more and more just how important it is to humans. But what if we find the smell of our own baby aversive, as can sometimes happen? First, we would notice this, and then bring our compassion to this experience, both for ourselves and our baby. Then we can set about with our compassionate mind to use smell as a way of moving closer to our baby. Perhaps at first we need to find a baby shampoo and bubble bath that smells wonderful to us. We might just take in the smell as we bath our baby. We might wrap them in a towel washed in washing powder that we have deliberately chosen for its smell, and just spend time holding them and smelling them while they are snug and content. As we begin to associate their closeness with a pleasurable smell, we might find over time that we come to enjoy more and more their natural smell too.

With regard to sounds, again we can start where this is easiest, perhaps just sitting near our baby or holding them when they are asleep and listening to their tiny quick breaths, their irregular deep in-breaths, the pause (that can seem alarmingly long – notice the threat mind creeping in here and just bring compassion to it) and the out-breaths. Listen to their 'talking' if they have moments of quiet wakefulness, and their 'belly laughs' as they get older.

As a real challenge, see if you can bring your compassionate mind to your baby's cries. You may become aware their cries trigger some anxiety or annoyance within you. Bringing your compassionate mind to yourself first can help to calm you before you respond to your baby: that the cry of a baby is designed to evoke a strong reaction within you; that it may trigger body memories from your own childhood within you, which makes it doubly hard to bear but isn't your fault; that distress is generally hard to bear so it is no wonder you are finding it difficult. Giving yourself support and understanding, using a few moments of soothing breathing rhythm and also putting your hand on your heart can calm you enough to enable you to bring your compassionate mind to your baby.

It can help to contrast how you might respond to your baby from your anxious mind, compared to your angry mind, and then compared to your compassionate mind.

You might also try different music for you and your baby and just notice with an interested awareness how you both respond. Try singing, nursery rhymes and reading with your baby. Although we may feel very self-conscious, or have some strong negative emotional memories from previous experiences of this, our baby has actually been conditioned to our voice from before it was even born, and to our baby it is the most wonderful voice in the world. Even if you have shouted at, or been cross with your baby, the positive conditioning to your voice is very powerful. It is never too late to continue building on these early positive associations even if you fear you have 'messed this up' through your earlier struggles with your baby.

Taste is a trickier sense to use without licking the baby! However, we might focus on the taste from kissing our baby's head or have a go at sharing in some of the tastes they experience; perhaps the toy they chew, your finger or the milk you give them. Try really tasting it all, imagining you have the curious, non-judgemental mind of your baby. When your baby reaches the 'everything in the mouth' stage, they are gaining huge amounts of information about their world by using their mouth's sensitivity to touch and taste. We often neglect taste, eating really delicious food without even noticing it. Instead we could spend some time experiencing food and drink just as a baby might. (See 'Eating like a baby', page 234).

... to what connects us

Our threat system focuses us on disconnection from others because this is our great fear, so it will particularly illuminate anything that is concerned with disconnection from our baby. This sense of disconnection or separation from our baby could be triggered by many things, such as having a boy when you are only used to girls, having a girl when you never felt particularly comfortable with girls, having a baby with a temperament that you find hard to relate to, feeling your baby was the cause of difficulties during pregnancy, birth or postnatally and so on.

Our compassionate self brings validation of how hard it is to have these feelings and experiences, and wisdom as to why they are troubling us. It also brings non-judgement and acceptance: that we didn't choose to feel this way but nevertheless this is how we are feeling. The compassionate self can then help us to shift our focus from what disconnects us, to what connects or links us with our baby. So we can focus on, for example, the experiences we have shared already with our baby, such as a difficult labour and birth, being separated from each other at birth, enjoying being out in the countryside, enjoying listening or dancing to music, being loved by the same person (e.g. 'my mother, your grandmother'), having a shy temperament, enjoying stroking the cat, and so on.

This is not about over-identifying with or trying to force similarities that are not really there, but just opening to an awareness of anything that joins us to our baby in any kind of way.

This has been a powerful exercise for some women when they suddenly came to realise that rather than being separate from their baby, in some cases almost to the extent of feeling like 'enemies' on different sides, they had actually been through a very tough journey together. One woman suddenly shifted from feeling as though her baby had nearly killed her during the birth, to suddenly seeing that the two of them had been through something utterly terrifying. She felt a shift, as if her baby was now alongside her, and they were both looking out at the world together. She found herself moved emotionally, for both her and her baby.

Exercise: Moving together – synchrony

We can also create new moments of connection through 'synchrony' where we bring our movements, actions or intentions together with our baby. There is evidence that becoming synchronous with others regulates and calms the heartbeats of all involved and also promotes a feeling of connectedness and affiliation. This includes things like tapping, drumming or singing together.[3, 4] We can use this knowledge to really connect with our baby, for example by making the same noises as them, tapping as they tap, dancing in time with their jigs, trying to stop and start at the same time as them. As the baby gets older they will really enjoy noticing the impact they have on you, such as watching you change your rhythm as they do, or listening to you copying their ever more silly sounds, or getting quieter as they get quieter and louder as they get louder.

Exercise: Through the eyes of my baby

We may really struggle to just be 'in the moment'. However, our babies are masters at this. They can become mesmerised by trying to get 'hold' of a stream of water running from a tap, or investigating your eyes, or a tiny hole in a blanket. We can learn a lot by observing them when they are in a state of 'alert wakefulness'.

You might notice that if they are able to, our baby uses all senses to explore their world. This is also the state that best facilitates learning, playfulness and joy. We often miss these moments in our baby because our lives can be so busy that we seize these as rare opportunities to get jobs done. If we can spend a little time sharing these moments with our baby, no matter how briefly, then the rewards for us as well as for our baby can be significant; it can be incredibly calming and can bring a sense of stillness and also clarity, especially when we are feeling stirred up.

Compassionate attention to what we <u>have</u> done all day

Earlier we looked at how women can often struggle to find the words to describe just what it is they do all day with the baby. Because we can't find the words it can feel as if we haven't achieved very much at all. And of course our threat system will focus our attention on just what we *haven't* achieved. Part of the problem is the view that is taken of the job of creating a sense of 'home'. For many it has become devalued and seen as unimportant and of low status. However, as we have seen throughout this book, a sense of 'home' and safeness is absolutely fundamental to us all. It is of profound importance to the developing brain of our children and is critical in providing the bedrock that enables our children to move out into the world with confidence.

Exercise: Compassionate attention to what we <u>have</u> done all day

We can shift our attention to refocus on just what we are doing during the day rather than what we fail to achieve, particularly those aspects that contribute to this sense of home, a place where our baby (and other people who live in the home) feels loved, accepted and safe. With compassionate attention we are refocusing on those aspects that we do during the day that give this sense of a place of care and safeness. These include those multitude of tiny acts carried out by a mother that are taken for granted but form the foundation of safeness, that most important springboard from which our children can push off into the world, like a floor that holds us up without us being aware or appreciative of its importance.

These tiny acts include every bottle or cup that we make sure is clean, every item of clothing that is washed, dried, folded and put away, every worry about our child, every feed given, every moving of our baby out of harm's way, every cuddle, every noticing and commenting to our baby on what appears to be in their mind . . .

There will rarely be gratitude, because gratitude comes through conscious noticing; for example, experiencing first-hand the contrast of life in a household that is dirty or treacherous, where clothes are rarely washed and meals are rare. Instead, the not noticing, the taking for granted, is testament to the sense of inherent safeness, where the safeness feels so certain that it does not enter the mind that it could be anything other. (Although some appreciation is always welcome!)

We are therefore turning our attention to the possibility of taking pleasure in each act of safeness we provide, of carrying it out with warmth and kindness, and of taking joy in the inner knowing that we have just created another tiny nugget of safeness in the household.

Compassionate behaviour

We have the potential to act in all sorts of different ways according to the motivation of the 'self' we are in. So, for example, we can be competitive, vengeful, submissive, loving, critical or encouraging, depending on which self we are using to guide us in our interactions with others and with ourselves. In each moment, which self do we want to give authority to? When we allow our compassionate self to be our guide, it helps us to act according to our most deeply held values and to behave in ways that fit with the person we want to become.

Compassionate behaviour is about acting in ways that encourage us and others to face our struggles, to work with them rather than turning away from them, and to help us and others become the best versions of ourselves we can be.

So, for example, if we want to become a mother who is calm with her children then we take steps to help ourselves become more like that. This might involve taking time to understand what makes it hard to feel calm and bringing a commitment to help with that, or learning and practising mindfulness, or soothing breathing rhythm. It might be writing 'to be calm' on our hand or on notes around the house to remind ourselves about our intention to be calm, or taking time to read a book that might help, or to ask our partner for some time for ourselves or to go out with them each week.

It means acting in ways consistent with the person we want to become, even if this is difficult. So, for example, if our intention is to become a person who can go to the supermarket on our own, we might go to the supermarket, accept that we may well have a panic attack there, but stay through the panic attack and then carry on with the shopping. We use our compassionate mind to be with us during this difficult moment, so, rather than being alone, we have support, wisdom, strength and courage with us. The compassionate mind is also the part of us that will take us back to the supermarket the next day if we couldn't manage to stay the first time.

In can be helpful to think about what behaviour might help us:

1.   in a difficult moment;

2.   in the short term (the next few hours or days);

3.   in the long term (the next weeks, months or years).

When we are struggling in that moment, perhaps feeling very anxious, or angry, or depressed, we can consider what behaviour might most help us. First, we need to feel safe. Once we feel safer our levels of arousal can calm sufficiently to enable us to engage in more exploratory behaviour that might help us a great deal in the long run. What makes one person feel safe may be different from what makes another feel safe. We need to find what works best for us. For example, we may initially need to retreat, reduce stimulation, have some quiet, listen to some peaceful music, for example, but then, once we feel calmer, we may then need to seek out safe social contact.

An important part of compassionate behaviour when we feel very fearful or depressed may be to create some kind of gentle physical movement, because our body responds in a very physical way to threat. This might be something as small as changing our body posture from slumped or hunched up and tight to the embodiment of compassion that we have been using throughout the book; feet flat and grounded on the floor, head upright and supported on a straight but relaxed spine, shoulders dropped and open, hands relaxed. It might also include walking, gentle activity in the house, yoga exercises or gently dancing around the room with the baby. Below are some suggestions, which might also generate more ideas.

Examples of compassionate behaviour 'in the moment'

This might include:

- Pausing, taking time out for a moment, and engaging in soothing breathing rhythm.

- Making sure the baby is safe and then moving away for a moment to allow ourselves some space to settle, perhaps by walking around the garden or going to a different room.

- Placing your right hand on or over your heart, feeling the rise and fall of your breathing and the comfort of the warmth from your hand.

- Bringing your compassionate self to the fore – changing your posture to one that is grounded, strong and open, steadying your breathing and slowing your out-breath, noticing your breathing with mindfulness, bringing your wisdom and acceptance to how you are feeling; that this is due to the minds we have evolved, and the experiences we have had, which makes this moment so hard, and that this struggle is what connects us to other people; we are not alone in this struggle. We just relate to ourselves with kindness, strength, wisdom, warmth and kindness.

Examples of compassionate behaviour 'in the short term'

- Imagining your compassionate image being here with you and noticing how it would help you.

- Making a cup of tea mindfully – see if you can focus on each aspect: filling the kettle, putting in the teabag, watching the effect of the water on the teabag, taking out the teabag, adding the milk, stirring the tea, holding the cup, smelling the tea and tasting the tea.

- Going outside for the higher light levels that help to lift our mood (even on a rainy day the light levels are much higher outside than indoors, even with all the lights on).

- Walking round the garden with the baby.

- Walking round the park or up the street and back with the baby.

- Putting our coat and wellies on and going out in the rain with the baby snug in the buggy under the rain cover.

- Phoning somebody – friend, family, GP, health visitor, a helpline.

- Going on the internet – Netmums or Mumsnet, for example.

- Getting something in order, even if it's tiny, e.g. smooth the bed covers, fold the tea towels or brush your hair.

- Putting on some music. Try different types of music.

- Smelling something nice, e.g. washing-up liquid, washing powder or soap – close your eyes and let the smell flow into you.

- Looking from a different perspective, e.g. out of a top window you don't usually look through or (carefully!) stand on a stool – imagine looking down at your situation from the clouds.

- Distracting yourself.

- Watching a film.

- Writing a compassionate letter to yourself.

- Going to a coffee shop.

- Going to something completely different that you don't usually go to, e.g. your local museum, the library, the children's centre, a church or a temple.

- Walking among trees, even if it is raining or cold (wrap up warm!)

- Sitting near some water.

- Feeding the ducks.

- Petting an animal.

- Going for a walk or a drive around an area you don't usually go to. Look out for something new that you wouldn't have been aware of if you hadn't gone.

- Noticing the moment without judging it; not just what you are feeling inside but what you see, hear, smell, touch or taste.

- Moving about, e.g. gentle exercise, yoga, Tai Chi, dancing to the radio, dancing with the baby, walking, or gentle stretching.

Examples of compassionate behaviour 'in the long term'

- Setting up some regular time each week that is just for you, even if it can only be an hour initially; for example, for a walk around the block while someone looks after the baby.

- Planning regular times of being with people each week, e.g. mother and toddler group, meeting a friend, going to the supermarket or doing a course at a children's centre.

- Setting up a regular compassionate mind practice, e.g. decide on a place, make it a place that feels good (clear a corner for sitting, with a nice light, an inspiring picture, some words that help, a comfortable chair, warmth – whatever will help you to look forward to being there). Decide on a time each day. Make a commitment that this is important for you and your family.

- Asking for your health visitor to come each week for a while, or go to a weekly health visitor clinic.

- Writing down the part of you that you most want to grow; how might your life be different, how might it be the same, as you begin to grow that part? What might help it to grow? What steps can you take to help it to grow? What will help you to take those steps?

- Going on a course that interests you and may help you, e.g. at a local children's centre, or at an evening class or local university (sometimes there may be help with childcare), or an online course.

Summary

Whereas our minds will naturally move to things that provoke our anxiety or anger, we can consciously shift our attention to things that stimulate our compassionate mind. When we consider the concept of 'what fires together wires together' this is important, given the mind that we are trying to foster. This is not to ignore what might need to be focused upon, or a way of just 'looking on the bright side'; it is developing the ability to choose with wisdom what is the most helpful and supportive focus of our attention in each moment.

Compassionate behaviour often takes courage because it is about behaving in ways that might involve facing suffering and taking action, which may not be easy.

STAGE THREE

Bringing our compassionate mind to our struggles

Introduction

In Stage One, we looked at how our evolved brains and our experiences can have such a bearing on our experience of having a baby. We didn't choose these, yet we can end up feeling that we are somehow to blame when we struggle. The purpose of Stage One is to help us shift from a position of shame, blame and self-criticism to one of acceptance and understanding; of having a deep sense that this is 'not your fault'.

> *Often when we struggle, we can feel alone. One of the aims of developing our compassionate mind is to give ourselves a deep sense of being 'with' ourselves.*

We also looked at the impact of blaming and shaming, which can have really problematic consequences for us. We do, however, also have evolved capacities to respond to warmth, compassion, support and kindness in ways that create powerful and positive responses at a biological level within us. Importantly, this occurs whether the compassion is coming from somebody else or from ourselves. In Stage Two we looked at the particular qualities that make up a compassionate mind and how to develop these so that we develop a relationship with ourselves and others of affiliation; a sense of having somebody who travels on our journey alongside us, with an intention to help, support and encourage us, even if that 'somebody' is ourselves.

In Stage Three we are bringing our compassionate mind to the struggles identified in Stage One. The aim here is not to eradicate our struggles, because these are part of the human mind. When we try to eradicate anxiety, anger or self-criticism, for example, or even physical pain, we couple frustration and fear with the original difficulty, so inadvertently adding to our suffering rather than alleviating it. If we bring understanding, acceptance and a deep desire to help the part of us that feels anxious, or angry, then, because of our wiring, we feel safer, and therefore calmer, and we are more likely to find a way through the struggle. We are in effect linking the struggle with the feeling that comes from being related to it in a compassionate way. If we do this repeatedly, we become more and more likely to meet future struggles with a greater calmness and steadiness, and a sense of being able to move forward and find solutions, rather than feeling beaten down and defeated.

This section gives examples of bringing different compassionate mind skills to some of the struggles identified in this book. Whatever the struggle, the principle is always the same: bring our compassionate mind to the struggle, rather than our anxious, angry or self-critical mind. To see the difference this makes, contrast the possible outcome of bringing an anxious or self-critical mind, rather than a compassionate mind, to whichever struggle is troubling you at the moment.

17 Using compassionate thinking, letter writing and imagery to help with our struggles

Compassionate thinking

Our thoughts are influenced by our current emotional state, so if we feel angry we think angry thoughts; if we feel anxious we think anxious thoughts; if we feel at peace we think peaceful thoughts. As we have seen, shifting out of threat-based emotional states into an encouraging and supportive compassionate state is difficult but becomes easier with practice. Here we are practising balancing thoughts triggered by our threat system with thoughts from our compassion system.

There is evidence that reading positive words such as 'to laugh', 'to be happy', generates those feelings in us by triggering our facial muscles into a smile as we read them. In this section we can fully consider just what it is we want to feel and then write those words for ourselves.

When we are generating compassion-focused thoughts, we need to first bridge across to our compassion system using the five steps: posture; soothing breathing rhythm; mindfulness; warm, kind facial expression; and warm voice tone. Then we engage our compassionate self using our deep commitment and motivation to help ourselves with this struggle, our wisdom (understanding the influences of our evolved brain and our experiences) and our strength. When we have generated the compassion-focused thoughts it can be helpful to write them down and then read them through with our warm voice tone and allow them to really sink into us so that they become felt in the body rather than simply being something we understand at an intellectual level. Experiment with reading the words through with a neutral or critical tone of voice, and then contrast how you experience the words when saying them to yourself with a really warm, kind voice.

Exercise: Compassion-focused thought balancing – an example

NB: SBR stands for 'soothing breathing rhythm'

Trigger	Unhelpful / distressing thoughts	Helpful / kind thoughts (try to create warm tone)
Leaving my baby crying and walking away.	I really am a horrible person to be able to do this to my baby.	**Empathy**: It is very distressing to me when I hear my baby cry and it is also distressing to feel like this about myself. This is very hard. **Evolved brain**: The cries of my baby stir up a lot of feelings in me, first because I have a human brain that is wired up to be bothered by the cry of a baby, **Experiences**: but also because the cries trigger memories of me being very upset in the past. I didn't have anyone to help me with my distress then, so the feelings became overwhelming and scary. This is why I am finding the cries of my baby so hard now. This doesn't mean I am horrible, just overwhelmed. I remember now that I would cope then by going and shutting myself in my room. Perhaps this is why I am trying to cope again by walking away. **Exercises**: Compassionate skills: I get now that attacking myself doesn't make me into the person I want to be, it actually brings me down and makes me feel worse. Instead of attacking I am going to try to give myself some kindness, support and understanding. I will spend some time with my compassionate image and perhaps write a compassionate letter to myself. I could also do with hearing how others cope with their crying baby because I bet I'm not the only one who finds this hard. Perhaps I will go along to that mother and toddler group after all or go on the internet to the Netmums forum (SBR).

I don't feel anything for this baby.	There must be something wrong with me.	**Empathy**: This is scary for me to feel that I have become somebody who I imagine is not normal or acceptable. It is a horrible feeling. I really am suffering in this moment.
		Evolved brain: I see now that our deepest fear is of being cast out of the group, so no wonder this experience is so frightening to me. I can see that I feel a deep sense of fear and also shame about this. It feels very lonely too. This is not something I have deliberately chosen to feel; my hope and intention was to feel love for this baby, but sadly at the moment, I am struggling to find any feelings.
		Experiences: There might actually be many reasons why I don't feel anything for my baby, and I am beginning to realise that this experience is more common than I thought. I am not alone in this, in fact I bet there are others feeling this way right this moment. Reading through this book I remember now that some of the reasons for having no feelings are postnatal depression, having a difficult birth, lack of support, tiredness and exhaustion, and also fear of becoming attached to someone who we might lose. I can relate to all of these to some extent. Whatever the reason, it is not something I have chosen, and although it can feel like it is my fault I am beginning to really see that it is not my fault; it is just very sad.
		Exercises: Compassionate skills: There are lots of things that can help (including giving this time) so I will start by reaching out and talking to my health visitor, and perhaps even my sister, about it. I understand now that if I can be compassionate to myself then this might help with my feelings for my baby, so I am going to practise these compassionate mind exercises each day. I really hope I start to find some feelings for him but in the meantime I will be the best mum to him that I can be in this moment (SBR).

Note: Remember to focus on the emotional tone of warmth and kindness even if we can't quite believe what we are saying to ourselves. We might not be able to change what has happened because life can be very difficult, but the aim is to try to find a way through with compassion, encouragement and support.

See Appendix C for a blank form for you to use.

Here is an example of a much more detailed way of working through difficult thoughts, which pulls together many of the skills we have been addressing in this book:

Form for more complex work[1]

Triggering events, feelings or images	Depressing, upsetting thoughts	Feelings	Compassion-focused alternatives to self-critical thoughts	Understanding and change in feelings
Key questions to help you identify your thoughts. What actually happened? What was the trigger?	What went through your mind? What are you thinking about others, and their thoughts about you? What are you thinking about yourself, and your future?	What are your main feelings and emotions?	What would you say to a friend? What compassionate alternatives might there be? What is the evidence for new view? (How) are these examples of compassion, care and support? Can you think these through with warmth?	Write down any change in your feelings.
Not being able to get out of the house because the baby keeps crying and I don't want people to see that I am a useless mother. Feeling trapped,	**External shame (what I think others think about me):** People will think I am selfish – can't put my baby first. They will be shocked to see how cross I am – in my job I am supposed to be a caring person. They might see that really I am not up to being a mum or to doing my job.	Ashamed Angry Scared Sad Lack of motivation, hard to think clearly, hard to try and do something that might help.	**Empathy for own distress:** Understandable that I would have all these feelings because I just want to feel accepted by others and to feel happy with my baby. I had really looked forward to becoming a mother and it is really disappointing to feel like this. Soothing breathing rhythm and just noticing the feelings mindfully. Bringing a real warmth, acceptance and understanding.	Feel calmer and able to refocus my feelings towards being warm with self. In my heart I know I can get through this if I can accept and work with my fatigue and anger.

Triggering events, feelings or images	Depressing, upsetting thoughts	Feelings	Compassion-focused alternatives to self-critical thoughts	Understanding and change in feelings
	Key feared consequences: Disconnection. People will not want me looking after this baby, or working in my job. **Internal shame (what I think about me):** Horrible person. Selfish. A fake – pretending to be nice when not really. **Key feared consequences:** Will be 'found out' and end up alone. **Image and emotion:** Female, tall thin, contemptuous, wagging finger at me, looking down on me. **Function:** Making sure I stay a 'nice girl' so that people like me and don't reject me.		**Compassionate attention:** Although it is understandable to focus on times when I struggle, there are also many times when I have done okay as a mother. Bringing specific memory to mind. Even when I was really tired and feeling really stressed I still managed to feed him and we both settled down. I can also remember many times when I have done well at work and people have found me to be helpful to them. **Compassionate thinking:** **Evolved** – We have evolved to need acceptance from others to feel part of the group, so it isn't surprising I worry about what others think. We have also evolved to be around people, so no wonder I feel trapped when I can't get out among people. I also really appreciate now that we have evolved to need help to be able to mother as best we can, so no wonder I feel like this when I am trying to do this all on my own. It really isn't my fault that I feel this way.	

Experiences – this feeling of being trapped also brings back memories of having to look after my younger brother when mum was ill and I just wanted to go outside and play with my friends. Now I can see just why this has made me feel so resentful.

Compassionate behaviour: Actually I see now that it is normal to need help when you are a mum so I think I am going to ask for a bit of help rather than trying to do it all myself. Perhaps my partner and I can start with agreeing a couple of hours when the other one looks after the baby – just so I can have a coffee and read a magazine without feeling responsible. I might also try practising my compassionate imagery while I am feeding him and seeing what that is like.

Image and emotion: Large old lady who has been around for many years (hundreds of years?) Has looked after many children and many mothers. Kind, wise, but strong, 'no nonsense'. Just here for me, to help and guide me. Understands the struggles of all mothers including me, knows we all need help and guidance and this is what she is here to do.

Function: To help guide me through difficult times, to develop my confidence and help me to find my own unique way as a mother. To support me and encourage me. To value me and help me to value myself.

Compassionate letter writing

Many people have found writing to be really helpful – whether a diary, a letter, poetry or a story – particularly when struggling with difficult emotions. A psychologist called James Pennebaker carried out research that demonstrated just how helpful writing can be,[2] even improving our physical health and immune functioning. Compassionate letter writing has been inspired by his work. Here we first need to move into our compassionate self or to bring to mind our compassionate image. We spend a few minutes doing this, using our posture, soothing breathing rhythm, mindfulness, and warm voice and facial expression, reminding ourselves of our compassionate motivation, intention or wish to ourselves, and then we write as our compassionate self, using 'I', or from our compassionate image, e.g. 'Dear Suzanne . . .'

> *Write from your compassionate mind with warmth and kindness. Write from the 'heart' rather than 'head'.*
>
> *In other words, let the pen flow rather than thinking too much about it.*

If we do not usually write then the act of writing in itself may trigger emotional memories of times when we were judged for our writing, such as at school or by our parents. We need to be aware of this possibility so that we can notice it with warm curiosity and without judgement, step outside of it, then move back into our compassionate mind and let that part just take hold of our pen or pencil and write for us. There is no right or wrong; poor grammar or spelling does not matter here. There is nobody to judge this, apart from our own critical mind if we allow it in. If it comes in, we can notice its presence with a respectful nod, and then refocus back onto writing from our compassionate mind.

There is some rough guidance below, but first just let your compassionate self or image write without thinking too much, and then if you wish you can have a look at the guidance to see if it can add anything to your letter.

Write about something that is important and deeply personal to you. Only write about what you feel you can manage at this time. Pennebaker suggests writing solidly for at least twenty minutes if you can, and to write each day for four consecutive days if possible.

Interestingly, Pennebaker discovered that the people who benefited the most from letter writing were those who had least worked through their difficulties. The process of writing seemed to serve to really unravel and make conscious their difficulties in a powerful way.

So just write in a heartfelt way, focusing on the warm tone and facial expression rather than the technicalities of the letter.

Once you have written the letter, have a look at this guidance. Your letter might have followed the two psychologies of compassion that we have talked about; i.e. engagement and alleviation. So it may have started with a turning towards your struggle, noticing and validating the distress, empathising with it and really understanding how our evolved mind and our 'lived in' mind with all its experiences contributes to the struggle. We become aware of all this with non-judgement. Then we might move to alleviation; what helps us to be free from the suffering.

So we might notice whether or not we have included something around the following skills and attributes, and if we have missed any we might see how it feels when we add them.

Engagement with suffering

1. Care for well-being (motivation, intention, wish towards oneself): *'I am writing to you because I want to help you with this.'*

2. Sensitivity: *'I am aware you are particularly struggling at the moment with your relationship with your baby. I can see that this is filling you with all sorts of painful emotions such as guilt, shame, anger, fear and sadness.*

Sometimes these come all at once and then you feel overwhelmed. I can see that it is starting to get you down.'

3. Sympathy: *'I am so sorry that you are struggling this way. I can feel how utterly disappointed you are.'*

4. Distress tolerance: *'These feelings really stir us up and I know you wish they would just go away. They will pass though as all feelings do.'*

5. Empathy: *'This would be a difficult situation for anybody; discovering that we are not feeling as we had hoped to feel towards our baby. Your fear is that there is something wrong with you or that you are a bad person inside. But as we start to look at this we see that these feelings are understandable and not your fault at all; as a child you were frequently let down by the people you had to rely on to survive. You learned to cope with this by using all sorts of safety strategies, such as keeping people at a distance, and blanking out feelings of hope and happiness because you were so often disappointed. It is not surprising then, when you have a baby who is so important to you, that you try to keep them at a distance to protect you and them from the potential pain of loving and then being hurt. On top of all this, you had an exhausting birth and you are struggling to talk to the people around you who could really help you with this. No wonder this is so hard for you, but now we know about it, we will find a way through it.'*

6. Non-judgement: *'This is very hard for you, but it is not your fault; you are not bad, or wrong, or crazy, just struggling with a very difficult set of circumstances, none of which you have chosen.'*

Alleviation of suffering

1. Compassionate imagery: *'Focus for a moment on the image of the compassionate person, or the compassionate part of you writing this letter to you. Bring to mind their warmth, kindness, wisdom, strength and heartfelt wishes for you. Hear their voice to you and notice the kind, warm expression on their face. Take in the feeling of them really wanting to help you. Hear the words they offer to you.'*

2. Compassionate thinking: *'You may feel you are the only one to feel this way, but this is more common than you might realise. Throughout history, animals and humans have struggled to bond with their babies and there will be many more in the future. There are women all over the world struggling with what you are feeling at this very moment. You are not alone in this.*

    'Thinking for a moment about these other women, what would you say to them from your compassionate mind? How would you relate to them? How would you feel towards them? What would your most heartfelt wish be for them? What might they say to you? How would they feel towards you? If the kindest person were here today, what would they say to you? How would they help you?'

3. Compassionate attention: *'You have come through many hard times in your life but when we feel this way our minds are naturally set up to focus on the bad rather than the good. We can forget what got us through these times. Remember how despite wanting to run away from it all, you stayed with it, when you felt so worried about being hurt you took the courage to still reach out again.'*

4. Compassionate behaviour: *'The particularly hard times for you are when your baby is crying. We are designed to be stirred up by this, but it is doubly hard for you because it also brings up for you your memories of crying and being left alone as a child. In that moment pause, and give yourself some space and time to slow down and bring compassion first to yourself before you respond to your baby.*

    'As a child you often felt alone with your struggles. This can still get played out in emotional memories; feeling deeply that you are alone and no one will come. But the situation now is different to then. Once we realise this it can be easier (although still very difficult) to try to reach out to others this time and to see if people can help. There is an entire world of people out there, so reach out to others again and again. Ring your health visitor or GP; go on internet discussion sites such as Netmums and Mumsnet, which have discussions sites on just your struggle. Reach out to your family and friends and give them a chance to help you if they can. Ask them

as wholeheartedly as you can. If they cannot help, this can be painful and disappointing and you will need to bring your compassionate mind to your disappointment. But keep reaching out. If you get knocked down 100 times then I am here to help you get up 101 times.'

Reading back your letter

When you read your letter back to yourself, notice the difference when you read it in a matter of fact or cold way, compared to reading it with a warm, kind voice tone and facial expression. Highlight or underline any parts that feel a little harsh or critical. We will be highly attuned to these parts so we can come back to them and rewrite them from our compassionate mind.

As James Pennebaker suggests, try extending this letter, or write a new letter, each day over the next four days and just notice how it feels.

Writing to your baby

A number of women have found it helpful to write to their baby from their compassionate mind. They have found that in explaining their struggles and their intention to their baby, it has clarified these for them too. They noticed an increase in softness and gentleness towards themselves and their baby, an inclination to say a heartfelt 'I am so sorry', and a motivation truly to try to make it better.

Here we may need to pay close attention to which self is writing the letter. When facing a person we feel we may have harmed in some way then the fearful, angry or ashamed part can easily creep in, producing a letter that has an attacking, justifying or generally defensive tone. We can check this when we read it back to ourselves. Our threat system is particularly sensitive to detecting even the slightest hint of criticism, so it will inform us of this by making us feel angry or anxious in response to particular words or phrases. We can then change these until we feel within ourselves a sense of safeness and of being encouraged when we read it. We may feel very moved by the words we hear.

Because the compassionate mind also enables us genuinely to step into our baby's shoes, it may well trigger feelings of guilt. As we discussed before, guilt resides in the compassion or soothing system, whereas shame comes from the threat system. Guilt arises when we really get in touch with the pain or distress we may have contributed to in someone else. This does not mean it is our fault (our wise mind helps us to genuinely understand this) but if we can use our compassionate mind to stay with us and help us bear these feelings then we can find ourselves moved to apologise, and repair, and try to make it better for both of us in the future.

If we are able to write from our compassionate mind then there is no blame, just understanding of what has created such a difficult situation. There may be sadness, grief, but also a sense of peace and often relief and joy. We can use our compassionate mind to allow us to sit with the emotions with kindness and warmth until they pass, as they will. There may be acceptance but also a desire to help both ourselves and our baby, so alongside acceptance there is also a forward momentum.

Writing to you and your baby

Writing one letter from our compassionate mind to ourselves and our baby ('Dear ... and ...') really helps to bring together an appreciation and understanding of the intertwined nature of ourselves and our baby.

Using compassionate imagery with the struggling 'parts' of our self

When we are working with parts of our self, such as our angry, anxious or self-critical part, it is just like encountering such a person in real life. This can, of course, stir us up, leaving us feeling anxious, helpless, frustrated or demotivated. It is therefore particularly important to spend a little time preparing ourselves by moving into our compassionate mind first:

- We need to anchor ourselves in our motivation; what is it that will really help that struggling part? What is our heartfelt wish for that part? What do we really want it to feel when it looks at us?

- We also need to anchor ourselves in our wise mind; our understanding of the difficult human mind we have that we didn't design or choose, our wiring for love, understanding and acceptance, just what it is that has tuned up this part of ourselves, and, importantly, the function that it came to serve. This latter consideration helps us to see that it often became so tuned up because initially it had a protective function, such as keeping in check emotions that would be unhelpful at the time, taking us away from difficult situations or keeping at bay people who might harm or ridicule us in some way. Once we see this, we develop a much deeper understanding and appreciation of that part of us that we might previously have wanted to eradicate, but we also see that it is no longer helpful to us. So, instead, we can help address its fears from our compassionate self, rather than allowing it to remain 'in charge'.

- We then need to embody our strength and authority, our decision to put our compassionate self 'in charge', by moving into our grounded, solid, open body posture.

- Then we bring our soothing breathing rhythm, our mindful awareness, and our kind voice and face.

Using the compassionate image alongside the compassionate self

When we are beginning to use our compassionate self to relate to the struggling parts of ourselves, it can initially be difficult, particularly when our compassionate self does not feel quite strong enough yet.

Because having a sense of affiliation is so powerful, we can manage difficult situations much better if we feel we are not going into them alone. It can therefore be very helpful to imagine having your compassionate image with you as a guide and a support when you are first bringing your compassionate self to meet your struggling 'selves'.

Exercise: Bringing compassion to our 'anxious self'

Imagine bringing compassion to your anxious self perhaps by imagining encountering it as you walk along or by looking down upon it. It is important first to anchor yourself in your strong body posture and your soothing breathing. Allow yourself to connect with the feelings coming from the anxious part while remaining anchored in your own sense of strength, wisdom, kindness and intention to understand and to help. Imagine these feelings flowing out of you to surround and fill up the anxious part. Notice how the anxious part feels to be held, understood and related to with compassion. We are trying to soften rather than take away the anxiety, and to validate, understand and try to help it. Imagine what you might wish for the anxious part, such as: 'May you be free of agitation and anxiety. May you find stability and peace.'

Exercise: Bringing compassion to our 'angry self'

This can be difficult because we can feel scared when faced with somebody who is angry, and our mind can respond to the angry part of ourselves just as if we are faced with an actual angry person. It may also bring up emotional memories in the body connected to being in the presence of angry people and this can make us feel small and submissive. This is why the posture and soothing rhythm breathing are important here, because rather than the automatic submissive posture (or overly aggressive posture) and quick breathing we may automatically adopt when facing an angry person; we are deliberately changing our body posture and breathing in such a way that we are fostering stability, confidence and a calmer and more open way of viewing the situation.

Anger is a protective emotion, so we can use the wise part of ourselves to be curious about how the anger part has been triggered off. It could be responding to hurt, shame, sadness, grief or fear, which can become buried below the anger. We can also truly begin to understand what would help bring peace to the angry part. We may have experienced anger as something that is shameful or harmful, so we may struggle with the acceptance that anger is part of us as it is for everybody. We can bring compassion to this struggle. The intention with this exercise is to find the capacity to allow ourselves to be with the angry part and to stay with it with kindness, understanding, acceptance and a real desire to help, as it rises and then falls and then fades away, as all emotions do.

If this feels difficult to do, then begin with an easier image, for example encountering a mildly disgruntled or irritated part of yourself, rather than a full-blown shouting, stomping part. Imagine encountering or looking down on your angry or irritated self or regarding it from a distance where you can see it but where you feel safe from it. Here, your strong posture is important. If necessary, imagine yourself becoming bigger and bigger until you feel confident in approaching your angry part. As we are using our imagination we can even imagine ourselves as huge in comparison to a tiny image of the angry part. The aim isn't to intimidate the angry part though, but to reach a state in which we feel safe enough to be able to relate with wisdom, understanding, acceptance, strength and kindness.

Relate to it with your compassionate motivation to come to understand it, to turn towards it with an interested awareness and a wish to help it, to look at the feelings that might be driving it, such as anxiety, grief, sadness or loneliness. Use your strength and confidence to help you stay with it. Our intention is to understand it and see what it needs rather than to condemn it, argue with it, try to beat it down or get rid of it.

There can be a fear that compassion will rid us of the protection or the energy that the angry part brings us. In actual fact, compassion does the opposite. It can transform anger into a determined, focused assertiveness.

Even if we struggle to feel compassion, because this can be difficult in the face of anger, we can anchor ourselves back into our intention to want to find peace and happiness. We can imagine sending out our heartfelt wish to it, with phrases such as:

'May you find peace. May you find stability. May you be free from suffering.'

Exercise: Bringing compassion to the part that struggles with your baby

Start as always with your strong, grounded, 'dignified' posture; and warm, friendly facial expression and voice. Then focus on your breath. Gently allow the out-breath to lengthen so that both the in- and out-breath are long and gentle. Imagine in your mind walking along as your compassionate self, noticing how you relate to anybody you see, both as you pass them and in the distance. Notice particularly your facial expression and how your voice might sound if you spoke. Become aware of your compassionate intention towards all those you encounter. Be aware, from your wise mind, of how they might suffer in their lives (just like you) and your wish for them to be free from suffering, to find peace and happiness, and to be at ease.

As you continue your journey, imagine you come across the part of you that is struggling in relation to your baby. Notice its shape, posture, facial expression and voice tone if it spoke. Become aware of its emotions.

You then simply approach it, as close as it needs you to be, and you just relate to it with compassion; with an intention to really care for its well-being, with a wise understanding of what its difficult human mind and its life experiences have brought to this struggle, and how it has tried to protect itself from its fears. See if you can become aware of what might have contributed to the struggle it has with the baby.

You just stay with it, with your strong, wise, accepting presence, and notice how it begins to respond to this; to being accepted and under-stood in this way. Allow it time to really begin to take in and fully experience your compassion. Stay with your understanding of any panic or resistance it may have. If necessary, move back a little, anchor back in your compassionate mind and then approach it gently again.

As you allow your compassionate mind to be with the struggling part of yourself, notice that there is a sense of space and time. There is no rush to do something about it. Often a need to find a solution is the threat self creeping in. If this happens, anchor back into your compassionate self, and use your out-breath to bring a sense of peacefulness and space again. If you stay with quietly understanding the suffering and the need behind it, a strategy may come to mind without effort.

Bringing compassion to our baby

There will times when we find it easier than other times to feel compas-sion to our baby. For some of us we may feel that we cannot experience any compassion at all. When we experience anger, frustration, hatred or anxiety towards our baby we can feel guilt, or shame. When this feels intolerable we can wall ourselves off from our experience and become cold or apparently indifferent. However, usually we are in a high state of arousal even when we imagine we don't care. These are really hard emotions to bear and often trigger feelings of deep disappointment or self-criticism within us.

But when we feel like this, what is our deepest wish for our relationship with our baby? We are designed to love and be loved and our biology and mind is set up this way. However, the circumstances of our lives can make this difficult. This is not our fault and is very sad indeed. By realising that our relationship with our baby often stirs us up so much precisely because we wish it to be good, we can start with our intention, which is to find a way to make it better.

We do also need to hold in mind the potential to be worried about feeling compassion to our baby. This might be where we fear becoming engulfed by the feelings coming from our baby, or perhaps where we worry that if we let ourselves connect to them, they may reject us, or be taken away from us.

Whatever we feel, we first allow ourselves some space around our feelings, so we can let them arise within us and be viewed by us with an interested awareness and an intention to try and work it out and make it better. Shame instead keeps our feelings tucked away and inaccessible to be worked with. Guilt, however, arises from an awareness of feeling sorry that we have behaved in or felt a particular way and leads to a desire to repair, so although guilt can feel uncomfortable it is an important emotion in moving forwards to becoming more of the person we wish to be.

A 'ladder' of compassion: 'compassionate desensitisation'

We can practise bringing our compassionate self to times when it arises more easily within us in relation to our baby. It may help to write out a 'ladder' with easiest times on the bottom rung, and hardest on the top rung. If a step feels too high we can make smaller steps. For example, we may put on the bottom rung, 'times when my baby is asleep', or 'times when my baby is away from me'. Then it may be 'times when my baby is happy' or 'times when my baby is in someone else's arms'. Higher up may be emotions in our baby that we find harder, such as when our baby is anxious, crying, angry or even happy.

We also need to hold in mind that our own state of mind can make our ability to feel compassion harder or easier, so we can include this on our ladder. Fear and anxiety, stress, and fatigue all damp down our soothing system and will make it harder to feel warmth, love and kindness towards our baby and ourselves. So we might want to consider where to place 'times when I feel tired', or 'times when I feel alone', or 'times when I feel rejected/angry/scared/hurt'.

Then we can practise bringing compassion to our baby, starting with the lowest rung of the ladder and slowly and gently working our way up over time. When we struggle, we really need our compassionate mind with us to support, validate, understand and encourage ourselves to get back up, and to carry on with our endeavour to develop the relationship with our baby that we deeply wish for ourselves, and for them. If we find a 'rung' difficult we can drop down a rung or try again another time, but all the while bringing kindness and understanding to our struggle, and encouragement to try again when we feel ready to do so.

Proximity to our baby

We might also consider when it is easier to feel compassion to our baby in terms of how physically close or distant we are. Again, we can use the idea of the ladder here. So, for example, we might find it easier for feelings of kindness and warmth to flow when we are holding our baby, and can focus on the warmth and heaviness of the baby, and imagine the kindness and warmth flowing directly from our body into theirs. We might find it easier or harder when we are bottle-feeding or breast-feeding our baby, or when they are in their buggy or cot, when they are across the room, in a different room, or in a different house altogether. Draw up the rungs of the ladder without judging or condemning but with an openness and warmth.

Exercise: Bringing the compassionate self to your baby

Start as with all the exercises with your posture grounded and strong, close your eyes and begin your soothing breathing rhythm and let your body and mind settle ('body like a mountain, breath like the wind, mind like the sky'). Bring your warm voice and facial expression to mind. Imagine walking along as your compassionate self, with strength, wisdom, acceptance, a real desire to help and alleviate suffering. Imagine, for example, encountering your baby in a place and state that is best for you at this moment (see your 'ladder of compassion'). Again, as with the other exercises you need do nothing but relate to your baby with your compassionate intention, strength, wisdom, kindness and warmth. So you might imagine encountering your baby when they are in a state that you find the least difficult, such as asleep in another room, asleep in your arms or awake and happy. Just imagining approaching your baby to a comfortable distance, with your compassionate intention, your wise understanding, your strength and your acceptance. Imagine staying with your baby and sending out warmth, and kindness as light, colour or mist, which wraps around and fills up your baby. Become aware of your most heartfelt wishes for your baby; for example 'May you be well, may you be happy, may you live with ease'.

Notice how your baby might respond to being related to in this way. How might your baby be responding to your heartfelt wishes, to the warmth of your face and your voice if you speak? Notice how it feels within you to be able to relate to your baby in this way.

If you find that your anxious, angry, sad, or self-critical self comes in, just notice that that has happened, bring your compassionate self to its struggles for a moment and then refocus yourself on your compassionate self. You may need to bring your attention back to your strong body posture, your soothing breathing rhythm, and your warm voice and face, and then bring your compassionate self back to your baby.

Then turn your attention to your points of groundedness in your body; feel your feet in contact with the floor, the feel of the chair holding you up, the awareness of your breath, and, when you are ready, gently open your eyes.

Exercise: Bringing the compassionate self to you and

your baby

In this exercise you once again give body to your compassionate self and this time you encounter both your struggling self and your baby. You relate to both with your wisdom, your strength, your deep care for them both, and your acceptance. You just stay with them both, allowing them to take in your compassion. With your wisdom you can understand the struggle of both you and your baby and how you are both doing the best you can given the difficult human brain each of you have and the experiences you have had. Neither of you chose to be feeling and responding this way. The intention of both is to be able to love and be loved. You send out your deepest wishes to both, which might be 'May you both find peace, may whatever is hurting you both be soothed, may you both flourish and be happy.' Notice how both the struggling part of yourself, and your baby, respond to having your compassionate presence with them, with your intention to stay with them, to understand them, to help them.

Summary

With compassionate thinking, we can notice the impact of our self-critical thoughts, and then generate compassionate alternatives, imagining them coming from the compassionate part of ourselves, from our compassionate image, or from a very good friend, for example. We can end up feeling very differently inside when we do this, but because we can be much more creative when we feel safe and soothed, we may discover we come up with solutions we had never thought of before.

Compassionate letter writing can be a very powerful tool for coming to relate to our difficulties in a different way. For some people who struggle with imagery, they might find letter writing easier. It also gives a real sense of somebody else taking the time to think about us and help us, and so it can have a real impact. Just the process of 'letting the pen flow' without judgement and with a compassionate mind can help to untangle what previously seemed far too difficult to even consider.

The concept of bringing our compassionate self or our compassionate image to aspects that we struggle with helps us to realise that we are not trying to get rid of these difficult parts; indeed, we often see that they had an important role when they first came into existence in terms of keeping us safe in some way. Instead, we are learning to relate to them with understanding, acceptance, kindness and compassion, and a willingness to help that part of ourselves with whatever causes it to react as it does. We are making a decision to give authority in dealing with the struggles of life to our compassionate self, rather than our self-critical, angry or anxious self, for example. This is why the concept of strength, courage and authority that we practise physically embodying is particularly important when we are working with aspects that we find particularly challenging. We don't have to find solutions, or get rid of these parts, but simply relate to them with compassion.

18 The journey from self-criticism to self-compassion

Earlier in the book we looked at shame. In this section we will focus on a strategy that many of us adopt as a way of protecting ourselves from becoming a 'shameful' person; self-criticism. As we shall see, though, our self-critic can cause us far more problems than it is trying to solve. Here we will look at how we can develop self-compassion rather than self-criticism as an antidote to shame.

We all have the capacity to criticise ourselves; however, the emotion driving the self-critic can vary over time and can be stronger or milder in different people. The response of our self-critic can range from a 'tut' of frustration to a full-blown horrifying attack on ourselves. It can operate like a different voice or person within us.

We have looked in detail at the importance of building self-compassion to be able to help us through the difficult times and to help calm our threat system. We are going to look now at self-criticism; why we knock ourselves down, the impact that this has on our mind, and how we can help ourselves to develop a compassionate mind that understands and potentially calms our self-critic and can provide us with a more powerful way of becoming the person we want to be than our self-critic ever can.

We might imagine that as we become more self-compassionate then our self-criticism will start to fade. This can happen. However, self-compassion and self-criticism come from different systems, the first from the soothing system, and the second from the threat system. They can therefore act independently. Moreover, self-criticism can have a number of different functions, some of which may disappear with increased self-compassion, but others to which we hold on tight. So, not only do we need the exercises that we have covered so far on building our compassionate mind, we also need to be able to bring our compassionate mind to understanding and relating to our self-critic.

Why do we criticise ourselves?

When something has happened which is a threat to us in some way (let's say we have just spilt milk on the floor), our threat system within our brain and our body reacts to this so we might jump back a little or cry out 'Oh no!' (or words to that effect). We might then criticise ourselves for the behaviour ('You clumsy idiot!'). From the exercise we did near the beginning of this book looking at the impact of 'the voice on our shoulder', we know that when we criticise ourselves it stimulates our threat system further. We now have a 'double-whammy'; the original threat plus our self-criticism. So why do we criticise ourselves, causing greater threat to ourselves when we are already under threat?

> *Our self-critic can develop as a safety strategy.*
>
> *One aim of the self-critic can be to try to stop us becoming the kind of person who might be rejected by others.*

We gained some insight into this earlier in the book where we imagined a 'shameless' person. Imagine for a moment that there is something magical and powerful within the pages of this book which removes our ability to criticise ourselves for evermore; what would that be like? It might initially feel like a wonderful relief. But what might the niggling fear be that comes on the heels of the relief?

Here are some of the fears that people have expressed about no longer having a self-critic:

'I will never get dressed in the morning and I will become a lazy slob.'

'I will say things to people that upset them.'

'I will do rubbish work.'

'I will leave my baby in front of the telly and not even feed him.'

Somehow we have developed a sense that our self-critic prevents us from becoming the kind of person that other people wouldn't like to know. Our self-critic then becomes a crucial part of our identity; without it, we fear we will become unpleasant, unlovable people who run the risk of being ignored, ostracised, cast out. Once we understand that we believe the self-critic helps us (albeit in a bullying kind of way) to stay safe, we can see why we can feel so worried about letting it go. But, in reality, how helpful is our self-critic? Let's look at what actually happens when our self-critic takes hold of us.

What does your self-critic look like?

Imagine what our self-critic might look like if we were to see it in front of us. We can try this now by thinking of some of the things it says to us. Imagine it is standing in front of us (if this feels difficult, imagine shrinking it or placing it further and further away until it feels more manageable). What are the emotions it directs at us? What is the tone of its voice and the expression on its face? What does it say to us? How big or small is it in relation to us? What shape is it? What colour is it?

Now notice how you feel in your body when it directs these emotions at you and when it says these things to you.

Become aware of whether it has your welfare at heart. Does it want you to grow and flourish? Does it want to help and encourage you? Does it have a heartfelt wish to help you become you at your very best?

Often we discover that actually our self-critic makes us feel small, vulnerable, deflated, demotivated and sometimes quite upset. Rather than helping us to become the best person we can be, it actually takes us further away from our goal, and can make us feel so horrible that we can struggle to pick ourselves up and try again. What we see instead is that the self-critic comes from a place of threat, panic and fear. It is focused on the harm that might come to us and reminds us of all the mistakes we have made in the past and the consequences of these. It is therefore backward looking and focused on our deficits rather than forward looking, focusing on our positive attributes and what we want to become. Its emotions all come from the threat system and are focused around disappointment, contempt and anger rather than support, encouragement, kindness, warmth and joy. We can imagine it as a 'stop' rather than a 'go', an inhibitor rather than an encourager.

Moving from using a critical to a compassionate self-corrector

So how do we keep ourselves in check, prevent ourselves from becoming lazy, or unlikeable, and drive ourselves towards our goals if our self-critic isn't truly able to help us? We can tap into our own intuitive wisdom about this if we consider which type of teacher we would like for a beloved child or a really good friend, or ourselves struggling to master a particular subject when we were at school: a critical teacher or a compassionate teacher? Most of us have had personal experience of both types of teachers; which would we prefer to have to help us become the best version of ourselves? When we start to consider the attributes of the teachers we had when we were little, we can sometimes identify that the most compassionate teachers were not necessarily the 'nice' teachers. Sometimes they were, in fact, strict and firm but there was a sense that they were driven by a deep desire truly to help us, even if that occasionally meant pushing us hard or keeping us firmly on track. Sometimes 'nice' teachers are motivated by a desire to be liked rather than by the child's needs. Children are very adept at spotting this and can end up feeling frustrated and held back. This is the same for ourselves; compassion isn't about being 'nice', rather it is about the determination and intention to help ourselves flourish, even if this means facing difficult things.

> *Our self-critic beats us down and inhibits us, whereas a compassionate guide, coach or self-corrector helps us to grow and flourish.*

So instead of growing a critical self-corrector, how about growing a compassionate self-corrector instead? We can think about it as a kind of coach, guide or teacher. A bit like a very wise, kind and experienced sports coach who sits on our shoulder or stands just behind us to guide us through life. When we struggle, what would they say to us? How would they be with us? How would their voice sound? What would the expression be on their face?

Critical parent, nice parent, compassionate parent?

We can think about this too in our mothering. If we spend a while just noticing with curiosity and non-judgement how we parent our children, we can notice the times we use our critical corrector with them, and the times when we use our compassionate corrector. (We really need our compassionate self rather than our critical self with us when doing this exercise. Our intention with this exercise is to look clearly and accurately, but also with kindness and understanding at how we are trying to guide our children as they grow. By using mindfulness and compassion when we observe ourselves, we can work out what our intentions are in our words and actions, why the critic may have jumped in, and how best to move instead to our compassionate guide or corrector).

Sometimes our panic or fear for our children drives us to parent in a critical way, particularly if this is the model of parenting we have experienced.

The exercise below ('Compassion for our self-critic') can help us truly to see what causes the critic to pop up.

We can assume as mothers that the alternative to critical correction of our children is to be 'nice' to them. As with teachers, 'nice' doesn't necessarily equate to compassion. If our child is distressed because they want the sweets they see at the supermarket checkout, what might be a compassionate way of responding? We might want to be seen as a 'nice' mother, so we let them have them. A compassionate response might be different. We will rapidly be weighing up many variables in a short space of time in that moment, but we can check back to our motivation as a guide to us. Compassionate motivation is a real intention to care for that person, to notice their suffering, and to help alleviate it in a way that helps them to grow and develop. We might therefore decide that we don't want them to eat sweets, or that they've had enough sweets that day, or perhaps we feel it would be fine for them to have just one small packet. We might then need our wisdom and our empathy towards them to help us genuinely to understand the utter frustration of having somebody else stop you from getting what you want. We can thus try to help them with that while remaining clear that it is not in their best interests to have the sweets. We might need to validate them, soothe them, give them space with kindness and warmth, distract them and so on. So we are helping them through their distress in a compassionate way.

When it's hard to say 'no': being nice as a safety strategy

If we do become aware that we have a strong need to be perceived as 'nice' mothers, then what is driving this? It may have come from experiences of learning that in order to be loved, or in order to stop criticism or aggression, we had to be 'nice'. 'Nice' then became a safety strategy that protected us. If we are being 'nice' through fear, this is an indicator that we need compassion to our self first in that moment in order to understand and calm our fear. Once we feel less fearful we are then better able to give a compassionate response to the other person (this is the 'oxygen mask' principle (see box).

Oxygen Mask Principle

During the safety announcements on a plane, cabin staff impress upon us that in an emergency you must put an oxygen mask on yourself first, before you put one on others, including your own children. This is, of course, because if you become unconscious you cannot help yourself or anyone else. It is the same principle with compassion; in an emergency you need to give this to yourself first before attempting to give it to others.

No matter what we are doing we can hold in mind our compassionate motivator/guide/self-corrector to help us. We can contrast it with our experience if we were to use our critical guide, motivator or self-corrector. We will put this part of us to work a surprising number of times in each day; from getting out of bed when we are tired, trying to be calmer as a parent, dealing with competing demands, losing a bit of weight, exercising more, learning a new skill, keeping going when we are tired, stopping when we are tired and so on. If we think about it in terms of our drive system, it is about bringing compassion rather than threat as the motivator for this system.

So, when we are feeling compelled to be 'nice' we can just check in with our body. Which system are we in? If we are feeling tense, anxious or angry then the chances are we are in our threat system and are being nice for fear that something difficult will happen if we're not. This is not our fault. We don't choose to have this response. But once we notice it, then we can choose whether still to respond from our threat system, or whether to have a go at bringing our compassionate corrector on board. How would that part guide us with this? How would it help us?

Compassion to the self-critic

As we develop our compassionate self we can begin to bring it to other people and to different aspects of ourselves. This is a skill, and like any skill can be learned. As we have seen in Buddhism there is a particular meditation designed to cultivate compassion called 'loving-kindness meditation'. Here the meditator starts off by sending out wishes that are as heartfelt as possible along the lines of: *'May you be well. May you be free from suffering. May you be happy. May you be at peace.'*

As with any new skill, a helpful way to learn it is to start with easier exercises and move to harder ones. Therefore these wishes are first directed to 'easy' people whom we love, or to animals such as pets, if that feels easier. Then it is directed to 'neutral' people whom we know little about, such as a shop assistant or people passing by in cars. Finally it is directed to 'difficult' people who have perhaps upset us or made us angry. We can also do this for ourselves; bringing compassion to easy emotions before difficult ones, easy problems before difficult ones, and easy before difficult parts of ourselves. A difficult part of our self is often the self-critic, particularly if the voice of the self-critic assumes that of somebody who was imposing and frightening to us. We need to appreciate this if we struggle with this exercise. We may need to move to an easier practice, particularly if the voice of the self-critic assumes that of somebody who was imposing and frightening to us first, so we could try easier parts of ourselves (our hurt part, or sad part, for example) or easier people first. Once we are more practised at these, we might want to revisit this section to bring compassion to our self-critic.

First, we need to be clear why we would want to bring compassion to our self-critic. It can seem intuitively wrong to be compassionate to something that can be so destructive and hateful towards us. As with any aspect of the processes in this book, we don't have to choose compassion, we are just giving ourselves choices and therefore greater flexibility in how we can respond, particularly when things get difficult. One of the reasons for turning our focus to the self-critic is that, even as we build our self-compassion, this doesn't necessarily mean that our self-critic will get smaller. We can find, particularly when we feel low, depressed or under the weather, that our self-critic can come back loud and strong.

If we imagine our self-critic as a real person we can imagine what it would be like to have them with us night and day with no escape, ready to attack us when we are at our lowest ebb. Sadly, for some this may be akin to reality. We can then appreciate how we move into all kinds of strategies to keep ourselves safe: be quiet, good, submissive, appeasing, avoid, blank out, attack first. This rarely resolves the problem however. As a result, we may live in a perpetual state of heightened anxiety or fear.

> *We are more likely to quieten our self-critic by trying to under-stand and alleviate the fear driving it, rather than trying to beat it down.*

This might seem counterintuitive, and we might kick against it initially, but what if, instead, we learn to become aware of the fear and unmet needs of the self-critic? This is where we search deep into our wise mind and look at the needs that connect all human beings, including our self-critic. We come to realise that our needs are in fact universal; to be heard, understood, connected to, loved, kept safe. Once we start truly to connect with empathy and compassion to the self-critic, we find that we move out of 'rank'-related threat-based strategies in which we are either trying to dominate or submit to the critic in order to protect ourselves. Instead, we move into our soothing/affiliative system, which is about strength, wisdom and a desire to care for and be cared for. Here we feel connected to and equal to the self-critic. Our motivation is to do what we can to help the suffering of both ourselves and the self-critic.

As with a real-life bully or critic, we also need to anchor our self into our strength, confidence and assertiveness, which is why our strong, grounded posture is so important. As we look at what has brought our self-critic to life in the first place, we might genuinely come to understand what makes the critic hit out. We might see that this comes from a place of pain and fear. However, this does not mean we have to take on board the criticism. Instead, our compassionate self can lean in and take charge. This part may also want to help the self-critic with their pain where we can.

So let's be clear that this is not about letting the critic or bully 'off the hook', free to carry on bullying us – a fear some have with moving to a compassionate point of view. Instead, we are moved to strong, courageous, compassionate action driven by an awareness of the needs of the other and of ourselves. In the case of living with a real-life extreme critic such as a violent or bullying partner, our compassionate self might enable us to understand the pain and vulnerability that might be driving this behaviour. As Marshall Rosenberg says in his work on non-violent communication: *'Violence is a tragic expression of an unmet need.'*[1] But our compassionate self also helps us to realise our own need to be safe and loved too, which can give us the support and encouragement we need to leave the relationship.

Understanding this doesn't mean we need to continue listening to the words of the self-critic. However, there can be real value in understanding the self-critic as alerting us to the pain of an unmet need which has just been triggered off. It is as if we have a wound. The self-critic is the shout of pain when that wound has been touched. Seeing the self-critic as in pain and suffering is much more likely to pull up our compassionate response towards it compared to seeing it as an aggressive bully. This is also far more likely to allow the self-critic to fade compared to trying to fight it or submit to it. Remember the 'two wolves' story? Which wolf do we want to feed? We can put our energy into feeding the wolf of self-compassion rather than the wolf of self-criticism.

Exercise: Bringing compassion to the self-critic

1. As always, begin with a strong, open grounded posture, gentle, long out-breath, and mindful awareness ('body like a mountain, breath like the wind, mind like the sky'). In addition, allow your face and voice to become kind, gentle and friendly, or imagine this happening.

2. It might help to imagine a time you felt real warmth towards someone or something, or to remember experiencing warmth and kindness from someone else. Allow the feeling to grow and grow inside of you.

3. Bring to mind a compassionate person, perhaps from a film, a book or from history, and imagine that you are practising to play them in a film. You are noting how they understand people, their wisdom, how they can be non-judging through understanding the difficult human minds we have and the experiences we have been through as we've grown up.

4. You might notice how they hold themselves, their sense of solidity, strength and inner confidence, coming from knowledge that nothing is too much for them to bear.

5. You become aware of their facial expression and voice tone of warmth and kindness.

6. Now imagine that, as this compassionate person, you walk along and come across the self-critical part of you. All you do is approach it (as near or far as feels comfortable) and relate to it with compassion; sending out your wishes that whatever causes it to be hurtful and hit out can be eased, that it could be at peace, that it could be free of suffering. Keep yourself anchored in your motivation or intention in this moment; this comes from the compassion or soothing system rather than threat system; to understand, to empathise with its suffering, to wish to alleviate its suffering.

7. It can be hard to trust that we will not get hurt again as we approach it. If we become scared or overwhelmed by our self-critic we need to move back until we feel safe, adjust our posture again to make sure we feel strong and anchored into the floor. Once we feel stronger we can approach the self-critic again. Notice any fears or judgements you may have, perhaps that bad people should be punished, that it will be let 'off the hook' and then attack again, that it doesn't deserve your compassion or that physically it just seems so scary. These are signs we have moved out of our compassionate self into our angry or anxious self. If so, we need to bring ourselves back into our compassionate self by genuinely coming to understand the needs behind the angry attack and then sending out our most heartfelt wish that these needs can be met, that it can find peace, that it can come to feel cared for and connected to other people. If an attack comes then we need first to apply our strength, wisdom and compassion to ourselves and then search again for the need or vulnerability that has set off the attack. So we send out our compassion to that wound, even if it is from what feels like a safe distance.

8. We might notice how we are with the self-critic, and how it responds to our kindness, our non-judgement, and our wise understanding of what has brought it into being in the first place, and what triggers it off now.

9. Become aware of its fear and unmet needs which trigger the attacks on us. We might notice if it is trying to protect us, in its own, very primitive, threat-focused way. Perhaps we can understand what it would be like for us if we were to try to get rid of it – what does it fear might happen to us, or what might we become?

10. We might be able to step into its shoes for a moment and appreciate the panic or unmet need that has fuelled it. We might also be able to get in touch with how it has felt trying to protect us as best it can for all these years but being hated or feared

by us. Notice any fear, any loneliness and any sadness behind the anger.

11. Once we can get in touch with the suffering of our self-critic, this is more likely to trigger off our compassionate self. We might bring an appreciation of how hard and how long it has worked to try to keep us safe but without a sophisticated set of strategies to do this well, particularly if it came about when we were only a child. We can bring our real heartfelt intention to help it find peace, and to be free from its suffering.

12. Notice how the self-critic responds to our wisdom, strength, non-judgement, acceptance, kindness and warmth. Notice how it responds to being in the presence of someone who just wishes to help and understand it rather than judging, condemning, and trying to fight or eradicate it. What happens to it? How does it feel in you to be able to relate to it in this way?

13. When it pops up in the future, how might we relate to it?

When the critic comes again, this exercise can help us to take note of the threat and the fear behind its anger; so rather than ignoring the critic we are appreciating that it is responding to the triggering of our threat system. We can turn towards the problem but we then make our compassionate self the authority that will deal with the threat rather than allowing the self-critic free rein to deal with it in its unsophisticated threat-based way.

Self-criticism to keep emotions in check

As well as trying to keep us on the straight and narrow, our self-critic can also be a way of keeping feared emotions in check. Feared emotions might include sadness; for example, where we fear we might appear weak, open to humiliation, or about to tip into depression if we get sad.

They might even include 'positive emotions' such as happiness and joy, where, for example, these have been linked or conditioned to subsequent disappointment, dashed hopes or being ridiculed for being happy; a kind of 'don't get too happy because then there is further to fall when it all goes wrong'.

A common source of self-criticism is where it has developed as a safety strategy to keep our anger in check. If we watched a child being shouted at and criticised by a parent, we might feel real anger towards the parent. As children, when we are shouted at and criticised by a parent we might feel small and scared but we also might feel anger at them too. But what might have happened if we had been angry with our parents when we were little? Some children do feel safe enough to be angry towards their parents but others know that the parent is likely to become enraged and possibly violent. Children learn very quickly to blame themselves instead; they keep their behaviour and anger in check as the best means of staying safe. It also gives us some feeling that we can control our own safety: 'I just need to be more quiet, more good, then I won't get criticised', whereas admitting that we have no control over threats to ourselves can be very scary indeed.

'Don't wake the sleeping lion'

Imagine a child trying to creep past a sleeping lion. To stay safe she needs to be as quiet as possible. If she steps on a stick then the she might angrily blame herself: 'You idiot, be quiet! You will get us eaten!' Although, of course, it would have been the lion's fault if it had eaten her, imagine what would have happened if she got angry with the lion. This is how self-criticism and self-blame can start – we blame ourselves to make sure we don't get angry at somebody who is bigger and scarier than us. Self-criticism can therefore begin as a safety strategy for protecting ourselves from a powerful other.

We can check out this notion that our self-critic is a safety strategy by taking note of when our critic appears. If we imagine our self-critic suddenly disappearing, what emotion might we be free to express in that situation? What if we were to express that emotion? This allows us to see if a particular emotion might have arisen in that moment, were it not for our self-critic. We also become more aware of any fear associated with having that emotion. This enables us to understand the function of our self-critic; its intention is to keep us safe, even if we end up feeling attacked by ourselves.

Once we understand its function, we can start to experiment with using our compassionate self to help us instead of our self-critic. So, for example, if we are feeling angry because somebody is treating us unfairly, we might use the strength, courage and assertiveness that comes from our compassionate self to help us to get our needs met.

If I don't have my self-critic I fear I will have nobody: our need for affiliation

When we are criticised as children, as well as experiencing fear and anger, often nobody comes to help us. We feel alone. We come to learn that as well as feeling we are wrong in some way, we associate it with aloneness. As our self-critic develops it can come to feel like a constant companion by our side. In their fascinating paper 'Living with the "anorexic voice"',[2] Stephanie Tierney and John Fox noted that people who developed anorexia had a kind of affiliation to their 'anorexic voice'. They felt it helped and protected them in its initial stages. However, later on it became more hostile and unhelpful. What is so striking is that for those who felt alone, it became a constant presence in their lives that initially shielded, motivated and guided them. If this is the case, we can understand how very difficult it is to just 'give up' the self-critic. This is why it is important to focus instead on growing the compassionate protector (or guide or coach if you like) rather than focusing on getting rid of the self-critic. At first we will have both the critical self-corrector and the compassionate self-corrector as different parts of us. But as the compassionate part gets stronger, the need for the critical self-corrector will fade and the self-critic will begin to disappear.

Having our compassionate self alongside us as an alternative to our self-critic

The drive for having a sense of not being alone is so strongly evolved within us that we would rather keep something that may not be helping us rather than get rid of it and feel totally alone. In many of the difficult experiences we have during our life there is a sense of aloneness, of having nobody 'on our side'. This is one of the important reasons why developing a compassionate part of ourselves is so powerful; we are developing a sense of having a part of ourselves *with us* that can be wise, strong, encouraging and supportive.

The journey to self-compassion: navigating the potholes and bumps in the road

This section gives thought to some of the difficulties that may arise as we take the journey from self-criticism to self-compassion. As we get going with the exercises, for many people it doesn't take long before difficulties pop up. These are in fact a normal part of the journey, but if we are not aware of them they can make it feel as though we are not doing things right, or that we have taken the wrong path, or that this is the wrong course for us. So the irony is that engaging in compassionate mind practices can end up initially firing up rather than calming down our threat and self-criticism if we are not aware that the potholes and bumps we encounter are to be expected on this journey.

In a paper looking at this journey from self-criticism to self-compassion for people who received compassion-focused therapy for traumatic experiences,[3] Verity Lawrence and Deborah Lee identified the steps that people commonly described. These are:

Table 18.1: Steps from self–criticism to self–compassion

1. Dominance of self-criticism/feelings of hopelessness.
2. Fear of self-compassion.
3. Emotional experience of compassion.
4. Acceptance of self-compassion.
5. More compassionate to self, leading to an increase in all positive feelings.
6. Increasing ability to manage self-criticism.
7. Changed outlook on life/increased hopefulness for the future.

Adapted from V. Lawrence and D. Lee, *An Exploration of People's Experiences of Compassion-focused Therapy for Trauma, Using Interpretative Phenomenological Analysis. Clinical Psychology and Psychotherapy*, (2013)[3]

Initially, there is usually great hope that this approach will be the solution to our difficulties, but this can swiftly be followed by disillusionment when we encounter the next struggle. In their research Lawrence and Lee noted that participants talked about a real sense of effortful 'pushing through' the difficulties with a need to keep getting back up and trying again. When depression is affecting motivation and the self-critic is still dominant and beating us down, it is very difficult to keep going, however. This is the 'chicken and the egg' problem, where to develop self-compassion when it is hard, we need our compassionate self to give us encouragement and keep us going; the very thing we haven't got! All we have to start with is the intention and motivation to build compassion and the knowledge that the journey is usually hard to begin with. However, it is like getting a boulder moving; once it starts to move then it picks up ever-increasing speed (see below). So as we build our self-compassion, this provides us with a source of encouragement through the difficult times, allowing us to further build our compassionate mind.

Support

One of the themes of the research was the importance of the therapist in providing genuine compassion and encouragement. Lawrence and Lee also gave a model or 'map' of what clients were moving towards, and provided the felt experience of what it was like to be regarded in this way. So, for people undertaking this journey with just this book as a guide, you may find this journey is slower and harder without the support of other people; this is to be expected rather than seen as evidence of some personal failing. Seeking out a therapist may be needed, but also sharing this model with one's partner, family, close friend or health visitor have all been found to be helpful for people learning the compassionate mind approach.

The 'positive feeling snowball'

Lawrence and Lee also noted that as self-compassion increased, it also enabled people to experience not just feelings of warmth and support from their compassionate mind but also other positive feeling states such as happiness and joy. This often came as a surprise when people realised they had not allowed themselves any positive feelings before, through believing they didn't deserve to feel that way, or that if they did it would lead to disappointment when it ended. As the positive feelings increased it made it much easier for people to keep going.

It's a bit like making a snowman. We start with a little bit of snow squashed into a ball. Then we start rolling it, and as we do so, more and more snow sticks, making it bigger and bigger. If we roll the snowball down a hill, the bigger it gets, the faster it gets, which makes it bigger, which makes it faster . . .! This is just how positive emotions work. The more we feel them, the more we exhibit them. And the more we exhibit them, the more positive we are to ourselves and the more positive others are towards us, which makes us more positive towards ourselves, which makes us exhibit more positive emotions towards others and so on and so on ... The message therefore is that it is hard to keep going at the beginning, but this difficult beginning is an inevitable part of the process. There is no way round it, only through it. But if we persist with it, we do get through it and then it eventually becomes easier and easier and the positives build and build.

Here are some of the fears that people have expressed, both in the research by Lawrence and Lee and in my own work using compassion-focused therapy. This is not a complete list but it just introduces the idea that fears and blocks to self-compassion are to be expected and that getting through them is usually the biggest part of the journey. We can then prepare ourselves to watch out for the potholes and bumps.

A fear of loss of identity: 'If I am not self-critical then who am I?'

The self-critic has, for many people, been with them as long as they can remember. In fact it is often described as the only consistent presence in their lives; it may be bullying and unhelpful but at least it is always there and always responsive. This demonstrates the power of being wired for social contact – that it can feel better to have a bully who also gives you a sense that you exist than to feel invisible and completely alone.

As we saw above, without the critic people can feel as if there will be a void, but there is also a fear that the self-critic prevents us from becoming something awful. This can be a very difficult fear to shake off. It can be helped by understanding that the compassionate voice can be built alongside the critical voice rather than focusing on just getting rid of the self-critic. It is like having the self-critic on one shoulder but building a compassionate voice on the other shoulder. Rather than losing the self-critic it is the gaining of another voice. This gives us the possibility of making a choice rather than having the self-critic as our only option. It also enables us to experiment with which one seems the most helpful to us.

Self-compassion as an alien experience

Common comments have included 'I don't know how it will feel.' 'I don't know how I will react if I feel it.' 'I am scared I might start to cry and never stop.' 'I am scared I will become angry.' 'I am scared that it might bring up painful memories.'

Whereas self-criticism may be familiar, with self-compassion there may be no map or template of what it looks like in action, what it feels like, and what might happen to us, particularly if compassionate experiences or role models were few and far between. It is therefore difficult to know what we are trying to develop and it can also be scary as we don't quite know what it will 'do' to us. At the beginning it can feel safer to start looking around for compassion in others, perhaps on the television, in films, on the news and in books to get an idea of what it looks like, how people act, speak, appear to feel and the impact their compassion has on themselves and others. This in itself is helping to stimulate our compassionate mind in a gentle way because we are refocusing our attention from people who might be threatening to compassionate people.

Self-compassion is an aversive experience

Sometimes we can feel we are just holding things together with great effort and fear that if someone says 'are you okay?' we will let it all go and fall apart. When we start to touch the edges of compassion, this worry can surface on a grand scale, particularly if it feels like we have spent a lifetime 'holding things together' and that inside is a lifetime of grief. As we develop ourselves as a compassionate presence, it can bring up memories of earlier attachment experiences with people who gave us compassion but who are no longer with us, or who are no longer able to give this to us, or it can bring up the realisation that we never had it.

There can be a real fear about whether or not this grief is possible to bear. As the compassionate self is developed, this is what does help us through the grief but at first it can feel like it is an unsafe place to go. As always with this approach, we take it gently with little steps.

As well as sadness, as we develop compassion we may find associated feelings of fear, aloneness, anger and trauma, for example. Indeed, research has found that the amygdala (part of the threat-detection system) becomes activated when highly self-critical people attempt self-compassion imagery.[4] With the compassionate mind approach we are learning to approach these fears as we would any fear that we want to overcome, such as a fear of heights or open spaces. So we approach rather than avoid, and, rather than the usual phobia treatment of linking a feeling of relaxation to the target (e.g. if we are trying to conquer a fear of going into an open space, traditional desensitisation couples each step with becoming relaxed), we are linking the fear to feelings of warmth and encouragement instead. Here the targets are sadness, trauma, aloneness, anger and anxiety, so we are learning, tiny step by tiny step, to link warmth and encouragement to these fears.

Self-criticism of attempts to be self-compassionate

When people begin the journey to self-compassion common worries include 'I can't do this', 'I'm no good at it', 'Everyone else can get this except me', 'I will fail at this.' Of course just because the issue we are working on here is self-compassion, it doesn't mean that our self-critic for once is going to have nothing to say on the topic. Our self-critic has become so strong for a reason, perhaps to protect us from trying and then failing, or from getting our hopes up and then being disappointed, so it is not surprising that it is likely to pop up with this endeavour too. The section on working with our self-critic is helpful here. Rather than fighting with or giving in to our self-critic we learn to bring an understanding to why it has come to exist and why it is so hard to let go of.

Eventually we can bring our compassionate self to the self-critic (see above, p. 320).

I don't deserve it

Our early experiences can give us a strong sense that we are bad or wrong in some way (see Chapters 10 and 11). Our self-critic can serve to keep punishing us because we feel that's what we deserve, and it can serve to keep the 'badness in' or to keep us distant from others so they don't get to see the real 'us'. It is therefore understandable that we can struggle with being compassionate to ourselves if we feel we don't deserve it. Really understanding our early experiences, how the human brain responds and how we learn to keep ourselves safe, can help with this sense of 'don't deserve', which can then allow us to begin to open up to compassion.

Keeping a focus on where we are going

So, all in all, it really isn't surprising that it can be so easy to give up this journey to compassion when fears seem high, feelings unpleasant and rewards low, particularly at the beginning of this journey. It is therefore important to hold on to why we are going on this journey; to develop ways of helping ourselves and others to alleviate and prevent suffering and to develop a part of ourselves that helps us grow and flourish. And, although it may seem impossible at first, to help us understand that these difficulties are part of rather than detractions from the journey.

As one lady said, she imagined that the 'back seat driver' in her car was her compassionate image who guided her back on track whenever she came off the road, who encouraged her when she became fearful on her journey and who helped to restart the car when she stalled, no matter how many times it happened.

I wish you well on your journey.

Summary

1. We can develop a part of ourselves which keeps us in check to make sure we don't do anything that might be regarded as shameful by our social group. This is our self-critic.

2. If we imagine our self-critic could be suddenly removed from us, we start to see its function. We might fear that we will no longer make an effort, might make mistakes and not care, and might become rude or upset people. We see that actually our self-critic is often a safety strategy.

3. Our self-critic can also serve to keep emotions suppressed if in the past these emotions have been responded to with criticism, anger or rejection. For example, we might learn from a very young age that it is safer to blame oneself than get angry at a parent who might get even angrier in return.

4. If we look at how the self-critic relates to us we start to see that actually it can be quite hostile and unhelpful, and that rather than helping us to grow and become the best version of our self, it in fact has the effect of making us feeling beaten down, anxious and demotivated.

5. A more effective self-corrector is the compassionate rather than critical one. Like a compassionate teacher or sports coach, this helps to encourage us, pick us up when we are down, look to the future, and guide us, rather than criticising us and beating us down.

6. As in the 'two wolves' story, we don't need to fight our self-critic, but rather to turn our attention to growing our compassionate self-corrector instead.

7. We can bring our compassionate self to our self-critic to understand the fear that is behind it, to help it and to take charge so that the critic feels safe enough to 'stand down'. The compassionate self has the wisdom to hear the need behind the angry attack of the self-critic and is motivated to help in any way it can to meet that need and to

alleviate its suffering. It won't however take on board the words of the self-critic.

8.   Our journey from self-criticism to self-compassion follows a similar course in many people. As we begin the journey we still have a strong self-critic which can undermine us. If we can understand that these fears, blocks and resistances to developing the compassionate self are normal, to be expected, and just part of the journey, then we are far less likely to be derailed by them.

Appendix A: A twelve-week 'exercise programme' for developing our compassionate mind

It can be daunting being faced with a whole book, particularly when we are struggling. It is even harder when we have a new baby. What follows is an example of a step-by-step journey to take you through the key stages of developing and strengthening your compassionate mind.

Notes on the 'exercise program'

- It is important that this isn't embarked on as an alternative to reading Stage One of the book, because the exercises will not have the power or impact without the fundamental understanding, wisdom and acceptance that develops during Stage One. I would recommend that you combine the daily exercise programme with reading a little of Stage One each day if that is at all possible.

- Although the 'programme' is divided into twelve sessions, this is likely to be the minimum time that somebody could work through it. It has just been divided this way to provide some clarity and structure. There is no hurry or time limit for completion. We are our 'life's work'.

- I would suggest that once you come to the end of the programme you try additional exercises in Stage Two and Three of the book not included in the programme, and then cycle through the programme again as many times as you wish. Each time will be a slightly different journey.

- Before you start the programme, read or revisit the section on 'The journey to self-compassion: navigating the potholes and bumps in the road' (see page 325). This helps to remind us that the fears, blocks and resistances we will encounter are an inevitable and important part of the journey, rather than an indication that we are 'doing it wrong'.

- This is just a guide. We are all different and you might prefer to do this a different way. Just play around and discover what works best for you. Hold the programme as a loose guide rather than a prescription.

- Seek additional help if necessary. Reaching out to others is an important part of developing our compassionate mind.

- If some parts feel too difficult, return to exercises you feel more comfortable with. Keep revisiting exercises that are more challenging though, as these are likely to be the most valuable to you in the long run.

Week One

1. One-off experiment: 'Awareness of restless mind' (Chapter 13)

2. One-off experiment: 'Spotlight of attention' (Chapter 13)

3. 'The five stepping stones' (Chapter 14)

    - Spend about ten minutes on (1) and (2) just to see what you notice. Spend a few minutes on each step of (3), long enough to allow your body to settle. You may enjoy taking your time over this as you settle into the practice.

    - Set aside some time when not in midst of strong emotions (i.e. practise 'learning to swim' in shallow end of pool rather than diving into stormy seas).

    - Try when you feel reasonably alert to begin with rather than just before going to sleep, aiming for a state of stillness and calm rather than relaxation and sleep (although you may feel sleepy just because you have stopped 'doing').

- Practise daily, even if you don't feel like it; these are core practices that are used at the beginning of each exercise. With practice they become more automatic.

- Be aware of your critical voice blocking practice. Notice it, set it to one side, and practise anyway.

4. Soothing breathing rhythm (SBR) (Chapter 14)

- Straight after 'five stepping stones' spend five to ten minutes daily (or longer if you wish) just sitting with soothing breathing rhythm.

- If you cannot manage five minutes then aim for just one to three minutes per day. SBR is core to all the exercises and is a powerful stand-alone exercise in its own right. Sometimes it is easy, sometimes it is hard. Repeated practice is key. Extend the time for this if you can.

- Put in place reminders to practise daily (see Chapter 13).

Week Two

1. Mindfulness to breath, sounds, body (Chapter 13)

- Three separate ten-minute sessions per day (one for breath, one for sounds, one for body), or one after the other in one longer session.

2. Mindfulness 'on the go'

- Try carrying out everyday activities in a mindful way, e.g. cleaning your teeth, washing up, pushing the buggy, drinking coffee or feeding your baby.

- Choose one particular activity each day for a week or try repeatedly through the day with different activities.

- Use reminders, e.g. stickers, reminder on mobile phone, notes to self or wearing a particular bracelet or wrist band.

Week Three

1. Safe place (Chapter 15)

   - Allow this some time to develop, playing and experimenting with changing different aspects. You may want to allow a good twenty minutes initially.

   - Practise daily for about ten to fifteen minutes.

   - Hold the images 'loosely', allowing them to change if necessary. Eventually it may become more solid and stable, or you may develop several 'safe places' that you can then choose from.

2. Mindfulness to thoughts (Chapter 13)

   - Allow fifteen minutes or so initially to get the hang of identifying thoughts, noticing that we get caught in thoughts repeatedly, and that we need to return again and again to just observing them.

   - Then practise daily for ten minutes.

3. Mindfulness to thoughts 'on the go'

   - Practise just noticing thoughts throughout the day, perhaps labelling them as 'thinking', 'worrying', etc.

   - Set up reminders as prompts.

Week 4

1. Compassionate colour: flowing in/flowing out (Chapter 15)

   - Practise ten minutes 'flowing in', then five minutes 'flowing out'.

   - Practise daily.

2. Compassionate attention: gratitude journal (Chapter 16)

- Write down three things each day that you are grateful for.

- These need to be three new things that you haven't included on previous days.

Week 5

1. Compassionate self (Chapter 15)

- Twenty to thirty minutes for initial practice.

- It may be hard to access feelings initially. Instead focus on your intention/motivation/heartfelt wish.

- Practise focusing the compassionate self. Start with something that feels easy for you. This might be an animal, a pet, a plant or tree, someone you care about, or your baby when they are asleep, for example. Imagine sending out your most heartfelt wishes to the object of your focus.

- Practise daily for ten minutes or so.

2. Compassionate self 'On the go'

- Practise daily.

- Go about your daily activities while 'in' your compassionate self, e.g. walking around the house, pushing the baby in the buggy, putting on face cream or body lotion, checking on the sleeping baby or making a cup of coffee for yourself or someone else. Start with activities that feel easy.

- If this is initially hard to imagine, try carrying them out 'as if you are' or 'if you could be' a compassionate person. Try the 'method-acting approach'; imagine you are a method actor playing the part of a compassionate person in a film.

- Put in place reminders to bring your attention to this practice throughout the day.

Week 6

1. Compassionate image

   - Twenty to thirty minutes for the initial practice.

   - You may want to write down qualities that you want the image to have, e.g. how you know that they are wise, strong, with a motivation to care for you and help you, warm, kind and accepting. Are they male, female, genderless? What is their height, clothes, appearance? How does their voice sound if they speak? What is the expression on their face? How do they move? How do they relate to you?

   - Hold the image loosely, allowing it to change as necessary, and experiment with different aspects. Eventually, it may settle into a particular image. Sometimes it might change after a few weeks/months/years of practising according to your needs.

   - Don't worry about having a clear image; just the sense of it is enough.

   - Practise daily for ten minutes or so.

2. Compassionate image 'on the go'

   - Practise daily.

   - Imagine how the image might help you as you go through your day. Initially practise with things that feel relatively easy to you, e.g. minor dilemmas, where you need a little encouragement, when you feel slightly bored, or a little 'flat'.

   - Set reminders, e.g. pictures, words or postcards.

Week 7

1. Compassionate self (Chapter 15)

    - Begin each day with this for five to ten minutes. Imagine sending out heartfelt wishes exercise (e.g. *'may you be happy, may you be well, may you be free from suffering'*) to people who are 'easy', for example people you care about (even animals, plants, pets), then to neutral people, e.g. neighbours you don't really know, other people in other streets or towns, and then to the image of yourself sitting doing this practice.

2. Compassionate thinking (Chapter 17)

    - Twenty minutes or so for initial practice.

    - Practise first off with an issue you want to think about which is not too emotive.

    - Use the more complex form to start with.

    - Then practise daily using the simpler thought-balancing form.

Week 8

1. Compassionate self or compassionate image (Chapter 15)

    - Practise daily on waking if possible.

2. Formulation (Chapter 10)

    - This needs a chunk of time to complete, or take a few goes at it.

    - It doesn't have to be our whole 'life story', it can just be focused on a few key experiences each time. The aim is to learn the *process* of understanding our struggles in a way that is ultimately non-blaming or shaming; how we have best tried to protect ourselves over the years. These ways might have downsides but they are 'not our fault'.

- Read through with the warm voice tone and facial expression of the compassionate self or compassionate image.

- Allow the compassionate self or image to help you consider how you move forward towards the person you want to become, given the experiences we have had, and the difficult human mind we all possess.

- If you feel stirred up by the exercise, use soothing breathing rhythm/safe place to bring a sense of space around the 'stirred up' feelings. Spend some time on 'five stepping stones' (Chapter 14) to help steady yourself.

3. Compassionate letter writing (Chapter 17)

- This can be helpful to do soon after formulation if there is the opportunity.

- It needs twenty minutes or so, or as long as you wish.

- Write from the heart rather than the head.

- Re-read with a warm voice tone and facial expression.

- Amend as necessary.

- Continue with the same letter, or write a new one over a period of four days if possible.

Week 9

1. Compassionate self/image (Chapter 15)

- Practise daily for ten minutes, on waking if possible.

2. Bringing compassionate self to a struggling part of the self (Chapter 17)

- Pick an issue that is not too troubling to begin with, e.g. a minor anxiety, a minor frustration, feeling a little fed up or flat, or getting mildly irritated with the baby.

- Finish with soothing breathing rhythm / safe place.

- Practise daily.

Week 10

1. Compassionate self (Chapter 15)

   - Practise daily, at the start of day if possible.

   - Send out compassionate wishes to all in the house, then to easy, then neutral, then difficult people.

   - Finish with soothing breathing rhythm / safe place.

2. Working with the self-critic (Chapter 18)

   - Twenty to thirty minutes for this one-off exercise:

   - Imagine what we fear we might become if we didn't have our self-critic. It can help to write this down.

   - Then imagine the self-critic in front of you, noticing how they appear, speak, their voice tone, facial expression, feelings they direct to you, how they relate to you and what they say to you.

   - Notice how you feel in relation to it.

   - How helpful is it to you? Does it encourage you, support you, help you to become you at your best, take joy in your well-being?

   - Compare a critical self-corrector to a compassionate self-corrector (or critical teacher or coach versus compassionate teacher or coach). Which would you recommend to a child or a person you care about? Which do you intuitively feel would help you to grow and flourish?

- From the 'two wolves' story; we are just focusing on growing, or 'feeding' the aspects of ourselves that we want, rather than fighting with or trying to get rid of the aspects that we don't want. We are merely shifting attention and intention, and changing the focus of our effort.

3. Bringing compassion to self-critic (Chapter 18)

- Twenty to thirty minutes for initial exercise.

- Then ten minutes daily.

- Start and end with 'five stepping stones' and compassionate self.

- Bring in your compassionate image for support if necessary.

Week 11

1. Choose your own daily practice.

- Remember, often the harder exercises will prove to be the most helpful to you in the long run.

- Decide when and for how long to practise.

- Set reminders.

2. Diary of a day in the life of your future compassionate self.

- Pick a time period, e.g. one year, five years, ten years, thirty years from now.

- Write a diary entry as if written by your compassionate self going through their day.

- Consider how they relate to others, how they carry out

activities and their chosen occupation, how they relate to themselves.

- Consider what commitments you can make now to help you get closer to the self you would like to be, or, if you feel you are there now, what will help you to best maintain this? It can be helpful to write these down. This might be something relatively small, e.g. 'do soothing breathing rhythm for five breaths each day', or 'read that book', to something larger, e.g. 'take steps to do that training course', 'do the baby massage course', 'go to the parent and toddler group' or 'speak to my health visitor about . . .'

- Decide whether you would benefit from going through some of the other exercises in the book. If so, you might want to plan in when you will do them.

- Decide whether or not you would like to have another run through all, or part, of the 'exercise programme'. (Each 'run through' will be a different experience and will give different insights).

- You may want to try some time without doing any exercises, to experiment with the impact of practising or not practising, perhaps trying a week without, and then a week with formal sitting practices. If so, you might want to decide when you would like to begin the practices again and make some kind of commitment to begin again on that date.

Week 12

This is the first week without a prescribed outline.

- You might want to use your compassionate self or compassionate image to decide what will be most helpful to you during this week.

- You may decide you want to try with a plan or with no plan.

- You may want to 'off-road' and do something completely outside of the suggestions in this book to help develop and maintain your compassionate self.

- Or you may want to see what it is like not to think about it at all!

Hopefully, what you will be finding by now is just how worthwhile it is to develop your compassionate mind.

Appendix B: The four-part formulation

Background	Threat or fear	Safety strategy	Unintended consequences
Example: Critical mother.	I am not good enough. People are attacking.	Try to be perfect. Be quiet and nice to other.	Impossible to be, so always feel in danger of failure. High anxiety. Never get own needs met. Get 'walked over'. Feel angry and resentful.

Appendix C: Compassion-focused thought balancing

Trigger	Unhelpful/ destressing thoughts	Helpful/kind thoughts (try to create warm tone)

Notes

Chapter 1: 'All going well?' Understanding the influences upon our experience of having a baby

1. Rosenberg, K. and W. Trevathan (2002), 'Birth, obstetrics and human evolution', *BJOG: An International Journal of Obstetrics & Gynaecology*, 109(11): 1199–206.

2. Odent, M. (2004), 'Knitting midwives for drugless childbirth?' *Midwifery Today*, 71: 21–2.

3. Hodnett, E., S. Gates, G. Hofmeyr and C. Sakala (2013), 'Continuous support for women during childbirth', *Cochrane Database of Systematic Reviews*, in *The Cochrane Library* (9).

4. K. Robson and R. Kumar (1980), 'Delayed onset of maternal affection after childbirth', *The British Journal of Psychiatry*, 136(4): 347–53.

5. Wolke, D., S. Eryigit-Madzwamuse and T. Gutbrod (2013), 'Very preterm/very low birthweight infants' attachment: infant and maternal characteristics', *Archives of Disease in Childhood: Fetal and Neonatal Edition*, (online, available at: http://dx.doi.org/10.1136/archdischild-2013-303788).

6. Blaffer Hrdy, S. (1999), *Mother Nature*, 1st edn, New York: Pantheon Books.

7. Blaffer Hrdy, S. (2009), *Mothers and Others*, 1st edn, Cambridge, MA: Belknap Press of Harvard University Press.

8. Cant, M. A. and R. A. Johnstone (2008), 'Reproductive conflict and the separation of reproductive generations in humans', *Proceedings of*

the National Academy of Sciences of the United States of America, 105(14): 5332–6.

Chapter 2: 'Where is the joy?' Understanding how I feel after having a baby

1. Beck, C. T. (2001), 'Predictors of postpartum depression: an update', *Nurs Research*, Sept./Oct., 50(5): 275–85.

2. Dennis, C. L. (2005), 'Psychosocial and psychological interventions for prevention of postnatal depression: systematic review', *British Medical Journal*, 2 July, 331 (7507): 15.

3. Gilbert, P. (2006), 'Evolution and depression: issues and implications', *Psychological Medicine*, 36(3): 287–97.

Chapter 3: 'I struggle to feel love for my baby': Our mixed emotions and how we try to manage them

1. Laurent, H. and J. Ablow (2012), 'A cry in the dark: depressed mothers show reduced neural activation to their own infant's cry', *Social Cognitive and Affective Neuroscience*, 7(2): 125–34.

2. Lee, D. and S. James (2012), *The Compassionate Mind Approach to Recovering from Trauma*, 1st edn, London: Robinson.

3. Levendosky, A., G. Bogat and A. Huth-Bocks (2011), 'The influence of domestic violence on the development of the attachment relationship between mother and young child', *Psychoanalytic Psychology*, 28(4): 512–27.

4. Shebloski, B., K. J. Conger and K. Widaman (2005), 'Reciprocal links among differential parenting, perceived partiality, and self-worth: a

three-wave longitudinal study', *Journal of Family Psychology; Special Issue: Sibling Relationship Contributions to Individual and Family Well-Being*, 19: 633–42.

5.   Parker, R. (1995), *Torn in Two: Maternal Ambivalence*, 1st edn, London: Virago Press.

6.   Raphael-Leff, J., 'Healthy Maternal Ambivalence', www.mamsie.bbk. ac.uk/documents/raphael-leff.pdf (MaMSIE is a website created by members of Birkbeck, University of London for discussions about motherhood and 'the maternal').

7.   Raphael-Leff, J. (1986), 'Facilitators and regulators: conscious and unconscious processes in pregnancy and early motherhood', *British Journal of Medical Psychology*, 59: 43–55.

Chapter 4: Understanding postnatal depression

1.   Gotlib, I., V. Whiffen, J. Mount, K. Milne and N. Cordy (1989), 'Prevalence rates and demographic characteristics associated with depression in pregnancy and the postpartum', *Journal of Consulting and Clinical Psychology*, 57(2): 269.

2.   Josefsson, A., G. Berg, C. Nordin and G. Sydsjö (2001), 'Prevalence of depressive symptoms in late pregnancy and postpartum', *Acta obstetricia et gynecologica Scandinavica*, 80(3): 251–5.

3.   Kendall, R. E., J. C. Chalmers and C. Platz (1987), 'Epidemiology of puerperal psychoses', *British Journal of Psychiatry*, 150: 662–73.

4.   Blaffer Hrdy, S. (2009), *Mothers and Others*, 1st edn, Cambridge, MA: Belknap Press of Harvard University Press.

Chapter 5: How we are shaped: the foundations of the compassionate mind approach

1. Gilbert, P. (2009), *The Compassionate Mind: A New Approach to Life's Challenges*, London: Constable (the original book detailing Professor Paul Gilbert's compassionate mind approach).

Chapter 6: Our brain: A mix of old and new

1. Wilson, D. (2007), *Evolution for Everyone*, 1st edn, New York: Delacorte.

2. Porges, S. (2011), *The Polyvagal Theory*, 1st edn, New York: W. W. Norton Press.

3. Doidge, N. (2007), *The Brain that Changes Itself*, 1st edn, New York: Viking, p. 427.

4. Siegel, D. (2014), *Brainstorm: The Power and Purpose of the Teenage Brain*, 1st edn, Brunswick: Scribe Publications.

5. Soon, Chun Siong, Marcel Brass, Hans-Jochen Heinze and John-Dylan Haynes (2008), 'Unconscious determinants of free decisions in the human brain', *Nature Neuroscience* 11(5): 543–5.

6. Kabat-Zinn, J. (1994), *Wherever You Go, There You Are*, 1st edn, New York: Hyperion, p. 4.

7. Davidson, R., J. Kabat-Zinn, J. Schumacher, M. Rosenkranz, D. Muller, S. Santorelli, F. Urbanowski, A. Harrington, K. Bonus and J. Sheridan (2003), 'Alterations in brain and immune function produced by mindfulness meditation', *Psychosomatic Medicine*, 65(4): 564–70.

8. Davis, D. and J. Hayes (2011), 'What are the benefits of mindfulness? A practice review of psychotherapy-related research', *Psychotherapy*, 48(2): 198.

9. Gilbert, P. and G. Choden (2013), *Mindful Compassion*, 1st edn, London: Robinson.

10. Zilcha-Mano, S. (2014), 'The effects of mindfulness-based interventions during pregnancy on birth outcomes and the mother's physical and mental health: integrating Western and Eastern perspectives', in A. Le, C. Ngnoumen and E. Langer (2014), *The Wiley Blackwell Handbook of Mindfulness*, 1st edn, Hoboken: Wiley, pp. 881–97.

Chapter 7: Understanding our emotion systems

1. Gilbert, P. (2009), *The Compassionate Mind: A New Approach to Life's Challenges*, London: Constable.

2. Bracha, H. S., T. C. Ralston, J. M. Matsukawa and A. E. Williams (2004), 'Does "fight or flight" need updating?' *Psychosomatics*, Sept.–Oct., 45(5): 448–9.

3. Lieberman, M., N. Eisenberger, M. Crockett, S. Tom, J. Pfeifer and B. Way (2007), 'Putting feelings into words: affect labeling disrupts amygdala activity in response to affective stimuli', *Psychological Science*, 18(5): 421–8.

4. Depue, R. A. and J. V. Morrone-Strupinsky (2005), 'A neurobehavioral model of affiliative bonding', *Behavioral and Brain Sciences*, 28: 313–95.

5. Porges, S. (2011), *The Polyvagal Theory*, 1st edn, New York: W. W. Norton Press.

6. Bowlby, J. (1988), *A Secure Base: Parent–Child Attachment and Healthy Human Development*, 1st edn, New York: Basic Books.

Chapter 8: How the threat, drive and soothing systems change in response to pregnancy and new motherhood

1. Glynn, L. and C. Sandman (2011), 'Prenatal origins of neurological development: a critical period for fetus and mother', *Current Directions in Psychological Science*, 20(6): 384–9.

2. Pearson, R., S. Lightman and J. Evans (2009), 'Emotional sensitivity for motherhood: late pregnancy is associated with enhanced accuracy to encode emotional faces', *Hormones and Behavior*, 56(5): 557–63.

3. Entringer, S., C. Buss, E. A. Shirtcliff, A. L. Cammack, I. S. Yim, A. Chicz-DeMet, C. A. Sandman and P. D. Wadhwa (2010), 'Attenuation of maternal psychophysiological stress responses and the maternal cortisol awakening response over the course of human pregnancy', *Stress*, 13: 258–68.

4. Matthews, K. A. and J. Rodinn (1992), 'Pregnancy alters blood pressure responses to psychological and physical challenge', *Psychophysiology*, 29: 232–40.

5. Glynn, L. M., C. Dunkel Schetter, P. D. Wadhwa and C. A. Sandman (2004), 'Pregnancy affects appraisal of negative life events', *Journal of Psychosomatic Research*, 56(1), 47–52.

6. Glynn, L. M., P. D. Wadhwa, C. Dunkel-Schetter, A. Chicz-Demet and C. A. Sandman (2001), 'When stress happens matters: effects of earthquake timing on stress responsivity in pregnancy', *American Journal of Obstetrics and Gynecology*, 184: 637–42.

7. Bublitz, M. H. and L. R. Stroud (2012), 'Childhood sexual abuse is associated with cortisol awakening response over pregnancy: preliminary findings', *Psychoneuroendocrinology*, Sept., 37(9): 1425–30.

8. Kendall-Tackett, K. (2007), 'A new paradigm for depression in new mothers: the central role of inflammation and how breastfeeding

and anti-inflammatory treatments protect maternal mental health', *International Breastfeeding Journal*, 2(6): 1746–4358.

9. Fredrickson, B., K. Grewen, K. Coffey, S. Algoe, A. Firestine, J. Arevalo, J. Ma and S. Cole (2013), 'A functional genomic perspective on human well-being', *Proceedings of the National Academy of Sciences*, 110(33): 13684–9.

10. Kim, P., J. F. Leckman, L. C. Mayes, R. Feldman, X. Wang and J. E. Swain (2010), 'The plasticity of human maternal brain: longitudinal changes in brain anatomy during the early postpartum period', *Behavioral Neuroscience*, 124: 695–700.

11. Dipietro, J., R. Irizarry, K. Costigan and Gurewitsch, E. (2004), 'The psychophysiology of the maternal–fetal relationship', *Psychophysiology*, 41(4): 510–20.

12. Kohl, J. V. and R. T. Francoeur (2002), *The Scent of Eros: Mysteries of Odor in Human Sexuality*, iUniverse Press.

13. Blaffer Hrdy, S. (2009), *Mothers and Others*, 1st edn, Cambridge, MA: Belknap Press of Harvard University Press.

14. Feldman R., A. Weller, O. Zagoory-Sharon and A. Levine (2007), 'Evidence for a neuroendocrinological foundation of human affiliation: plasma oxytocin levels across pregnancy and the postpartum period predict mother–infant bonding', *Psychological Science*, Nov., 18(11): 965–70.

15. L. Strathearn, U. Iyengar, P. Fonagy and S. Kim (2012), 'Maternal oxytocin response during mother–infant interaction: associations with adult temperament', *Hormones and Behavior*, 61(3): 429–35.

16. Shamay-Tsoory, S. G., M. Fischer, J. Dvash, H. Harari, N. Perach-Bloom and Y. Levkovitz (2009), 'Intranasal administration of oxytocin increases envy and *schadenfreude* (gloating)', *Biological Psychiatry*, 66: 864–70.

17. De Dreu, C., L. Greer, M. Handgraaf, S. Shalvi, G. Van Kleef, M. Baas, F. Ten Velden, E. Van Dijk and S. Feith (2010), 'The neuropeptide

oxytocin regulates parochial altruism in intergroup conflict among humans', *Science*, 328(5984): 1408–11.

18. Bartz, J. A., J. Zaki, K. N. Ochsner, N. Bolger, A. Kolevzon, N. Ludwig and J. E. Lydon (2010), 'Effects of oxytocin on recollections of maternal care and closeness', *Proceedings of the National Academy of Sciences*, 107: 21371–5.

19. Bartz, J., D. Simeon, H. Hamilton, S. Kim, S. Crystal, A. Braun, V. Vicens and E. Hollander (2010), 'Oxytocin can hinder trust and cooperation in borderline personality disorder', *Social Cognitive and Affective Neuroscience*, Oct., 6(5): 556–63.

20. Rockliff, H., A. Karl, K. McEwan, J. Gilbert, M. Matos and P. Gilbert (2011), 'Effects of intranasal oxytocin on "compassion focused imagery"', *Emotion*, 11(6): 1388–96.

21. Larsen, C. M. and D. R. Grattan (2012), 'Prolactin, neurogenesis, and maternal behaviors', *Brain, Behavior, and Immunity*, 26(2): 201–9.

22. Gerlo, S., J. R. E. Davis, D. L. Mager and R. Kooijman (2006), 'Prolactin in man: a tale of two promoters', *BioEssays*, 28(10): 1051–5.

23. Hsu, D., B. Sanford, K. Meyers, T. Love, K. Hazlett, H. Wang, L. Ni, S. Walker, B. Mickey, S. Korycinski, et al. (2013), 'Response of the μ-opioid system to social rejection and acceptance', *Molecular Psychiatry*, 18(11): 1211–17.

Chapter 9: Understanding shame

1. Rochat, P. (2003), 'Five levels of self-awareness as they unfold early in life', *Consciousness and Cognition*, 12(4): 717–31.

2. Trevarthen, C. and V. Reddy (2007), 'Consciousness in infants', page 50 in *The Blackwell Companion to Consciousness*, ed. M. Velmans and S. Schneider, Oxford: Blackwell.

3. Gonsalkorale, K. and K. Williams (2007), 'The KKK won't let me play: ostracism even by a despised outgroup hurts', *European Journal of Social Psychology*, 37(6): 1176–86.

4. Wesselmann, E. D., F. D. Cardoso, S. Slater and K. D. Williams (2012), '"To be looked at as though air": civil attention matters', *Psychological Science*, 23: 166–8.

5. Williams, K. D. (2009), 'Ostracism: effects of being excluded and ignored', in *Advances in Experimental Social Psychology*, ed. M. Zanna, New York, Academic Press, pp. 275–314.

6. Ahmed, S. (2004), *The Cultural Politics of Emotion*, Edinburgh: Edinburgh University Press.

7. Stadlen, N. (2004), *What Mothers Do: Especially When it Looks Like Nothing*, London: Little, Brown Book Group.

Chapter 11: 'How am I feeling, how are you feeling baby?' Understanding the minds of ourselves and others

1. Liotti, G. and P. Gilbert (2011), 'Mentalizing, motivation, and social mentalities: theoretical considerations and implications for psychotherapy', *Psychology and Psychotherapy: Theory, Research and Practice*, 84(1): 9–25.

2. Main, M. and E. Hesse (1990), 'Parents' unresolved traumatic experiences are related to infant disorganized attachment status: is frightened/frightening parental behavior the linking mechanism?', in M. T. Greenberg, D. Cicchetti and E. M. Cummings (eds), *Attachment in the Preschool Years: Theory, Research, and Intervention*, Chicago, IL: University of Chicago Press, pp. 161–82.

Chapter 12: The nature of compassion: What makes up a 'compassionate mind'?

1. Gilbert, P. (1989), *Human Nature and Suffering*, London and New York: Psychology Press/Guilford Press.

2. Sussman, R. and C. Cloninger (2011), *Origins of Altruism and Cooperation*, 1st edn, New York: Springer.

3. Cacioppo, J. and W. Patrick (2009), *Loneliness: Human Nature and the Need for Social Connection*, 1st edn, New York: W. W. Norton & Company.

4. Hamilton, D. R. (2010), *Why Kindness is Good for You*, London: Hay House.

Chapter 13: Preparing the compassionate mind: Mindful awareness

1. John Bowlby, *A Secure Base: Clinical Applications of Attachment Theory*, London: Routledge, 1988, p. 154.

2. Ericsson, K. A. (2006), 'The influence of experience and deliberate practice on the development of superior expert performance', in K. A. Ericsson, N. Charness, P. Feltovich and R. R. Hoffman (eds), *Cambridge Handbook of Expertise and Expert Performance*, Cambridge, UK: Cambridge University Press, pp. 685–706.

3. Hölzel, B., J. Carmody, M. Vangel, C. Congleton, S. Yerramsetti, T. Gard and S. Lazar (2011), 'Mindfulness practice leads to increases in regional brain gray matter density', *Psychiatry Research: Neuroimaging*, 30 Jan., 191(1): 36–43.

4. Germer, C. (2009), *The Mindful Path to Self-Compassion: Freeing Yourself from Destructive Thoughts and Emotions*, New York: Guilford Press.

5. Williams, M., J. Teasdale, Z. Segal and J. Kabat-Zinn (2007), *The Mindful Way through Depression: Freeing Yourself from Chronic Unhappiness*, 1st edn, New York: Guilford Press.

6. Kabat-Zinn, J. (1990), *Full Catastrophe Living: Using the Wisdom of Your Body and Mind to Face Stress, Pain, and Illness*, New York: Delta.

7. Teasdale, J. K., A. V. Segal, J. M. G. Williams, V. Ridgeway, J. Soulsby and M. Lau (2000), 'Prevention of relapse/recurrence in major depression by mindfulness-based cognitive therapy', *Journal of Consulting and Clinical Psychology*, 68: 615–23.

8. Van Aalderen, J., A. Donders, F. Giommi, P. Spinhoven, H. Barendregt and A. Speckens (2012), 'The efficacy of mindfulness-based cognitive therapy in recurrent depressed patients with and without a current depressive episode: a randomized controlled trial', *Psychological Medicine*, 42(5): 989–1001.

9. Kabat-Zinn, J. (1994), *Wherever You Go, There You Are*, 1st edn, New York: Hyperion, p. 4.

10. Williams, M., J. Teasdale, Z. Segal and J. Kabat-Zinn (2007), *The Mindful Way through Depression: Freeing Yourself from Chronic Unhappiness*, 1st edn, New York: Guilford Press.

Chapter 14: Preparing the compassionate mind: Activating the soothing system

1. Porges, S. (2004), 'The polyvagal theory: phylogenetic substrates of a social nervous system', *International Journal of Psychophysiology*, 42: 123–46.

2. Carney, D., A. Cuddy and A. Yap (2010), 'Power posing brief nonverbal displays affect neuroendocrine levels and risk tolerance', *Psychological Science*, 21(10): 1363–8.

3. Peper, E. and I. Lin (2012), 'Increase or decrease depression: how body postures influence your energy level', *Biofeedback*, 40(3): 125–30.

4. Gilbert, P. (2009), *The Compassionate Mind: A New Approach to Life's Challenges*, London: Constable.

5. Brown, R. and P. Gerbarg (2012), *The Healing Power of the Breath: Simple Techniques to Reduce Stress and Anxiety, Enhance Concentration, and Balance Your Emotions*, Boston and London: Shambala.

6. Kraft, T. and S. Pressman (2012), 'Grin and Bear It: The Influence of Manipulated Facial Expression on the Stress Response', *Psychological Science*, 23(11): 1372–8.

Chapter 16: Strengthening the compassionate mind: Using compassionate attention and behaviour

1. Emmons, R. (2007), *Thanks! How the New Science of Gratitude Can Make You Happier*, Boston, MA: Houghton.

2. Hanson, R. (2013), *Hardwiring Happiness: The Practical Science of Reshaping your Brain-and your Life*, Rider.

3. Kirschner S. and M. Tomasello (2010), 'Joint music making promotes prosocial behavior in 4-year-old children', *Evolution and Human Behavior*, 31: 354–64.

4. Anshel, A. and D. A. Kipper (1988), 'The influence of group singing on trust and cooperation', *Journal of Music Therapy*, 25: 145–55.

Chapter 17: Using compassionate thinking, letter writing and imagery to help with our struggles

1. Gilbert, P. (2007), *Counselling and Psychotherapy for Depression*: London: Sage.

2. Pennebaker, J. W. (2004), *Writing to Heal: A Guided Journal for Recovering from Trauma & Emotional Upheaval*. Oakland, CA: New Harbinger.

Chapter 18: The journey from self-criticism to self-compassion

1. Rosenberg, M. (2003), *Nonviolent Communication: A Language of Life*, Encinitas, CA: Puddle Dancer Press.

2. Tierney, S. and J. Fox (2010), 'Living with the "anorexic voice": a thematic analysis', *Psychology and Psychotherapy: Theory, Research and Practice*, 83: 243–54.

3. Lawrence, V. and D. Lee (2013), 'An exploration of people's experiences of compassion-focused therapy for trauma, using interpretative phenomenological analysis', *Clinical Psychology and Psychotherapy*; published online in Wiley Online Library (wileyonlinelibrary.com), DOI: 10.1002/cpp.1854.

4. Longe, O., F. A. Maratos, P. Gilbert, G. Evans, F. Volker, H. Rockliff and G. Rippon (2010), 'Having a word with yourself: neural correlates of self-criticism and self-reassurance', *NeuroImage*, 49: 1849–56.

Useful resources

Books

Compassion

Germer, C.K. (2009), *The Mindful Path to Self-Compassion: Freeing Yourself From Destructive Thoughts and Emotions*, New York and London: Guilford Press.

Gilbert, P. (2010), *The Compassionate Mind*, San Francisco: Constable and Robinson.

Gilbert, P. and G. Choden (2013), *Mindful Compassion*, London. Robinson.

Hanson, R. (2013), *Hardwiring Happiness: The Practical Science of Reshaping your Brain and your Life*, London: Rider.

Depression

Williams, M., J. Teasdale, Z. Segal and J. Kabat-Zinn (2007), *The Mindful Way Through Depression: Freeing Yourself from Chronic Unhappiness*, New York and London: Guilford Press.

Intrusive thoughts

Kleiman, K. and A. Wenzel (2011), *Dropping the Baby and Other Scary Thoughts: Breaking the Cycle of Unwanted Thoughts in Motherhood*, London: Routledge.

Lee Baer, L. (2002), *The Imp of the Mind: Exploring the Silent Epidemic of Obsessive Bad Thoughts*, New York: Plume.

Parenting

Gerhardt, S. (2007), *Why Love Matters: How Affection Shapes a Baby's Brain*, London: Routledge.

Stadlen, N. (2005), *What Mothers Do: Especially When It Looks Like Nothing*, London: Little, Brown.

Sunderland, M. (2007), *What Every Parent Needs to Know: The Incredible Effects of Love, Nurture and Play on Your Child's Development*, London: Dorling Kindersley.

Trauma

Lee, D. (2012), *The Compassionate Mind Approach to Recovering from Trauma: Using Compassion Focused Therapy*, London: Robinson.

Using the breath

Brown, R.P. and P. Gerbarg (2012), *The Healing Power of the Breath: Simple Techniques to Reduce Stress and Anxiety, Enhance Concentration, and Balance Your Emotions*, London and Boston, MA: Shambala.

Websites

Compassion

Compassionate Mind Foundation UK
www.compassionatemind.co.uk/
Information and videos about compassion-focused therapy and the science of compassion; links to other websites on compassion.

Compassionate Mind Foundation (USA)
www.mindfulcompassion.com
Run by Dr Dennis Tirch. It includes information and various downloads that can be used for guided practice and meditation.

The Center for Compassion and Altruism Research and Education (CCARE)
www.ccare.stanford.edu
Lectures and videos on many aspects of compassion.

Mindful Self-Compassion
www.mindfulselfcompassion.org
Run by Christopher Germer. It includes various downloads that can be used for meditation.

Self-Compassion
www.self-compassion.org
Run by Dr Kristin Neff. It includes research, measures and downloads that can be used for meditation.

Bereavement

Cruse Bereavement Care
http://www.cruse.org.uk
Helpline 020 7436 5881
Support for when someone dies. Also offers support to children, face-to-face support, and local support groups.

SANDS
https://www.uk-sands.org/
Stillbirth and neonatal death charity, help for anyone affected by the death of a baby. Offers information, telephone support, email support, local support groups, online forum.

Postnatal Mental Illness

Association for Postnatal Illness (APNI),
http://apni.org.uk
Helpline: 10.00am and 2.00pm on 0207 386 0868
Information, support.

Action on Postpartum Psychosis
http://www.app-network.org/
Telephone 020 3322 9900
APP is a network of people who have been affected by Postpartum Psychosis (also called puerperal psychosis, postnatal psychosis, postnatal bipolar disorder); online support forum (https://healthunlocked.com/app-network), information, one-to-one email support.

Netmums
www.netmums.com
www.netmums.com/parenting-support/drop-in-clinic, Monday to Friday: 9am–12 noon and 7.30pm–9.30pm; Saturday and Sunday: 7.30pm–9.30pm

Variety of parenting topics, online 'drop-in clinic'. Staffed by parent supporters, round-the-clock online support forum, information, online postnatal depression course.

PANDAS Pre and postnatal Depression Advice and Support
http://www.pandasfoundation.org.uk/
Helpline: 0843 28 98 401, 9am to 8pm, Mon. to Sun.
Information, support groups.

Royal Society of Psychiatrists
http://www.rcpsych.ac.uk/expertadvice.aspx
Information on mental health.

Samaritans
http://www.samaritans.org
Telephone 08457 90 90 90
'Samaritans provides confidential non-judgemental emotional support, twenty-four hours a day, every day for people who are experiencing feelings of distress or despair, including those which could lead to suicide.'

Parenting support

Cry-sis
www.cry-sis.org.uk
Helpline 08451 228 669, 9am to 10pm, seven days a week
Offers support for families with excessively crying, sleepless and demanding babies.

La Leche League
www.laleche.org.uk
Breast-feeding Helpline: 0845 120 2918
Support for women who wish to breast-feed their baby. Information, local support groups, online requests.

Mumsnet

www.mumsnet.com,

Variety of parenting topics, information, local groups, online support forum.

NCT

www.nct.org.uk

Helpline: The National Childbirth Trust Postnatal Line – 0300 330 0700

Antenatal and postnatal courses, local support, information.

Netmums

www.netmums.com

www.netmums.com/parenting-support/drop-in-clinic, Monday to Friday: 9am–12 noon and 7.30pm–9.30pm; Saturday and Sunday: 7.30pm–9.30pm

Variety of parenting topics, online 'drop-in clinic'. Staffed by parent supporters, round-the-clock online support forum, information, online postnatal depression course.

Acknowledgements

First, I would like to thank all the clients that I have worked with over the years who have shared their experiences, their wisdom and part of their life's journey with me. This book has been created from their stories and from what we have learned together.

I would like to thank Professor Paul Gilbert, for the compassionate mind model. This feels like a genuine gift to the world. Also, for his immense generosity of both time and sharing of knowledge as he taught me, supervised me, and painstakingly went through this book with me. And finally, for his compassion and support at a personal level.

I would also like to thank those in, and connected to, the Compassionate Mind Foundation and Community, a wonderfully warm, supportive and thought-provoking group of people. These include Mary Welford, Russell Kolts, Chris Irons, Deborah Lee, Jean Gilbert, Hannah Gilbert, Kate Lucre, Fiona Ashworth, Choden, Ken Goss, Ian Lowens, Neil Clapton, Tobyn Bell and Dennis Tirch.

My knowledge of the compassionate mind approach has been shaped and deepened by so many people. These include the Perinatal Mental Health Team in Derby, particularly Kim Sladen, who has worked with such wisdom and compassion alongside me as we run the compassionate mind groups for women referred to our service. These also include Wendy Wood, who runs and supervises on the Post Graduate Certificate in Compassion-Focused Therapy at Derby University, and Andrew Raynor, who supervises with me on this course.

An important part of my journey has been in taking this model out beyond the therapy world. This process has been deeply rewarding and has helped me to try to understand and convey the real essence of this model to those who haven't been trained as therapists. My thanks in this endeavour go to many people including Liz Andrews when she worked with me and Paul to include a compassionate mind module on the parenting support website Netmums, to La Leche League Great Britain, who in fact helped bring this book into existence when they asked for such a book a number of years ago, to Jane Elliott, Professor Steve Trenchard, and the staff at the Derbyshire Healthcare Foundation Trust for their support and involvement in the compassionate mind twelve-week course for staff. Thanks also go to the family nurses and staff at the Family Nurse Partnership, particularly Ann Rowe, Ruth Rothman, Mary Clarke and all those at Ripplez, the family-nurse team in Derby. These are truly inspirational and compassionate people who have worked tirelessly with such warmth and encouragement to bring the compassionate mind model to as many family nurses and young first-time mothers in the United Kingdom as possible.

My thanks also go to those who have supported me at a personal level on this journey into compassionate minds, including Mia Scotland, Sam Buckley, and all those in my book group.

I wish also to thank my children, who lost their mother to this book on many occasions, but I hope got a slightly better one back in the end.

Lastly, I must thank my family for all their encouragement and support, particularly my husband Neil, who has put so much thought and time into helping me with this book and looking after our children while I disappear, but who, most of all, has been such a steadfast and loving presence.

Index

abandonment 35–6, 138, 187
absent other, the 157
abuse *see* childhood abuse
achievement 102, 155
adaptability 200
adrenalin 9–10
affiliation xxxi, 104, 105, 123–31, 201, 247,
    248–9, 264, 274, 285, 301, 318, 324–5
aggression 130, 188
aloneness 324, 325
    see also loneliness
amygdala 98, 161, 168, 330
anger 43, 48, 83–4, 94, 96, 117, 128, 129,
    153, 181, 285–6, 298
    angry self 110–11, 113, 301–3
    baby's feelings of 97–9
    and compassion 199
    and compassionate motivation 207
    directing attention away from 264–5
    engagement with 186, 188–9
    feeling towards your baby 40–2
    internal 149
    keeping in check with self-criticism
        323
    and neuroplasticity 205
    as protective emotion 302–3
    regarding birth 184
    rumination on 87
    as scary emotion 163–4
    see also rage
anorexia nervosa 324
anxiety 19–21, 45, 48, 83–4, 94, 96, 102,
    120, 127–8, 163, 171, 188, 285–6
    anxious self 110–11, **112**, 113, 301
    baby's feelings of 97–9
    combined with depression 25, 51
    and neuroplasticity 205
    regarding birth 183–4
    rumination on 87
appetite loss 51
'as if', acting 197, 241, 339
Asperger's syndrome 166
assertiveness 303, 324
attachment 106, 123–31
    disorganized 12, 170–1, 172
    insecure 126–8, 166
    secure 126, 166
attachment figures, abusive 170, 172
attention *see* compassionate attention

authority 259, 300, 309
autism 166
awareness *see* mindful awareness

babies
    abandonment 35–6
    accepting the emotions of 165–6
    being scared to love 42–3
    bringing compassion to 268–72,
        298–9, 303–8
    characteristics 11–13
    compassionate letter writing to 298–9
    creating a 'safe place' for 253–4
    disliking your baby 37–40
    drive system of 103, 108
    early days with 14–18
    effects of postnatal depression on
        how you feel about your baby 53–4
    as the enemy 128
    'falling in love' with your baby 30, 100
    feeling concern over what other
        people think about your baby 155,
        164, 291–3
    feeling overwhelmed by your baby
        34–7
    feeling rejected by your baby 136–7,
        156
    feeling resentment towards your baby
        40–2
    feelings of disgust of 97–9
    harming 52, 56
    indifference to 9
    needy 15–16
    paying compassionate attention to
        268–9
    powerlessness and vulnerability 41–2
    proximity to 306
    scent of 27, 123–4
    and the six attributes of compassion
        185, 186–91
    and the six skills of compassion 191–5
    smiling 43–5
    soothing 105
    soothing systems of 107–8
    struggling with the emotions of 174
    struggling to feel love for 27–46
    and synchrony 274
    taking babies away from mothers
        52–3

threat system of 97–99, 103, 108
Through the eyes of my baby
(exercise) 274–5
understanding the influences of our
life experiences on having a baby
3–18
see also crying babies; mother-baby
bonding
'baby blues' 23, 50
Baer, Lee 56
balance
emotional balance 114–16, **114**, 223
thought balancing 287–90, 349
behaviour *see* compassionate behaviour
'better safe than sorry' strategies 80,
95–6, 136, 150, 153, 154, 158, 169
bipolar disorder 48, 49
birth 6–9, 45, 258
difficult/traumatic 9, 19, 34, 37, 184,
273–4
fear of 8–9, 183–4, 185
recovering from 14–15
and your feelings 19–26
see also post-birth experience
birth canal 6
birthing partners, male 7, 8
birthing positions 8
Blaffer-Hrdy, Sarah 14, 16, 54, 124
blame xxviii, xxx, 18, 40, 62–3, 65, 150,
285, 323
bodily sensations, impact of emotions on
110, **112**
body
bringing compassion to 229–30
bringing gratitude to 229–30
mind-body link 3
mindfulness of 227–8
settling 223
body memory 129, 157, 227
body posture 237, 238–41, 278, 301–3, 319
body shape 4–5
bonding *see* mother-baby bonding
borderline personality disorder 126
boredom 101, 102, 103
Bowlby, John 106, 205
brain 197, 258
amygdala 98, 161, 168, 330
changes during pregnancy and after
birth 117–31
changing your 205–6
evolution of the xxviii, 19–20, 25–6,
31, 34–5, 54–5, 59–63, 66, 67–70, 135,
144, 164, 200–1, 206–7, 292
and fear of rejection 135–7
frontal parts 171
limbic system 68, **78**
neocortex 72

neuroplasticity 73, 205, 208–10
old brain–new brain interactions
74–7, **76**, **86**, 87, 89–90, 218
prefrontal cortex 72–4, 90
reptilian 67, 68, 75–7, 89–90
and shame 133
thought balancing exercises for 288–9
breast milk 9–10, 15–16, 272
'coming in' 23
breast-feeding 15–16
difficulties 184
and medication 51
and oxytocin 124–5
and pheromones 124
positive effect on postnatal
depression 30
and stress 120
breathing 257, 300–3
activating the soothing system
through 237, 241–4
coherent breathing 243
Mindfulness to the breath (exercise)
224, 225, 244
shallow 242
soothing breathing rhythm (SBR) 121,
199, 241–4, 252, 254, 255, 257, 261,
262, 272, 277, 278, 287, 288–9, 291,
294, 300, 301, 307, 337
Brown, Richard P. 243
Buddhism 180, 202, 213, 317
bullying 319

calmness 70–1, 106
care-giving system 71, 107, 140, 197, 203,
219
care-receiving system 71, 197, 219
cartwheel diagrams 111, **112**
CFT *see* compassion-focused therapy
change 4–5, 117–31, 205–6, 258
child carers 157
childhood abuse 34, 97, 118, 120
'Chinese man' analogy 231
closeness 70–1
cocaine 130
colicky babies 31–2, 195
colostrum 23
colour, compassionate 254–6, 338
compassion xxviii–xxix, 45–6, 62–3, 65
basis for 87
benefits of 200–1
bringing to babies 268–72, 298–9,
303–8
bringing to the body 229–30
building our capacity for 249–63
creating patterns of compassion
within ourselves 196–8
for the 'dark side' 179–83

definition 177–8, 201–2
growing 207–9
ladder of 305–6
and mindfulness 85–8, **86**, 219
six attributes of 182, **182**, 183–91,
  195–6, 202, 248
six skills of 182, **182**, 183, 184, 191–6,
  202–3, 248, 288–9
three flows of 250
see also self-compassion
compassion face-lift 198
compassion-focused therapy (CFT) 43
compassionate attention 113, **182**, 185–6,
  191–2, 202, 218–20, 252–3, 264–76, 292
  to the breath 224
  and compassionate letter writing 297
  directing 220–5, 264–6, 281–2
  exercises for 266–76
  impact of emotions on 111, **112**
  paying attention to attention 81–4
  secure 106
  shifting the focus of 222
  turning inwards 162, 216
  to what we have done all day 275–6
  without judgement 244
compassionate behaviour 193–4, 203,
  276–82, 293
  and compassionate letter writing 297
  in the long term 277, 281
  in the present moment 277–9
  in the short term 277, 279–80
compassionate colour 254–6, 338
compassionate desensitisation 305–6
compassionate feelings 195–6, 203
compassionate imagery 192–3, 202, 248–
  63, 279, 293, 296, 299–309, 338, 340, 342
  impact of emotions on 111, **112**
  'on the go' 340
compassionate letter writing 294–9, 309,
  342
compassionate mind approach
  application to struggles 283–333,
    341–2
  compassionate imagery 299–309
  compassionate letter writing 294–9,
    309
  compassionate thinking 287–93, 308–9
  foundations 59–66
  from self-criticism to self-compassion
    310–33
  regular practice 281
compassionate mind development xxxi,
  175–282
  activating the soothing system 237–47
  compassionate attention and
    behaviour 264–82
  compassionate imagery 248–63

five stepping stones to 209, 237–47,
  255, 257, 266, 336–7, 342, 344
preparing the compassionate mind
  205–36, 237–47
strengthening the compassionate
  mind 248–63, 264–82
what makes up the compassionate
  mind? 177–204
see also body posture; facial
  expression, warm; mindfulness;
  soothing breathing rhythm; voice,
  warm
compassionate motivation 206–9, 210,
  259, 302, 326–7
compassionate posture 240–1
compassionate self 247, 248–9, 256–9,
  339, 341, 345
  Bringing the compassionate self to
    you and your baby (exercise) 308
  bringing to the fore 279
  and compassionate imagery 300–4,
    309
  focusing 260–1
  Imagining becoming your
    compassionate self 257–9
  'on the go' 339
  putting in charge 300
  and self-criticism 325
compassionate self-identity 247, 248–63
compassionate sensory focusing 195,
  203
compassionate thinking (reasoning) 193,
  202, 287–93, 297, 308–9, 341
compulsions 156
confidence, inner 259
conflict 200
confusion 170–3, 174
containment 189
control issues 135, 156, 185
cortisol 9–10, 118, 239
courage 194, 239, 248, 282, 309, 324
creativity 108–9, 167, 203–4
criticism 145, 155
  see also self-criticism
crying babies 12
  and compassionate letter writing
    297
  empathy for 189–90
  failure to calm 171
  intolerance of 128
  and mentalising 168–9
  'numbing to cope' with 30–2
  paying compassionate attention to
    271–2
  and postnatal depression 29
  sensitivity to 186
  sympathy for 169

thought balancing exercises for 288, 291–3
and threat systems 168–9

death 63–4
delusions 49
depression 87
   combined with anxiety 25, 51
   incidence 120
   and mindfulness 215–16
   recurrent 215–16
   see also postnatal depression
desensitisation, compassionate 305–6
deservingness 331
detachment 48
diagnosis xxxiii
diary writing 344–5
   gratitude diaries 267–8, 339
disapproval 141
disconnection 28
   fear of 273, 292
   health risks of 201
   and shame 138, 140
disgust 95–9, 117, 128
dissociation 33–4
distancing yourself 15, 164
distress, sensitivity to **182**, 185–6, 191, 295–6
distress tolerance 187–8, 191, 296
'doing', state of 216–17
dominance 132–3
dopamine 21–2, 27, 129–30
drive system (emotion system) 91–3, **93**, 99–103, 108, 109, **114**, 115, 116, 249
   how compassion shapes 198–200, **199**, 203
   and new motherhood 122, 123
drive-oriented societies 204

early life experience 63, 118, 120, 126–9, 181, 207, 258, 293, 297
   of being parented 46
   and disorganised attachment patterns 170–1, 172
   and distress tolerance 187–8
   empathy for 189
   and expression of scary feelings 162–5
   and safety strategies 145, 147–9, 151–8
early morning waking 24
earthquakes 118
eating disorders 324
'effortful control' 125
ejection 332
Elliott, Stephen 243
embodiment 238–41
emergencies, psychiatric 49
emotion systems 91–116

see also drive system; soothing system; threat and self-protection system
emotional abuse 97
emotional contagion 169–70
emotional detachment 48
emotional resilience 130, 201
emotions 293
   balance 114–16, **114**, 223
   and the body 227
   extreme 155
   functions of 92–3
   keeping in check with self-criticism 322–4, 332
   mindfulness to 82–4, 231–2
   and motives 91–2
   naming 98, 160–1, 162, 165
   and our multiple selves 110–16
   overwhelming 34–7
   positive 99–103
   struggling to feel love for baby 27–46
   and thoughts 287
   'three circle' model of 93, **93**, 264–5
   tone, kindness and warmth 259
   see also feelings; *specific emotions*
empathy 74, 188–90, 191, 288–9, 291, 296
endorphins 130–1
enemies
   babies seen as 128
   compassion for our 179
enjoyment
   loss of 50
   see also happiness; joy
envy 126, 146, 180
epigenetics 38
evolution, of the brain xxviii, 19–20, 25–6, 31, 34–5, 54–5, 59–63, 66, 67–70, 135, 144, 164, 200–1, 206–7, 292
excited self 110–11, **112**
exercises
   Bringing compassion to mindfulness 88
   Bringing compassion to our 'angry self' 301–3
   Bringing compassion to our 'anxious self' 301
   Bringing compassion to ourselves 260–1
   Bringing compassion to the part that struggles with your baby 303–4
   Bringing compassion to the self-critic 320–2
   Bringing compassion to someone you care about 260
   Bringing the compassionate self to you and your baby 308

Bringing the compassionate self to your baby 307–8
Bringing gratitude and compassion to the body 229–30
Compassion-focused thought balancing – an example 287–90, 349
Compassionate attention to gratitude 267–8, 339
Compassionate attention to memories 266–7
Compassionate attention to parts of our baby 268–9
Compassionate attention to times when it was easier 269–70
Compassionate attention to using all of our senses with our baby 270–2
Compassionate attention to what connects us 273–4
Compassionate attention to what we have done all day 275–6
Compassionate colour 255, 338
Compassionate colour flowing out 256, 338
Compassionate image 262, 340
Eating like a baby 234
Examples of compassionate behaviour 'in the long term' 281
Examples of compassionate behaviour 'in the moment' 278–9
Examples of compassionate behaviour 'in the short term' 278–9
Finding balance 114
Imagining becoming your compassionate self 257–9
Mindful coffee drinking 85
Mindfulness to the body 227–8, 337
Mindfulness to the breath 224–5, 244, 337
Mindfulness to emotions 232
Mindfulness to the senses 226
Mindfulness to sounds 225, 337
Mindfulness to thoughts 232–4, 338
Mindfulness to the washing up 235
Mindfulness walking with the pushchair 236
Moving together – synchrony 274
Safe place 251–3, 338
Safe place with your baby 253–4
Soothing breathing rhythm 242
The power of our mind towards ourselves 78–80
The spotlight of attention (1) 82
The spotlight of attention (2) 82
Through the eyes of my baby 274–5
Twelve week exercise programme for developing the compassionate mind xxxi–xxxii, 335–46

experiments
   'Awareness of the restless mind' 217, 336–7
   Finding a compassionate posture 240–1
   Neutral face, kind face 245
   Neutral voice, kind voice 246
   'Spotlight of attention' 220–2, 336–7
exploration 108–9
eye contact 10, 11, 173

facial expression 117
   warm 6, 237, 238, 257, 259
'Facilitators' 44
fatigue 101, 102
favouritism 38, 128
fear 31, 45, 48, 117, 129, 180–1, 186–8, 264–5, 285–6, 298, 313, 314, 318–19
   of abandonment 138, 187
   and birth 8–9, 183–4, 185
   of disconnection 273, 292
   'fear without solution' 170–1
   of rejection 135–7
   and safety strategies 144–5, 149, 151–3, 155–8, 170
feelings 291
   compassionate 195–6, 203
   and emotional contagion 169–70
   failure to think clearly when upset 166–73, 174
   feeling low 50, 102, 215–16
   'I don't know who I really am' 161–2
   'I have no idea how I feel' 160–1
   overwhelming 34–7, 170–3, 174, 187, 189
   'positive feeling snowball' 327–8
   scary 162–6, 169–70, 174, 179–80, 185–6, 187
   towards our baby 305
   understanding 19–26, 160–74
   see also emotions; specific emotions
'fight, fright, freeze or flight' response 75, 89, 90, 94, 95–7, 117, 171, 237
flashbacks 33
foetus 5
food, paying attention to your 226
Fox, John 324
Fredrickson, Barbara 121
friends xxix

genes 258
genetics 37–8, 48–9
Gerbarg, Patricia 243
Germer, Christopher 208
Gilbert, Paul 196
grandmothers 17–18
gratitude 229–30, 276
   gratitude diaries 267–8, 339

great apes 54, 67, 72
grief 41, 42, 299, 329–30
'growing a tulip' metaphor 208–9
guilt 51, 139–41, 142–3, 299, 305

habituation 103
hallucination 49
Hamilton, David 201
Hanson, Rick 270
happiness 323, 327
    pursuit of 65–6
    see also enjoyment; joy
harming babies 52, 56
health 201
hearing 212
    see also sounds
heroin 130
hierarchies, social status 68–9
home, sense of 276
hopelessness 23–4
hormones 3, 4, 117

identity 72, 247, 248–63
imagery see compassionate imagery
imagination 251
imprinting, mother-baby 27
in-groups 126, 127, 128, 128–9
indifference, feelings of 9
Inflammation Paradigm for Postnatal
    Depression 119–22
instincts 91
intention 218–20, 326–7
interest, loss of 50
intrusive thoughts 33, 56–7
irritability 21–3, 50

jealousy 41, 148
joy 323, 327
    see also enjoyment; happiness

Kabat-Zinn, Jon 214, 218
Kendall-Tackett, Kathleen 119, 120

La Leche League 30
Langer, Ellen 88
Lawrence, Verity 326, 327, 328
learning 108–9
Lee, Deborah 326, 327, 328
letter writing, compassionate 294–9, 309,
    342
life expectancy 64
life experience 32–4, 118, 144–5
    see also early life experience
limbic system 68, **78**
loneliness 129, 147–8, 150, 153, 155, 164,
    180–1, 201
    see also aloneness

loss, childhood 156
'lotus flower' metaphor 180, 202
love 201
    conditional 148–9
    'falling in love' with your baby 30, 100
    mother-baby rush of love 9–10
    struggling to feel love for your baby
        27–46
    unconditional 156
loving-kindness meditation 317
'lying in' period 14–15

Main, Mary 170
mammals 68–9, 70–1, 89
mania 49, 115, 180
maternal ambivalence 40–2
maternal instinct 13–14
MBCT see Mindfulness-Based Cognitive
    Therapy
MBSR see Mindfulness-Based Stress
    Reduction
meconium stool 23
meditation, loving-kindness 317
memories 265–6
    body memory 129, 157, 227
    Compassionate attention to memories
        (exercise) 266–7
    impact of emotions on 111, **112**
    traumatic 33
mentalisation 166–70
method-acting 241, 339
midwives, 'knitting' 6–7
mind
    Awareness of the restless mind
        (experiment) 217
    empty 216–20
    'nature's mind' 63
    restless 217–18
    settling 223
    understanding the mind of self and
        others 160–74
    see also compassionate mind
        approach; compassionate mind
        development
'Mind like the sky' (mindfulness) 213
mind-body link 3
mindful awareness 205–36
mindfulness 81–4
    benefits 90
    to the body 227–8
    and compassion 85–8, 219
    definition 81, 90, 218
    to emotions 231–2
    exercises 82, 85, 88, 224–6
    learning to become more mindful
        84–5
    to making a cup of tea 279

and new motherhood 88–9
'on the go' 234–6, 337–8
and pregnancy 88–9
and self-focus 162
and soothing system activation 237
to thoughts 232–4
see also mindful awareness
Mindfulness-Based Cognitive Therapy
(MBCT) 214, 215–16
Mindfulness-Based Stress Reduction
(MBSR) 214
mindlessness 220
mirror neurons 186
mirroring 170
mistakes, learning from 259
Mother and Baby Units 52, 53, 121
mother-baby bonding 10–13, 27
difficulties 27–46, 38, 53–4, 127–9, 184
'lack of fit' 38
and oxytocin 125, 127–9
and pheromones 123
and postnatal depression 28–30
mother-baby imprinting 27
motherhood (new) 9–14, 184–93
learning to mother 13–14
and mindfulness 88–9
and shame 139–41
and the threat system 117–22
mothers
attachment patterns 166
critical and unloving 153
'perfect' 155
voice of 11, 272
what mothers do 141–2, 275–6
motivation 91–2, 300
see also compassionate motivation
music 272

Native American Indian tradition 207–8
'nature's mind' 63
needs
overwhelming 157
unmet 157, 161
negative self-judgements 80–1
negative thoughts 51
neglect 156
neocortex 72
nervous system
parasympathetic 71, 105, 237–8, 242
sympathetic 95, 237
neuronal networks 197
neurons 73–4, 186
neuropeptides 124
neuroplasticity 73–4, 205, 208–10
'nice', being 313–14, 315–16
non-judgement 86, **86**, 99, 190–1, 218–19,
225, 244, 296

numbness 28, 30
numbing to cope 30–1
thought balancing exercise for 289
triggers 32–45

objectification 43–5
oestrogen 4, 50
openness 108–9
opioids 130–1
'orienting sensitivity' 125
out-groups 126, 128–9
overwhelming feelings 34–7, 170–3, 174,
187, 189
'oxygen mask' principle 316
oxytocin 4, 10, 21–2, 27, 30, 71, 124–9
and bonding 125, 127–9
dark side of 125–7
and mentalising 169

pain
of birth 8–9
chronic 215
mental 80
and rejection 137
worry about 215, 227
panic 145, 146–8, 155–7, 183–4, 188–9,
313–14
parasympathetic nervous system 71, 105,
237–8, 242
parents
angry 323
critical 314–15
'nice' 314–16
see also mothers
'peaceful contentedness' 104
Pennebaker, James 294, 295, 298
'people pleasing' 153, 161, 292
perfectionism 155
perinatal mental health teams 51–2
permanence, search for 64
personal growth 165, 180, 181–2, 313–14,
315
personality disorder 126
perspective-taking 167, 168–9, 189, 197
pethidine 9, 37
pheromones 123–4
physical abuse 97
physical exercise/movement 278
placenta, delivery 10–11
play 68, 157
positive thinking 80–1
post-birth experience 9–14, 184–93
post-traumatic stress disorders (PTSD)
33, 34
postnatal depression 47–58
effects on how you feel about your
baby 53–4

frightening thoughts of 55–7
and harming babies 52, 56
incidence 120
as 'just the blues' (myth) 50
medication for 51
and mother-infant bonding 28–30
myths surrounding 47–50, 58
onset 47
protective function of 25–6
rates of 24
slipping into 24
and support 53, 54–5
symptoms of 24–5, 47–8, 50–1,
    101
and taking babies away from
    mothers 52–3
treatment 51–2, 58
posture 237, 238–41, 278, 301–3, 319
poverty 36
predators 19–20, 31, 74, 97
prefrontal cortex 72–4, 90
pregnancy 258
    changes during 4–5, 117–31
    hormones 3, 4, 117
    and mindfulness 88–9
    onset of postnatal depression in 47
present moment 84, 218, 265, 275,
    277–9
professional help xxxiii
progesterone 4, 50
projection 128–9
prolactin 4, 21–2, 129–30
    as 'protect and defend hormone' 22
psychiatric emergencies 49
psychosis, postpartum (puerperal) 48–9
PTSD *see* post-traumatic stress disorders
pushchairs, mindful walking with 236

'quiet wakefulness' 108

rage 40–2, 45
Raphael-Leff, Joan 44
reciprocal relationships 11–12
'Regulators' 44
rejection 149–50, 156, 164, 311–12
    hard-wired fear of 135–7
religion 64
reptiles 67–8, 69, 70, 74, 89
reptilian brain 67, 68, 75–7, 89–90
resentment, feelings towards your baby
    40–2
resilience, emotional 130, 201
'rest and digest' system 71, 103
resting states 201
restlessness 217–18
reward systems 21–2, 28–9, 122
Rosenberg, Marshall 319

rumination 83–4, 87, 193, 205, 208, 215,
    218

sadness 41–2, 129, 166, 181–2, 299, 322
    mindfulness of 218–19
    spiralling into depression 215–16, 219
safe havens 106–7, 251–4, 338
safety, sense of 7, 13, 15, 22, 23–4, 31, 32,
    71, 237, 275–6, 278, 286, 323
    and distress tolerance 187
    and emotional contagion 169–70
    and mentalising 167–9
    'safe places' 251–4, 338
    social safeness 103–9
safety strategies 173
    being nice as 315–16
    and 'fear without solution' 170
    four-part formulation 151–8, 347
    and self-criticism 311–12, 323
    unintended consequences 144–59,
        164, 174
SBR *see* soothing breathing rhythm
schizophrenia 49
Segal, Zindel 214
self 80
    angry self 110–11, 113, 301–3
    anxious self 110–11, **112**, 113, 301
    excited self 110–11, **112**
    lack of a sense of 161–2
    multiple selves concept 110–16,
        276–7
    socially constructed self 61–3
    soothing/contented self 110–11, **112**,
        113
    struggling parts of our self 299–309
self-acceptance 122
self-awareness 72, 77–81, **78**
self-compassion 172, 183, 197, 208–9,
    342–3
    as alien experience 329
    as aversive experience 329–30
    bringing to your baby (exercise) 307–8
    journey to 325–7
self-criticism 77–81, **78**, 132, 149, 155, 180,
    208, 285, 343
    alternatives to 288, 291
    appearance of your 'self-critic' 312–
        13, 343
    compassion for the self-critic 317–22,
        344
    and compassionate letter writing
        298–9
    defining a new identity for the 'self
        critic' 328–9
    from self-criticism to self-compassion
        310–33
    motivations for 311–12

moving towards a compassionate
  self-corrector 313–14, 324–7, 332,
  343–4
of our attempts to be compassionate
  330–1
and our compassionate self 325
and our need for affiliation 324–5
and the 'positive feeling snowball'
  327–8
and support 327
to keep emotions in check 322–4
self-focus 162
self-hatred 180–1
self-identity 72
  compassionate 247, 248–63
self-kindness 40
self-monitoring 77–81, **78**
self-understanding 39–40
senses 252–3, 274–5
  mindfulness to 226
  paying compassionate attention to
    270–2
  see also sensory focusing; specific senses
'sensitivity to distress' **182**, 185–6, 191,
  295–6
sensory focusing, compassionate 195,
  203
settling mind and body 223
sex hormones 117
sexual abuse 34, 97, 118
shame xxviii, xxx, 9, 33, 35, 37, 40, 42–3,
  54, 56, 62–3, 70, 97, 128, 132–43, 285,
  298, 305, 332
  and compassion 179, 180
  definition 132–3, 137, 142
  and disconnection 138, 140
  external 134, 291
  and fear of rejection 135–7
  and guilt 139–41, 142–3
  internal 134, 292
  protection from 140
  reasons for the existence of 133–5
  and scary feelings 163, 164, 185–6
  and self-criticism 310
  trap of 138–9
shift-work 120–1
showing off 155
sight, sense of 211, 270
skin-to-skin contact 11, 71
sleeping problems 5, 24, 51
smell, sense of 123–4, 212, 253, 271, 280
smiling 43–5, 238, 245–6
social comparison-making 69–70
social contact 102
social control 135
'social engagement system' 238, 245, 246
social feedback 43–5

social isolation 164
'Social Mentality' 196–8, 203
social roles 196–8, 203
social safeness 103–9
social status hierarchies 68–9
soothing breathing rhythm (SBR) 121,
  199, 241–4, 252, 254–5, 257, 261–2, 272,
  277–8, 287–9, 291, 294, 300–1, 307, 337
soothing system (emotion system) 91–3,
  93, 103–9, **114**, 116, 121, 248–9, 310
  activation 237–47, 264–5, 287
  benefits of 201
  damping down 306
  and distress tolerance 187
  focusing on memories that build 267
  and guilt 139
  how compassion shapes 198–200, **199**,
    203–4
  and mentalising 167–9
  and new motherhood 123–31
  and self-criticism 318
soothing/contented self 110–11, **112**, 113
sounds 84–5, 212, 225, 252, 271–2
Stadlen, Naomi 141
stool, meconium 23
strength 194, 239, 259, 264, 300, 309, 324
stress 119–22
stress hormones 9–10, 118
stress management 117–18
stressful life events 118
submission 132–3, 137, 239, 301
suckling 10–11
suffering 63–6, 177–83, 258, 286
  alleviation of 181–3, **182**, 191–6, 202–3,
    216, 248–9, 296–7, 315, 331
  engagement with 181–91, **182**, 202,
    216, 248, 295–6, 315
suicidal thoughts 51
support 53, 54–5, 120–1
  after giving birth 14–15
  during birth 7
  in the early days of baby's arrival
    14–15, 16–17
  lack of 3, 24, 35, 36, 53
  and self-criticism 327
sympathetic nervous system 95, 237
sympathy 169, **182**, 186–7, 188–9, 191,
  196, 296
synchrony 274

taste, sense of 212, 253, 272
tea, mindful making of 279
tearfulness 50
Teasdale, John 214
temperament 37–8, 125
'tend and defend' stance 126
territorial behaviour 74–5

testosterone 130, 239
thinking (reasoning), compassionate 193, 202, 287–93, 297, 308–9, 341
thoughts
    balancing 287–93
    and emotions 287
    frightening 55–7
    impact of emotions on 110, **112**
    intrusive 33, 56–7
    mindfulness to 232–4
    negative 51
    positive 80–1
threat 29, 100, 185, 193
    and confusion 171–2
    perception 32, 34, 42–3, 75–7
    and shame 133, 142
threat and self-protection system (emotion system) 91–9, **93**, 102–3, 108, 109, 113–16, **114**, 165–6, 248–9, 316
    and attention 222, 223, 264–5, 268
    and breathing 242
    'bridging across' to the soothing system 237, 263, 287
    and disconnection 273
    ease of activation 218, 237
    how compassion shapes 198–200, **199**, 203–4
    and mentalisation 168–9
    and mindful awareness 213
    and naming emotions 160–1
    and new motherhood 117–22, 123
    and self-criticism 298–9, 310, 311, 318, 322
    and shame 136
    and the six attributes of compassion 185, 186
'three circle' model of emotions 93, **93**, 264–5

Tierney, Stephanie 324
tiredness 50
tolerance 131
touch, sense of 211–12, 252–3, 270–1
    see also skin-to-skin contact
tragedy 63–6
trapped feelings 41, 291, 293
traumatic experiences 32–4
Trevarthen, Colwyn 134
turning inwards 162, 216
'two wolves' story 207, 344

unlovable, feeling 156
urges/action tendencies, impact of emotions on 111, **112**

violence 319
voice
    anorexic 324
    maternal 11, 272
    warm 237–8, 246–7, 257, 259, 287, 290, 303, 328

washing up, mindfulness to 235
'weak' other, the 157
well-being
    eudaimonic 121
    hedonic 121
    motivation and willingness to care for **182**, 184–5, 191, 295
'what if' thinking 56
Williams, Mark 214
Wilson, David Sloan 67
wisdom 178, 181–2, 206–7, 258, 258–9, 300, 313
worry 56, 215, 218, 264–5